LEGENDARY LOCALS

OF

FAIR LAWN

NEW JERSEY

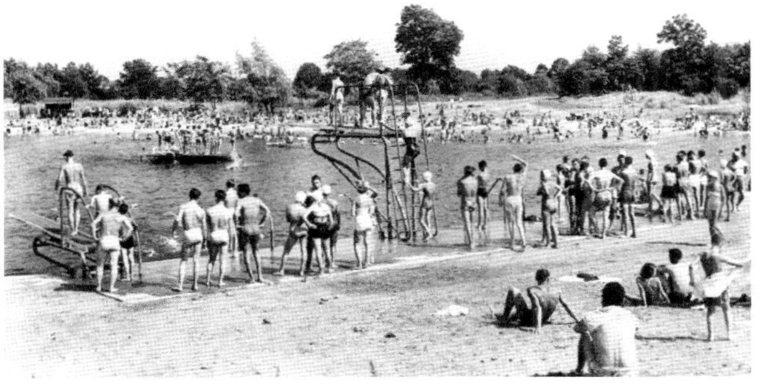

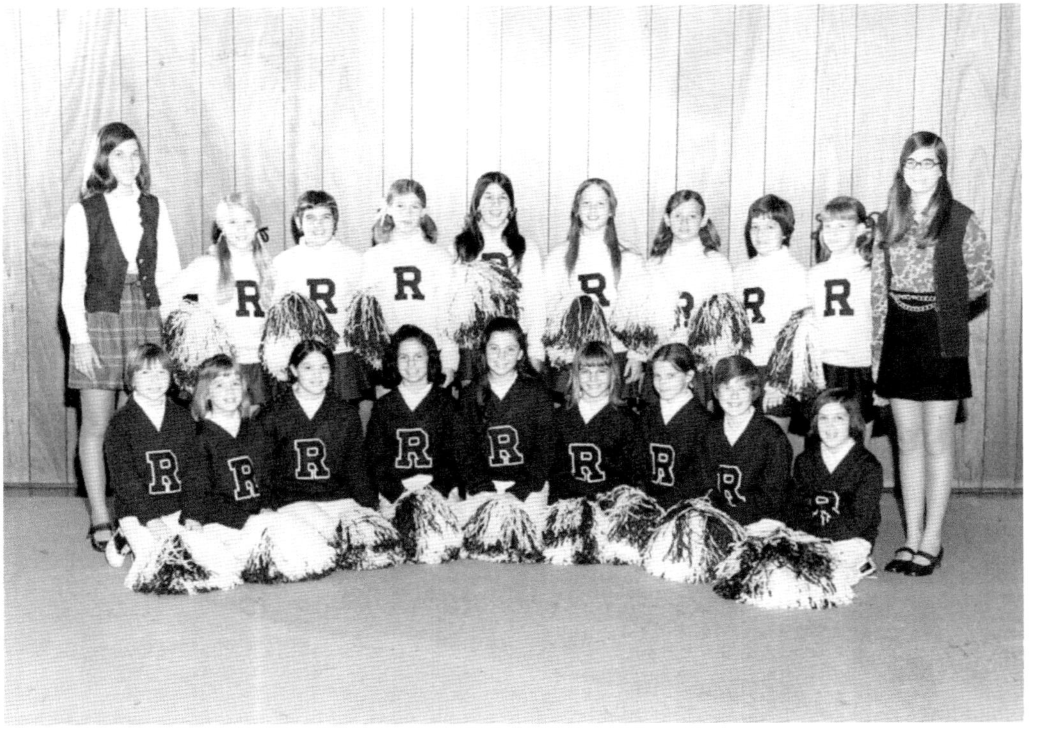

Cheerleaders
A 1970s cheerleading squad included, from left to right, (first row) Judy Lyman, Susan Cook, Joy Mancini, Phyllis Harris, Lynn O'Malley, Jill Muhr, Christy Andrews, Kristi Lamb, and Teri Fox; (second row) Maura Fox, Susie Enterline, Karen Ryan, Kitty McGovern, Mary McGovern, Kristen Kearney, Jodi Weissman, Karen Pizzo, Jenny Andrews, and Joanne Meade. (Authors' collection.)

Page 1: Memorial Park and Pool
The residents of Fair Lawn have been enjoying Memorial Park and Pool since it opened in 1949. Many people buy passes for the entire summer for swimming, diving, picnicking, playing sports, and just relaxing under the trees. (Authors' collection.)

LEGENDARY LOCALS

OF

FAIR LAWN

NEW JERSEY

CORNELL CHRISTIANSON
AND JANE LYLE DIEPEVEEN

LEGENDARY LOCALS

ISBN 978-1-4671-0106-6

Legendary Locals is an imprint of Arcadia Publishing
Charleston, South Carolina

Printed in the United States of America

Library of Congress Control Number: 2013938697

For all general information, please contact Arcadia Publishing:
Telephone 843-853-2070
Fax 843-853-0044
E-mail sales@arcadiapublishing.com
For customer service and orders:
Toll-Free 1-888-313-2665

Visit us on the Internet at www.arcadiapublishing.com

On the Front Cover: Clockwise from top left:
John A. Cosgrove, fire chief in driver's seat (Courtesy of John J. Cosgrove; see page 46), Lee Meredith, actress (Courtesy of Lee Meredith; see pages 58, 59), Hubie Brown, NBA sportscaster (Courtesy of ESPN; see page 85), Michael Vanore, first police chief (Courtesy of Cadmus House; see page 20), Robert M. Gordon, New Jersey state senator (Authors' collection; see page 46), Ron Perranoski, baseball player (Courtesy of Ron Perranoski, see page 79), Millie Perkins, actress (Courtesy of Millie Perkins; see pages 56, 57), Donna Vivino, actress (Courtesy of Donna Vivino; see page 65), John J. Cosgrove, Mr. Fair Lawn (Courtesy of John J. Cosgrove; see page 47).

On the Back Cover: From left to right:
Florence "Flossie" Dobrow, riding her tricycle with the borough council (Authors' collection; see page 41), the Radburn branch of Columbia Bank, housed in the Radburn Plaza Building (Courtesy of Columbia Bank; see pages 96, 97).

CONTENTS

ACKNOWLEDGMENTS

The authors wish to thank the many people who helped us with this book.

Neal Diepeveen provided invaluable technical assistance with the digital photographs and with computer problems. Our editor at Arcadia Publishing, Erin Vosgien, gave us patient guidance in the production of the book. Cathy Schofield and the Fair Lawn High School Athletic Hall of Fame Executive Committee provided contact information and biographies of the athletes. Peggy Norris of the Ridgewood Public Library helped us find images of some early notables. The Cadmus House Museum (CH) and James Graff of the Fair Lawn Recreation and Parks Department (RD) lent us photographs. Many other people also provided us with photographs. They are credited in the captions. Photographs from the Historic American Buildings Survey are noted as HABS. Unless otherwise noted, all images appear courtesy of the authors. Cornell Christianson shot 56 of the photographs in the book.

The authors have tried to provide accurate information about all of the people celebrated in this book. Any corrections needed as well as additional material on locals of note will be posted on Diepeveen's website, www.fairlawnhistory.com.

INTRODUCTION

This book celebrates the people who made Fair Lawn the community it is today. Located between two rivers with streams and fertile soil, this area attracted both Native Americans and Europeans. A part of Bergen County, it was first named Sloterdam, then Small Lots, and now Fair Lawn, but no matter the name, those who built the institutions of this community are the people who should be remembered.

The Lenape Indians were the first to settle the area of present-day Fair Lawn. Their land was given to two Englishmen in 1664, but the first European settlers were Dutch. David Danielse bought a tract in Sloterdam, as the area was then called, and probably farmed the land, but Peter Garretson built the first house after he bought the tract in 1719. By 1766, Garretson was joined by Jacob Vanderbeck at Dunkerhook, Dirck Ryerson at Wagaraw, Peter Hopper on Small Lots Road (Fair Lawn Avenue), and John Doremus at Zabriskie's Mills (now Arcola). These hardy pioneers built stone houses and farmed the land covering most of today's town. Their descendants inherited the farms and built their own houses. By 1861, there were five additional Hopper houses, including that of Henry A. Hopper, and two more, built by Adam and Isaac Hopper, were added later. Other farms were sold to newer residents, including a few wealthy businessmen, like George Morlot, who built elaborate mansions.

By 1924, Fair Lawn was still part of Saddle River Township. Some of the farms had been replaced by groups of modest homes, interspersed with small stores and factories. A cemetery had been established, and a bleachery and dye works were built. Peter Henderson, Martin Romaine, and Raphael Grunauer had turned their farms into housing developments. The Kuiken Brothers and the Landzettels had started their growing businesses. By now, there were many residents with children, and parents were not happy with the township schools. A successful movement to separate was started by John Greydanus, the Kuikens, and others, and the resulting borough took its name from the railroad station and neighborhood, which had been named after David D. Acker's estate, Fair Lawn.

A new government was formed with farmers and businessmen becoming the first councilmen and mayors. New schools were built, and more farms were replaced with housing developments, including the "Town for the Motor Age," Radburn. Other farms gave way to factories and additional dye works. Residents founded the Fair Lawn Building and Loan, today Columbia Bank, with headquarters in the borough, and the Fair Lawn–Radburn Trust Company. Fair Lawn was becoming a suburb.

Growth slowed during the Great Depression but exploded in the late 1930s. The borough grew from 9,000 to more than 13,000 people from 1940 until May 1942, making Fair Lawn reputed to be the fastest growing town in the country. A zoning board and a planning board were established in the 1930s to help guide the growth. There were now four population centers: Fair Lawn Center (at River Road and Fair Lawn Avenue), Warren Point, Columbia Heights, and Radburn.

When the United States entered World War II, young and middle-aged men volunteered or were drafted. Most were "lucky," but 38 local men gave their lives overseas. Troops were encamped on "Soldier's Hill" in Radburn, and there was an antiaircraft battery in Columbia Heights. Wright Aeronautical and other war industries moved into the brick factory buildings on Wagaraw Road and Maple Avenue. Almost everything was rationed, and "War Savings Time" meant walking to high school in the dark in the winter.

When the high school was opened in 1943, a competitive sports program was started. The program has produced famous athletes like Ron Perranoski and Dave Sime and notable coaches such as Frank Bennett and Hubie Brown. The list of Fair Lawn High School athletes who went on to make a mark in the sports world is long indeed.

The high school drama club also produced notable stage and screen performers such as Millie Perkins and Judith Lee Sauls, known in the show business world as Lee Meredith. Other high school alumni who became notable artists included Keith "Red" Mitchell, jazz bassist, and "Ace" Andrews, television director and producer. Many artists and entertainers have made their homes in Fair Lawn, including Donna Vivino of Broadway fame and L. Barry Tedesco, a music teacher at the high school, who developed the town's award-winning marching band.

After the war, the soldiers returned and created a huge demand for housing and for new schools, new businesses, and doctors and other professionals to serve the residents. A sewer plant and other municipal works were constructed. The population grew to almost 24,000 by 1950.

Fair Lawn needed a source of funds to pay for the necessary facilities. To bring in ratables, a modern "industrial park" was planned for the Croucher and Youngsman farms. Nationally known firms such as National Biscuit Company and Lea and Perrins were attracted, and the site became widely known as a model for modern industrial development. Today, these and other industries remain, but other plants have been redeveloped for office buildings and mixed residential/commercial projects, keeping up with changing needs.

The government has also changed. A movement was started by some town organizations to establish the municipal-manager form of government with a professional manager in charge of directing the department heads instead of a councilman being in charge of each division. In 1948, a referendum approved the new form, with nonpartisan elections. Today, there is still a manager in charge of running the town under policies set by the borough council, but a newer form, called council-manager, has been instituted and elections are now on a partisan basis.

The borough continued to grow, most rapidly through the 1960s. Apartments and townhouses were added to the predominant single-family homes. More schools, businesses and houses of worship were established. The famous Dietch's Kiddie Zoo was among the entertainment venues that came to town.

Today, Fair Lawn is a thriving community of many ethnic groups, named by a real estate firm as the "best city in New Jersey," based on amenities, low crime rate, and other factors. The residents owe a debt to those who came before to make their town a great place to live. Not all of them could be included here; those that are represent the town's legendary locals.

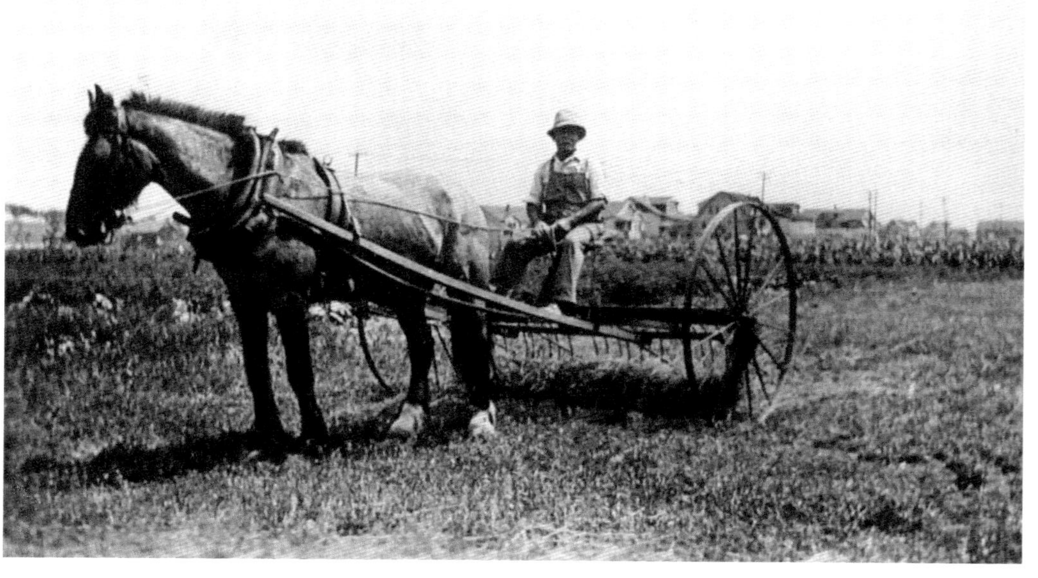

Small Town Fair Lawn
Fair Lawn began as a patchwork of farms. Pictured is Charles Vogel driving his horse-drawn farming machinery.

CHAPTER ONE

The Founders

After the Lenape Indians, Peter Garretson was the first settler in what is now Fair Lawn. Others soon followed him, and by 1766, large parts of the area were under cultivation. During the Revolutionary War, no battles were fought in the settlement, but Gen. Henry Lee was headquartered at Dirck Ryerson's stone house.

Farms were divided into smaller parcels; some were left to sons; others were sold to new residents. During the 1800s, wealthy businessmen and prosperous farmers built elaborate homes on the few roads. David D. Acker called his estate Fair Lawn, giving the area, and later the borough, its name.

In 1924, some of the newer residents and farmers from the Fair Lawn section were active in working for the separation of the town from Saddle River Township. William Croucher and Charles Vogel later served in the new government. Samuel Greydanus became head of the road department and worked to civil service status for his fellow borough employees.

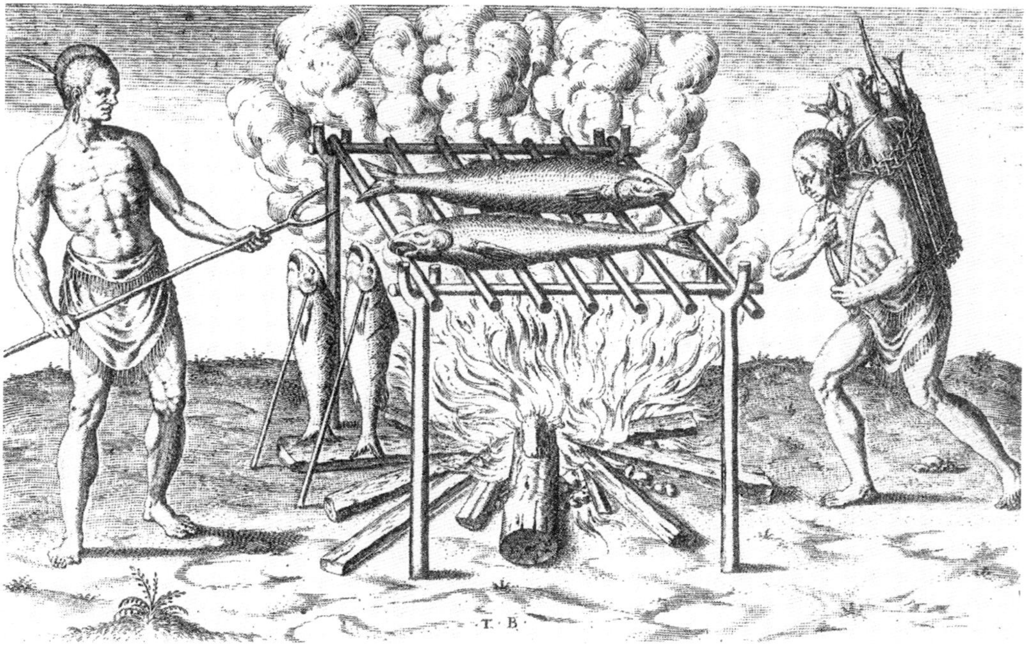

The Lenape Indians and River Road
The Lenape Indians were the first settlers in what is now Fair Lawn. By the time Europeans arrived, the Lenape were living in small villages and supplementing game with corn and vegetables, which they grew in small plots. Fish was also an important food. The Indians constructed a stone fish weir in the Passaic River to trap shad, bass, and other fish as they swam upstream to spawn, pictured below. The Lenape made a trail along the river leading to the great rock in Glen Rock. The trail was widened by the Dutch settlers and became today's River Road. Because of the dam, the road was originally known as Sloterdam Road, after the Dutch word for "closing dam." (Above, illustration from *Ancient North Americans*, edited by Jesse D. Jennings; below, photograph by Tony DeCondo.)

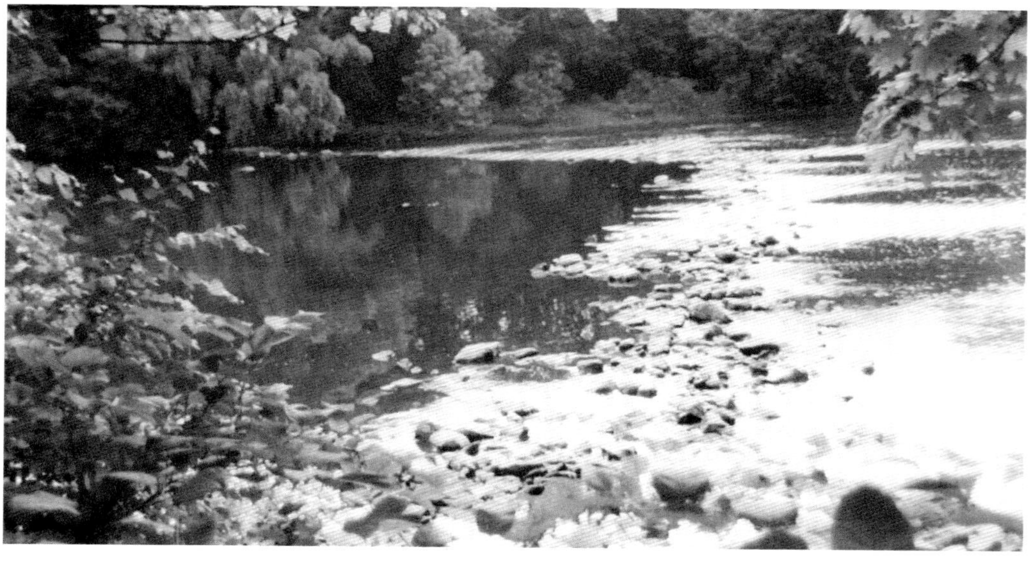

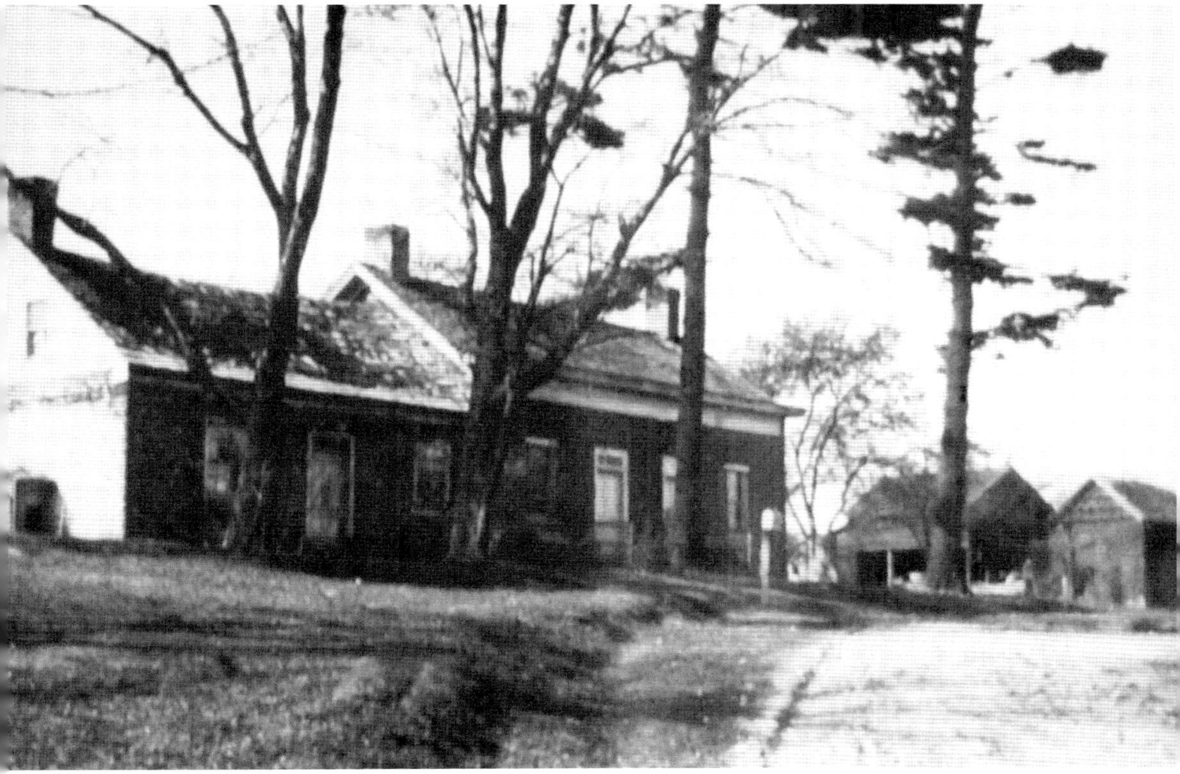

The First Settler

In 1719 or 1720, Peter Gerritse, with his father, Gerrit, bought a farm in a portion of the Sloterdam Patent. Soon afterwards, Peter built the small stone house that is the oldest building in Fair Lawn. The original building is now the smaller wing of the Garretson House; Peter or one of his sons later built a larger addition. Peter was a successful farmer and was prosperous enough that he owned six slaves at his death in 1766. His heirs anglicized the name to Garretson. The home remained in the family until 1950. Today, the house and several farm buildings are preserved as the Garretson Forge and Farm and are open to the public as a museum. (Courtesy of CH.)

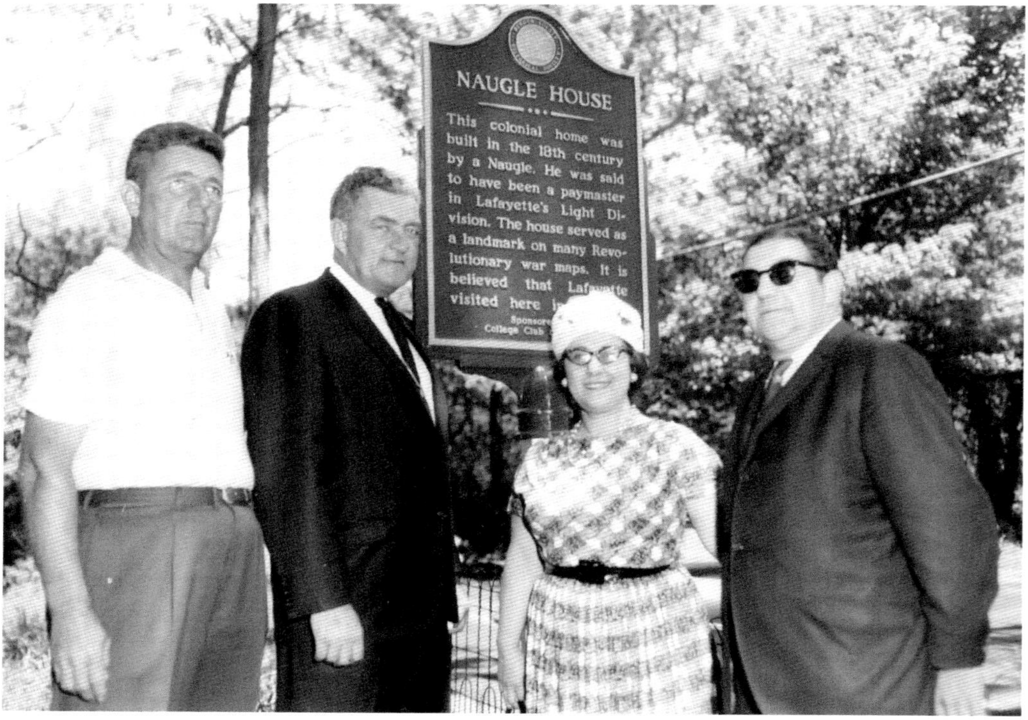

An Early Farmer

Jacob Vanderbeck bought farmland in Dunkerhook in 1734 and built the unusual stone house on the side of the hill near the Saddle River. He also built a mill nearby, the first mill in Fair Lawn. The house later was the home of several generations of the Naugle family and is known as the Naugle-Vanderbeck House. Mel Naugle—who is pictured (from left to right) with Mayor Richard Vander Plaat, an unidentified woman, and John Gottlieb—was the last to live in the house. The Marquis de Lafayette, a general in the American Revolution, is said to have visited his paymaster at this house on a trip to the United States in 1784. Jacob or his son Jan built another stone house nearby, pictured below, known as the Jacob Vanderbeck Jr. House. Both houses are in the New Jersey and National Registers of Historic Places. (Below, courtesy of HABS.)

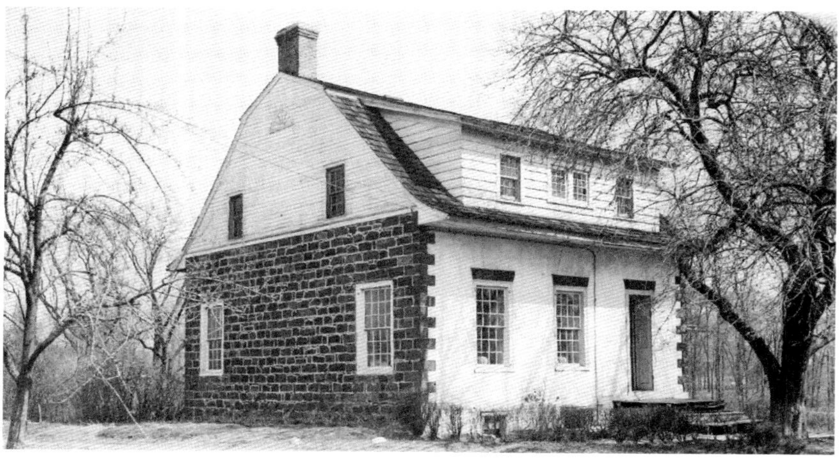

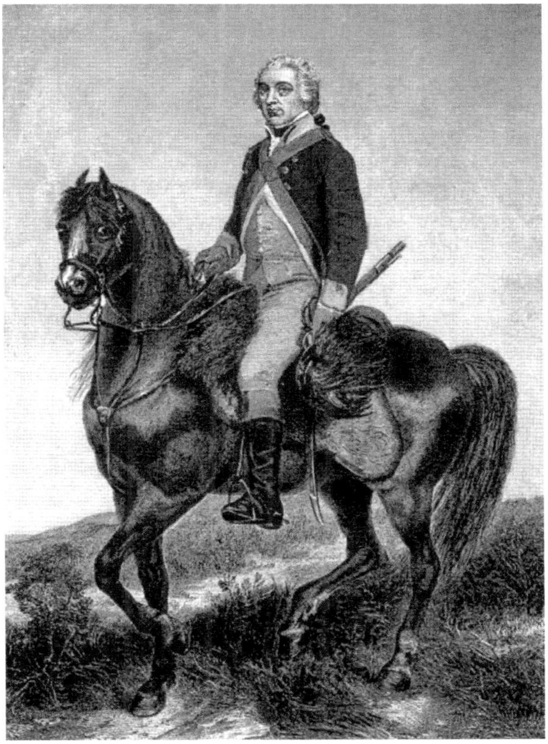

Maj. Henry Lee

Dirck Ryerson was another early farmer. He inherited his land at Wagaraw and, around 1750, built a one-room stone house on the Wagaraw Road. He also had a gristmill and pond nearby. In the fall of 1780, Maj. "Light Horse Harry" Lee, a Revolutionary War hero, was quartered at the house while his cavalry unit was guarding Lafayette's troops in Hawthorne.

An Early Developer

Peter D. Henderson Jr. inherited a farm and an ice pond, located next to Ryerson's land, from his father. Henderson Jr. became an early developer when, in 1912, he filed a subdivision plat on a portion of the farm bordering today's Maple Avenue. The pond, shown below with Henderson's house at the left, was later a bathing beach, and the stream that fed it became known as Henderson Brook. (Courtesy of CH.)

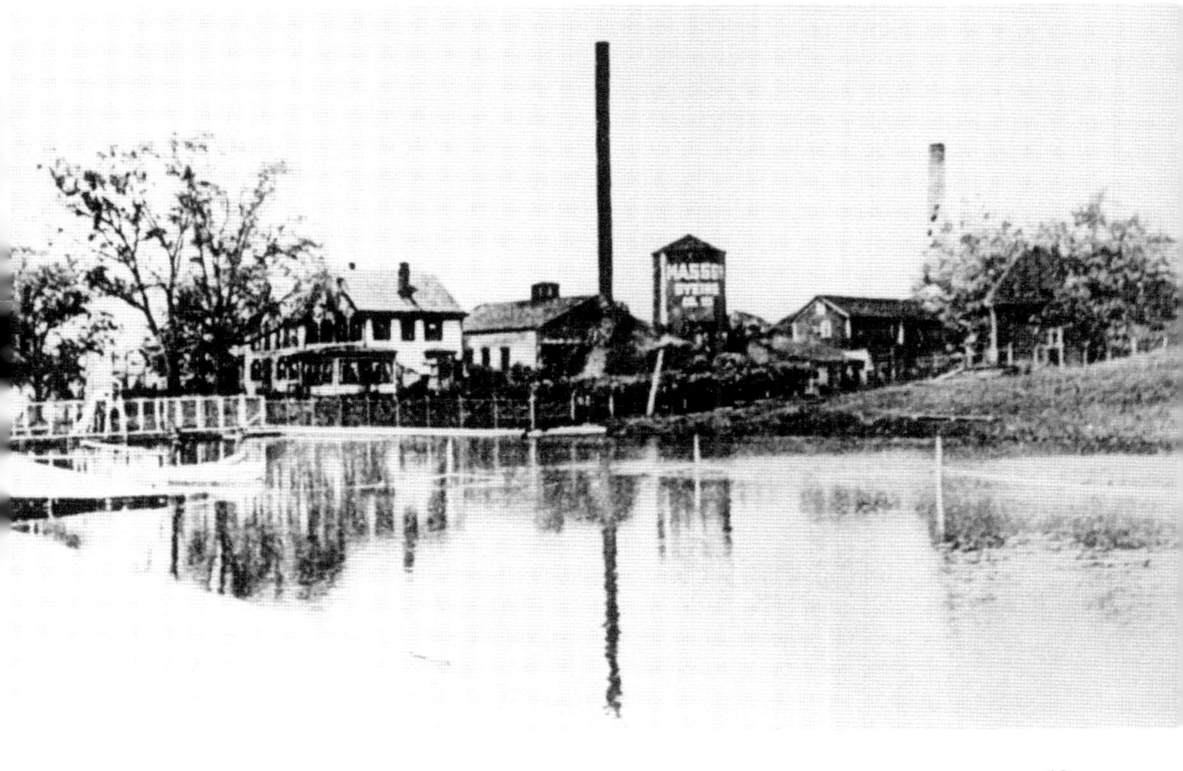

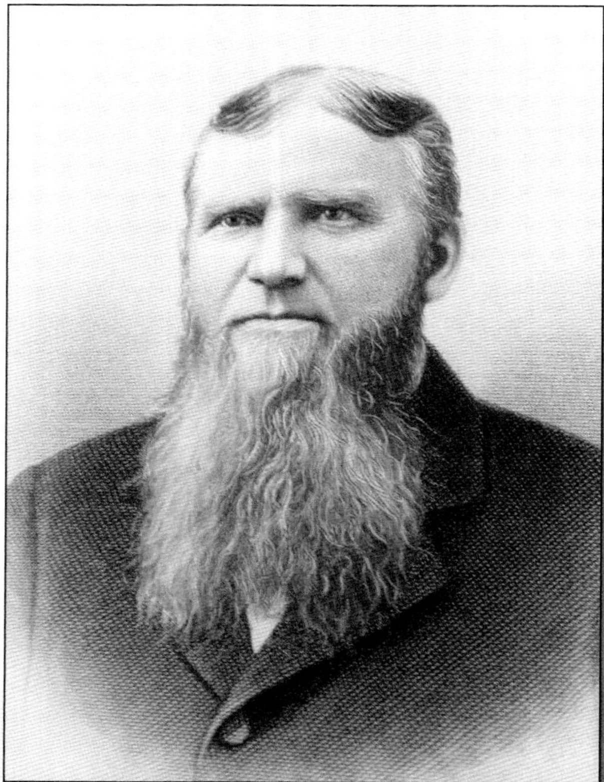

Fair Lawn Estate

David Depeyster Acker was a prosperous Manhattan merchant who bought a farm and, later, built a large house in the country on Small Lots Road. About 1863, he moved his family to the house at the top of the hill and put in a spacious lawn sweeping down to the road. He called his estate Fair Lawn. When the railroad was built through town in 1881, Acker built a shed where the road crossed the tracks and put up a sign that read, "Fair Lawn." When the railroad built a station there, it was also called Fair Lawn. Later, Small Lots Road and the Small Lots section of Saddle River Township were named after the station. When the citizens of the area separated from the township in 1924, they decided to call their new borough Fair Lawn. (Left, illustration from *History of Bergen and Passaic Counties, New Jersey* by Woodford Clayton.)

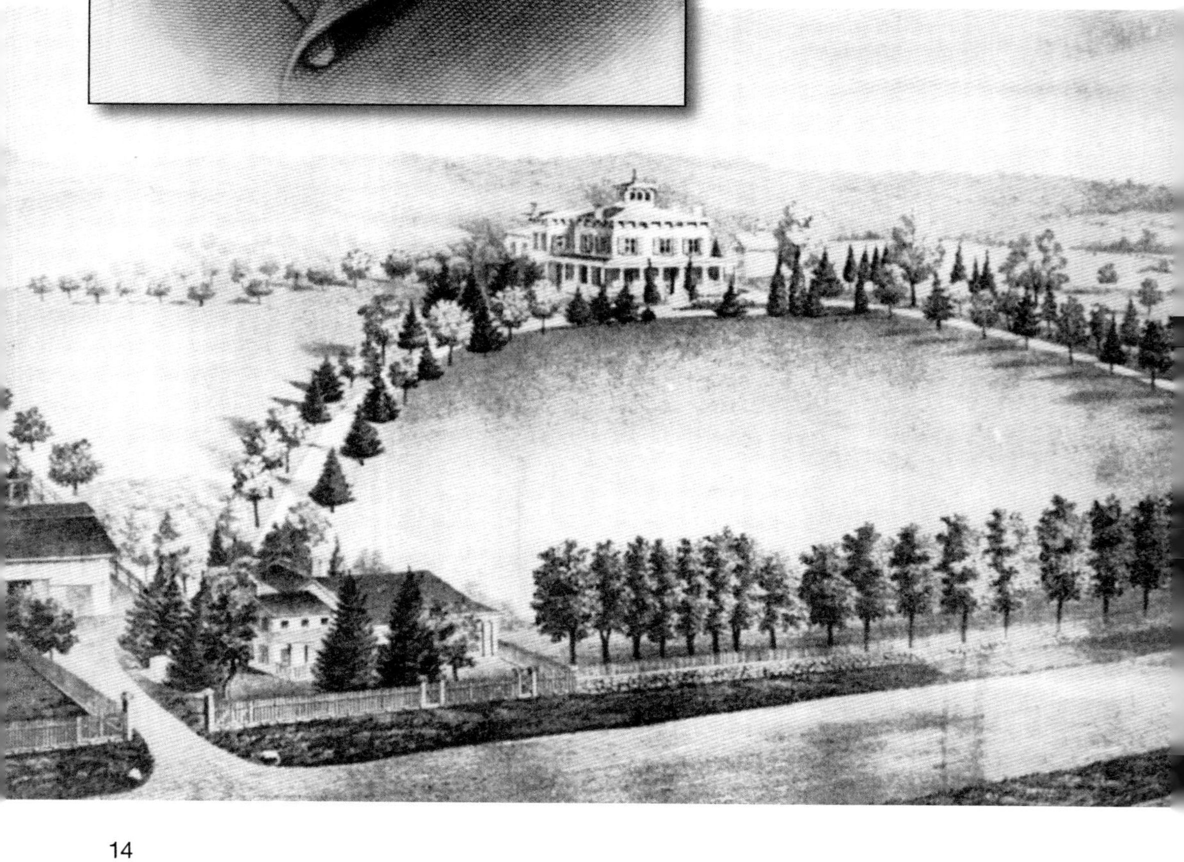

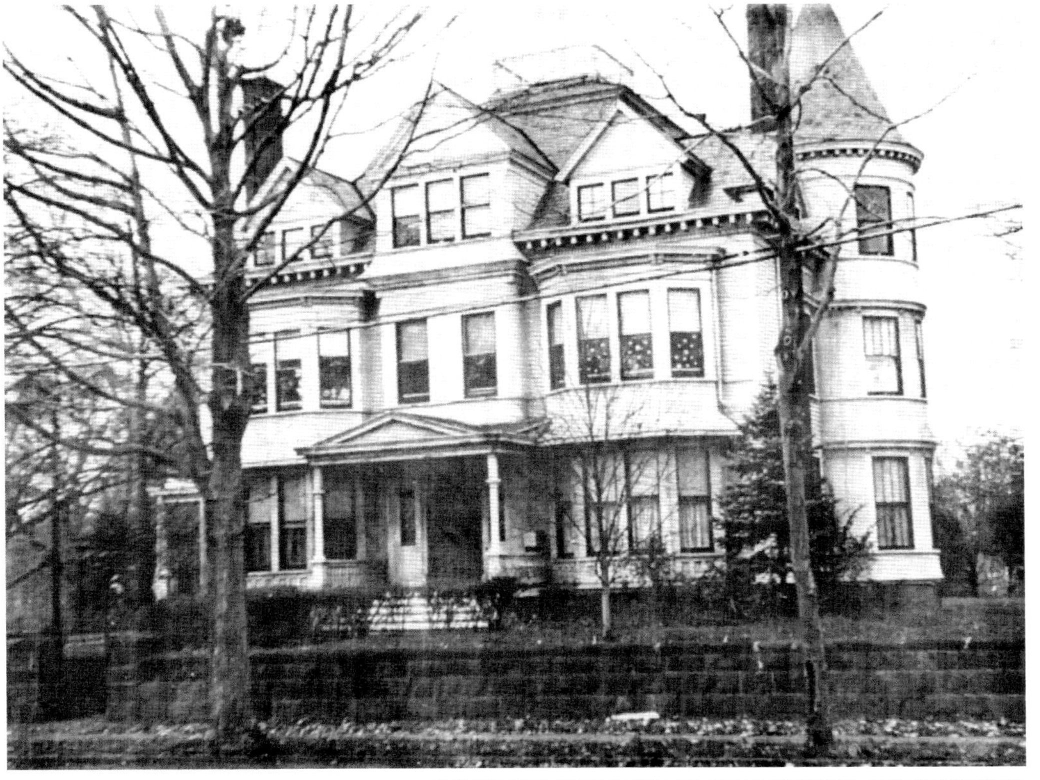

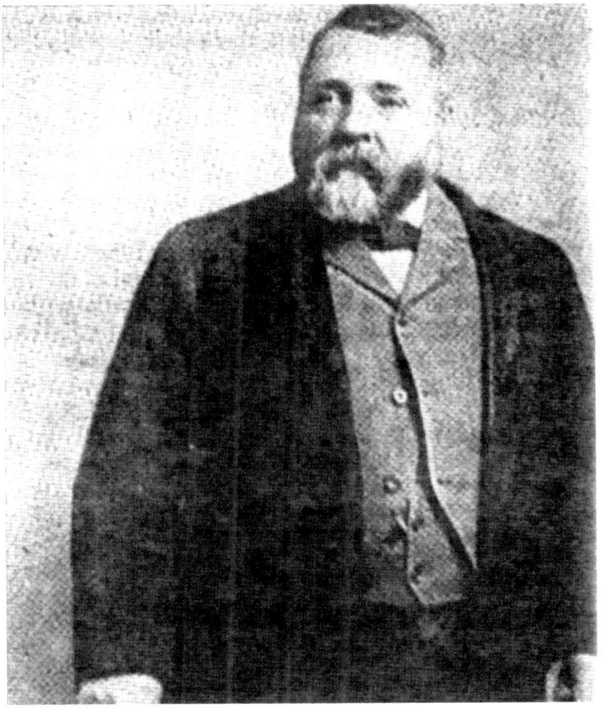

A Mysterious Disappearance
George Morlot was a prosperous silk dyer who built a 24-room mansion on the street now named for him. On a Saturday in March 1894, he withdrew $4,000 from his bank to pay his workers. But he did not go to his dye works; he boarded a train bound for Manhattan and was never seen again. A fellow passenger who looked for him said that he had vanished "as if the ground had opened and swallowed him up." Police conducted investigations on both sides of the Hudson River, but the mystery of his disappearance was never solved.

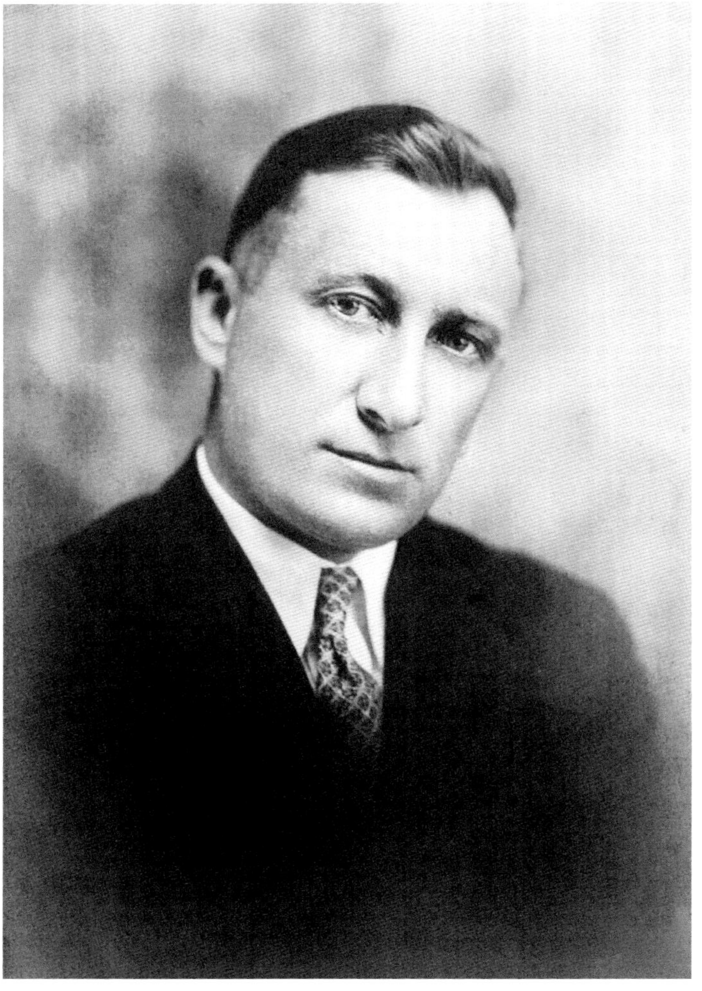

A Founder and His Family

Nicholas "Nick" Kuiken took an early interest in local government, starting when he was elected to the Saddle River Township Committee in 1922. He was one of the founders of the movement to separate from the township; many meetings of the separatists were held in the Kuiken store. Nick Kuiken served as the second mayor of Fair Lawn, from 1931 to 1937. He later was elected a Bergen County freeholder and held the office for three terms, serving as chairman of the public works committee. Nick Kuiken came to New Jersey with his family from Holland in 1898, moving to Fair Lawn four years later. He became a carpenter and joined his brothers and a cousin in the construction business, which they had founded in 1912 as Kuiken Brothers. Nick Kuiken was also active in business affairs. He was a founder of both the Fair Lawn–Radburn Trust Company, of which he was president, and the Fair Lawn Building and Loan Association, which is today the Columbia Bank. Many of the Kuiken family members were active in Fair Lawn affairs. Several Kuikens served as firemen with Fair Lawn Company No. 1, and Nicholas A. was an early president of the company. Evan Kuiken was a founder of the Fair Lawn State Bank, now Valley National Bank. Nick's brother Henry Kuiken was chairman of the borough's first planning board and was chairman of the Citizens Committee for Council-Manager Government, the group that led the drive for the new form of government for the borough. (Courtesy of Doug Kuiken.)

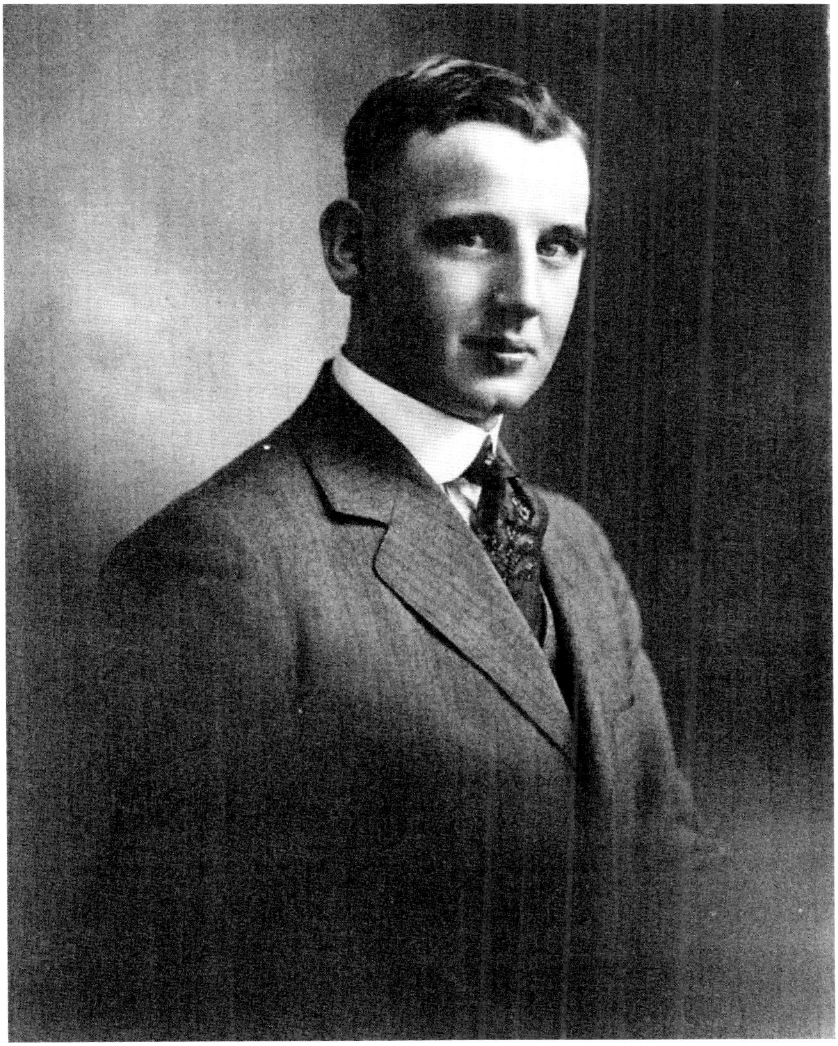

A Campaigner for Independence

Samuel Greydanus was born in today's Fair Lawn. Sam, as he was called, was one of the people who went to Trenton to lobby for Fair Lawn's separation from Saddle River Township. He was a captain of the marshals before there was a police department, a member of the first fire department, and a justice of the peace. Later, he served as president of the board of education. Greydanus was head of the borough road department and, later, first superintendent of the department of public works. In 1938, he became president of the Anti-Slavery and Aborigines Protective Association of Fair Lawn, a group of borough employees working for "freedom" from the patronage system. The group campaigned for the establishment of civil service to prevent the firing of workers whenever a different faction was elected to the council. (Courtesy of Carol G. Bennett.)

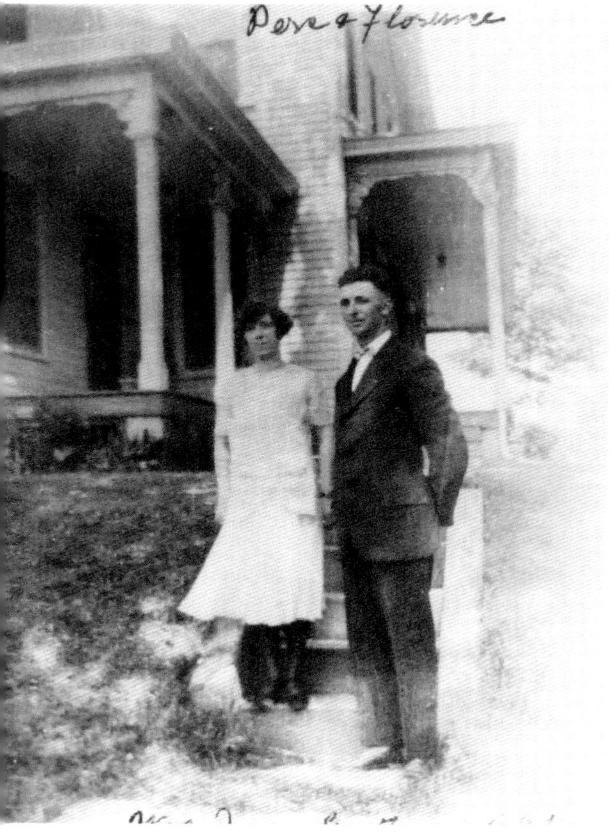

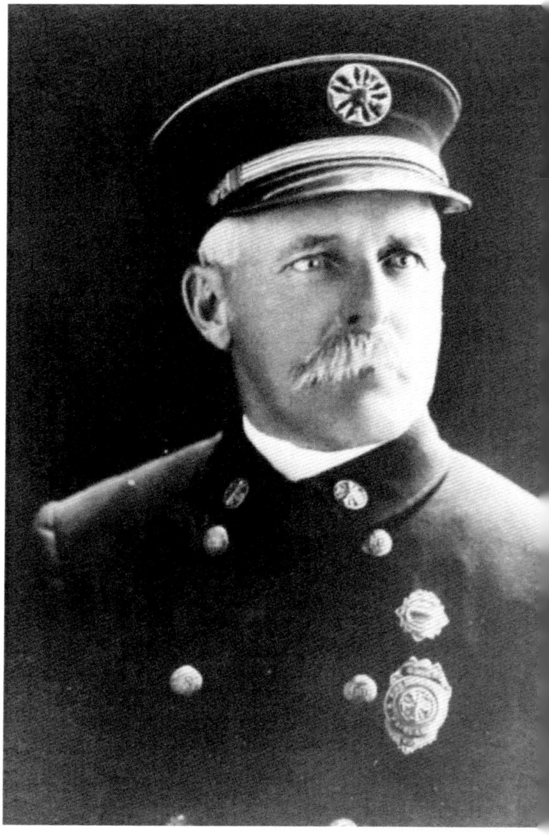

Two Civic-minded Founders

William M. Croucher Sr. bought the Henry Hopper farm in 1919 and was one of the founders of the borough in 1924. He served as councilman from then until 1930 and became the first police commissioner. He was instrumental in the paving of Fair Lawn Avenue so that the bus company could extend its Paterson route to Radburn. One of Croucher's sons, Percy (a volunteer fireman), married Charles Vogel's daughter Florence (pictured at left), uniting the two civic-minded families. Charles Vogel started the Fair Lawn Volunteer Firemen's Association in 1911 and was Fair Lawn's first fire chief. The fire truck was kept in his barn; when an alarm sounded, Chief Vogel would hitch his plow horses to the truck and gallop to the fire. Vogel was also an early councilman. (Left, courtesy of Jim Croucher; right, courtesy of CH.)

CHAPTER TWO

The Community Builders

Fair Lawn has always been know as a volunteer town, starting with the first volunteer fire company organized in 1911. It was volunteers who built the town into a community with cultural, civic, religious, and sports opportunities and services to keep the community safe.

The Fair Lawn Improvement Association, a Fair Lawn Center civic group, successfully agitated for borough water service in 1927 and a road department to pave the dirt roads in 1932. Volunteers started the Boy Scouts and the Girl Scouts; recreation organizations, such as the Athletic Club and the Boys Club; and many sectional and town-wide civic associations, including the League of Women Voters.

Many of the early houses of worship were started through the efforts of residents. Citizens worked tirelessly for new schools, the public library, a master plan, and the council-manager form of government. Volunteers staffed the many divisions of the civil defense and disaster control organization. Residents worked to establish Walsh Pool and Memorial Pool and Park, the Community School, and the Opportunity Center. The fire companies, the ambulance corps, and the rescue squad are all vital volunteer services.

Volunteers of another kind were the men who served the United States in the armed forces. Many of these were unsung heroes; the stories here are only a small sample of tales about servicemen from three wars.

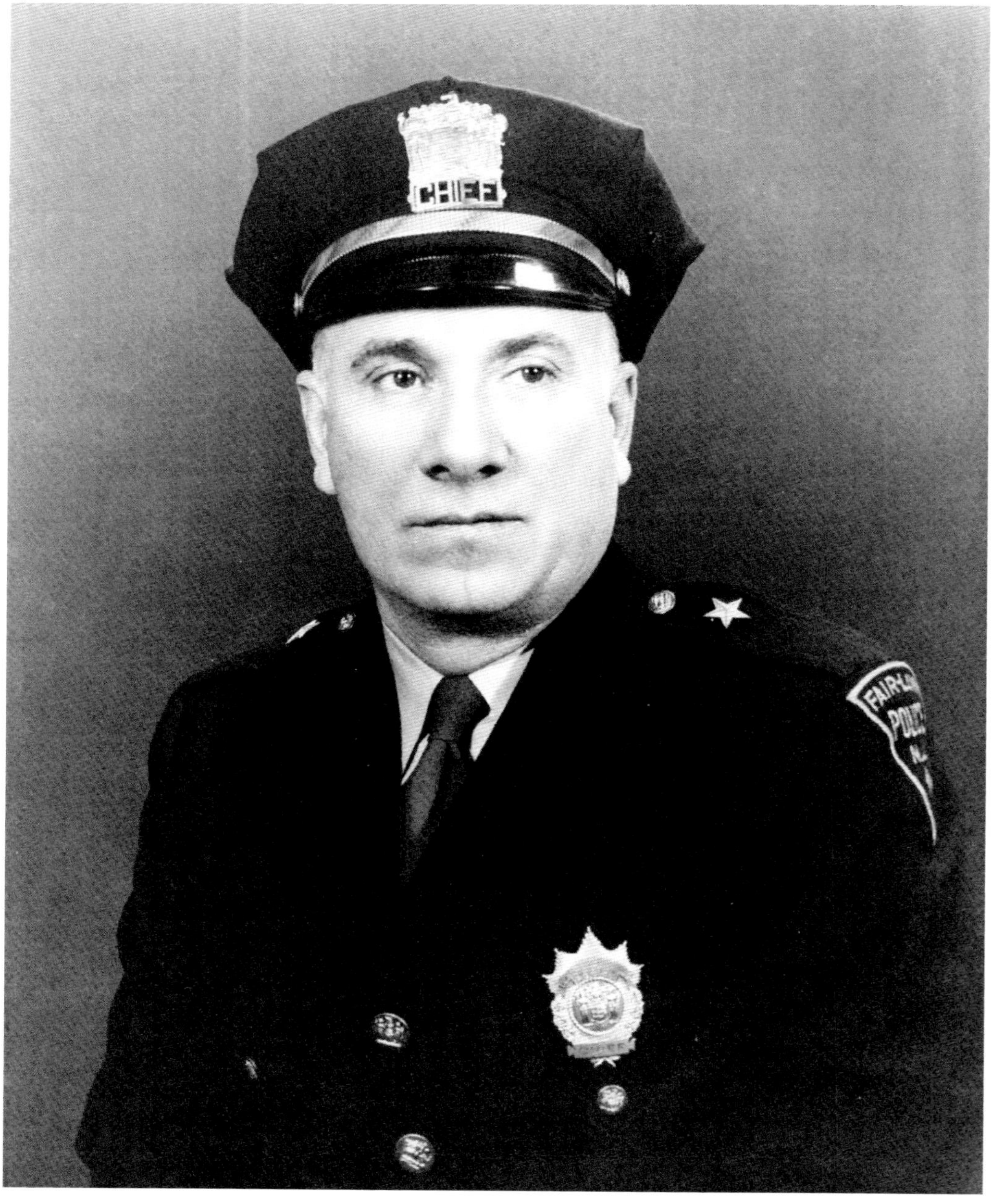

The First Police Chief

Michael Vanore was Fair Lawn's first police chief when the department was established in 1930. Before then, 13 part-time marshals on an on-call status served the borough. Vanore, who had been a constable for Saddle River Township, was appointed chief marshal when the force was created in 1924 at the borough's beginning. The building of Radburn and the opening of the Textile Dying and Printing Company, with resulting increased traffic, made a full-time department necessary. Chief Vanore guided the growth of the department from four full-time men in 1930 to 21 in 1949. He continued to serve as chief until his death in 1955. (Courtesy of CH.)

A War Hero

Harry Coppendyke volunteered for the Army during World War I at the age of 19. He was the first Fair Lawn serviceman lost in the war, killed in action in the battle of the Meuse-Argonne in October 1918. Very few members of his 114th Infantry Battalion survived the battle. When the local American Legion post was chartered, it took Coppendyke's name in his honor. Coppendyke's father, Cornelius, married into the Jim James family and lived in his father-in-law's house where Harry was born. The house was known as Elm Tree Farm and is still standing on Saddle River Road. (Courtesy of John Delaney, Harry Coppendyke American Legion Post No. 171.)

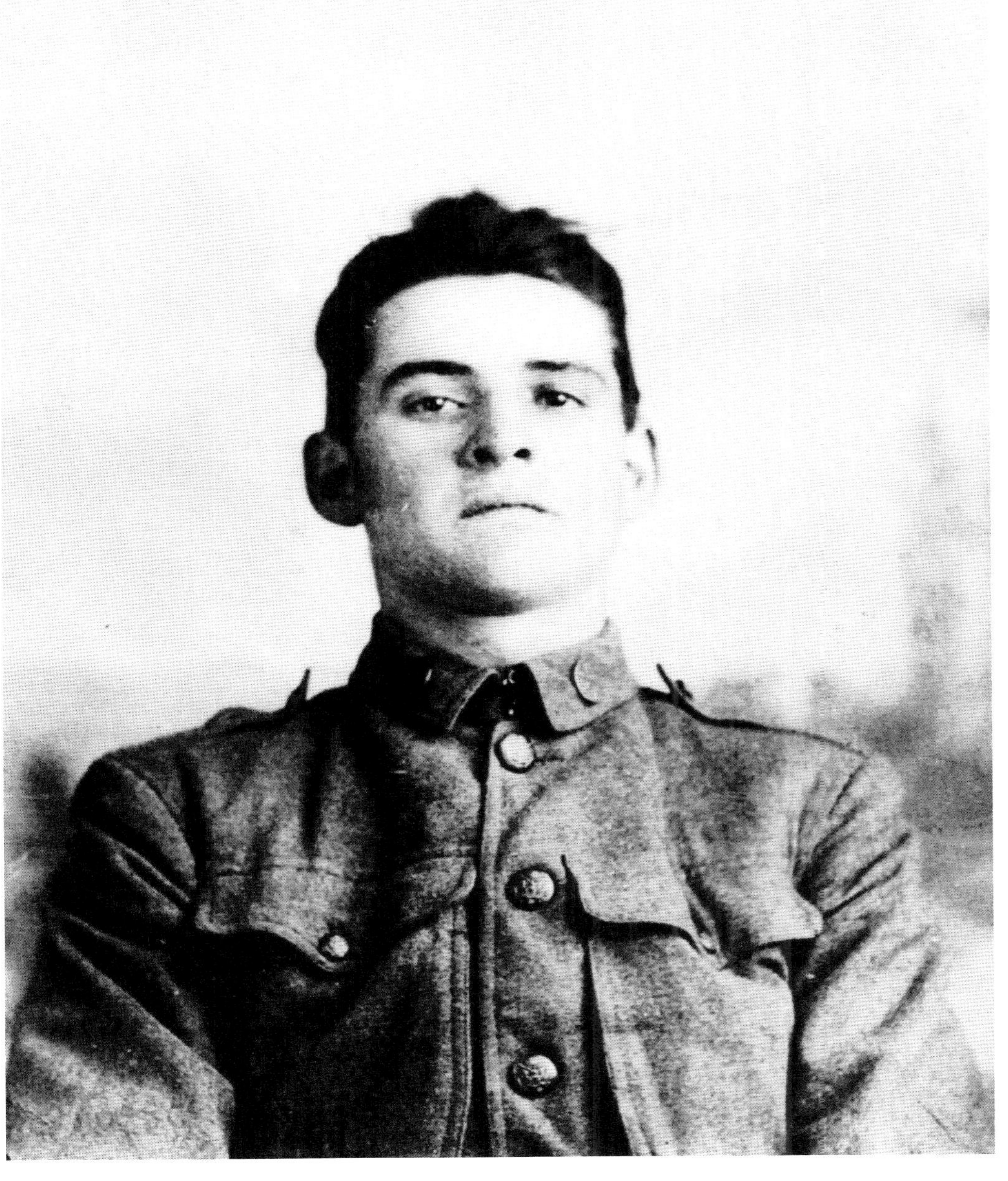

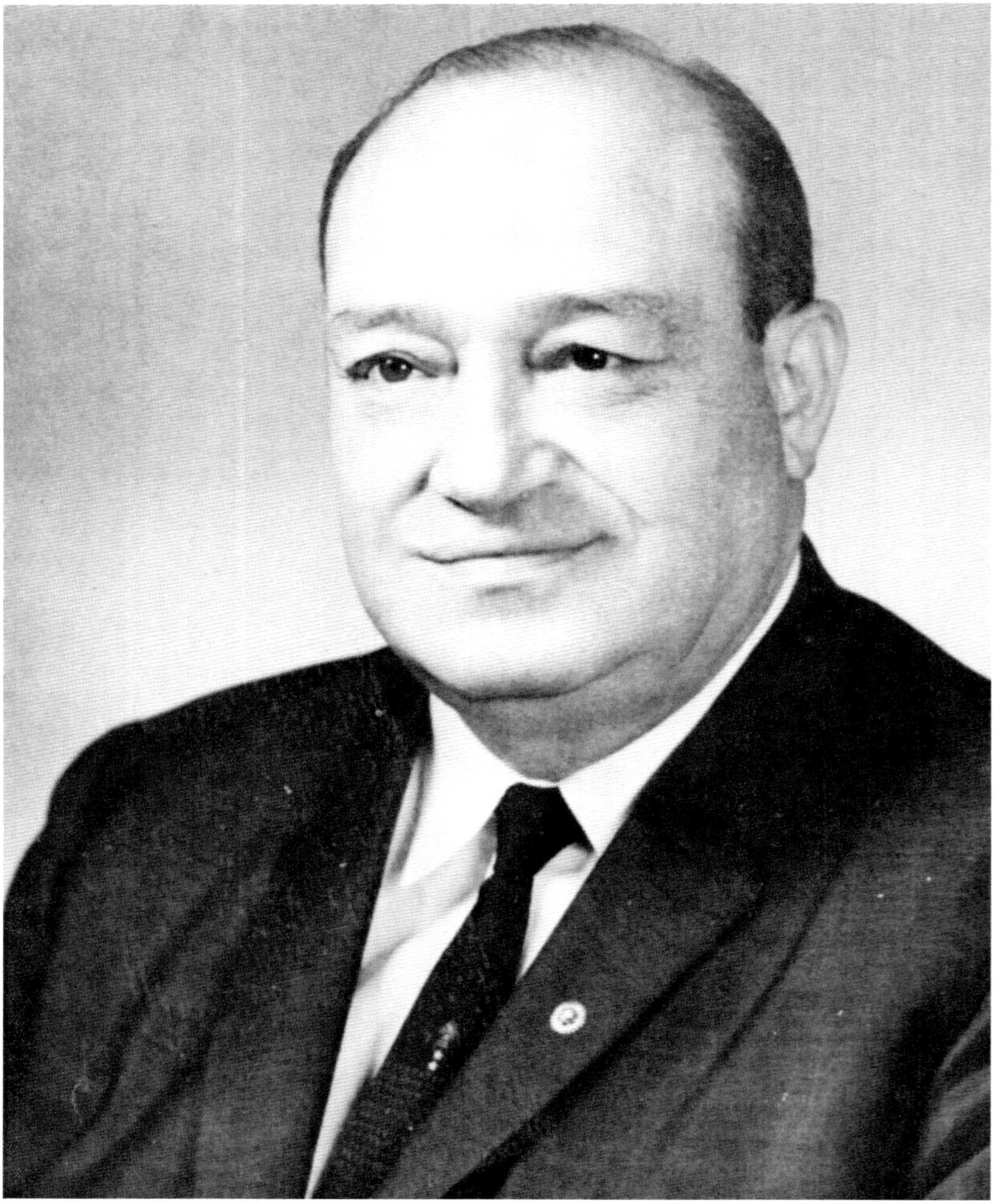

A Man Devoted to Fair Lawn

Michael Canger was a longtime member of Fair Lawn's first planning board, starting in 1939, and was instrumental in shaping the development of the town during its fastest-growing years. Later, he served as borough engineer and then as councilman and deputy mayor. Mike Canger was also a founder of the Cosmos Club and was active in many civic, fraternal, professional, and social organizations. When the founders of Memorial Park and Pool sought donations of equipment, labor, and services to construct the pool and surrounding parkland, Canger's firm contributed engineering services, and Canger Contracting donated labor and machinery. Canger served as master of ceremonies at the park's dedication.

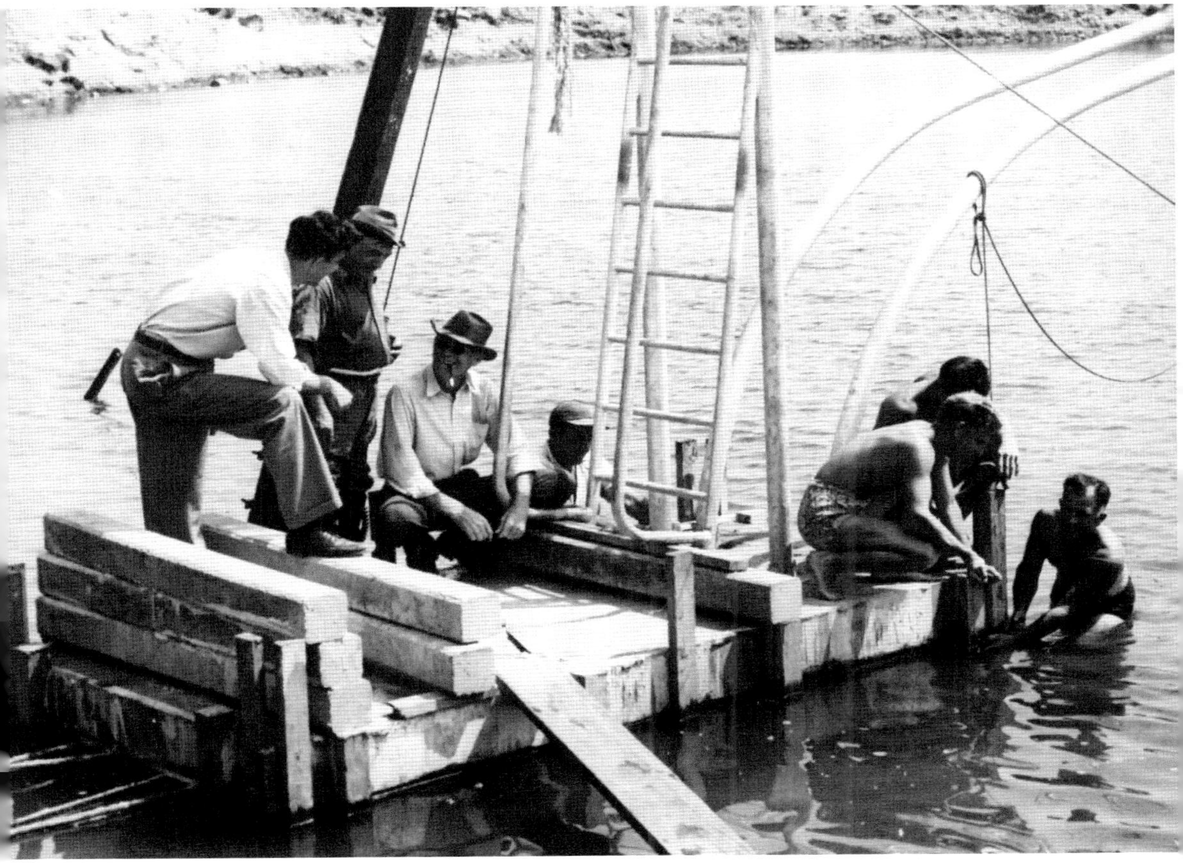

Memorial Pool Founders

Postmaster Cameron "Mac" McCurdy and his neighbor Bill Eaton were talking about the drownings at the abandoned sand pit, which had filled with water and was used as an unsupervised swimming hole. They thought the 33-acre property, owned by the borough, could be developed into a municipal pool and park with lifeguards to watch over the swimmers. The Memorial Park Civic Group was established in 1948 with McCurdy as its president. Because local government funds were not available, the group members persuaded contractors, builders, and other businesses to donate materials, equipment, services, and labor to clear and grade the land and pool bottom and to build roads and facilities. The United Organizations of Fair Lawn, a wartime coalition, suggested that the park be dedicated to the veterans of both World Wars and donated its remaining funds toward the project. The park was dedicated on Memorial Day 1949, and the pool was opened on the Fourth of July. In the photograph, Mac McCurdy is shown third from the left, and Bill Eaton is in the water at the far right. Recreation director Monte Weed is at the extreme left. (Courtesy of the Fair Lawn Recreation and Parks Department.)

Founder of the Library

Maurice Pine, known to all as "Piney," was a local dentist who founded the Fair Lawn Library Association in 1933 and established a small library next to his office. When the borough appointed the library board of trustees in 1936, Dr. Pine was chosen president, a position he held through the 1970s. He helped to guide the growth of the library in its many homes throughout his long tenure. In recognition of his service, the 185,000-volume library now bears his name. Dr. Pine also served as president of the board of education from 1955 through 1957. (Courtesy of the Fair Lawn Public Library.)

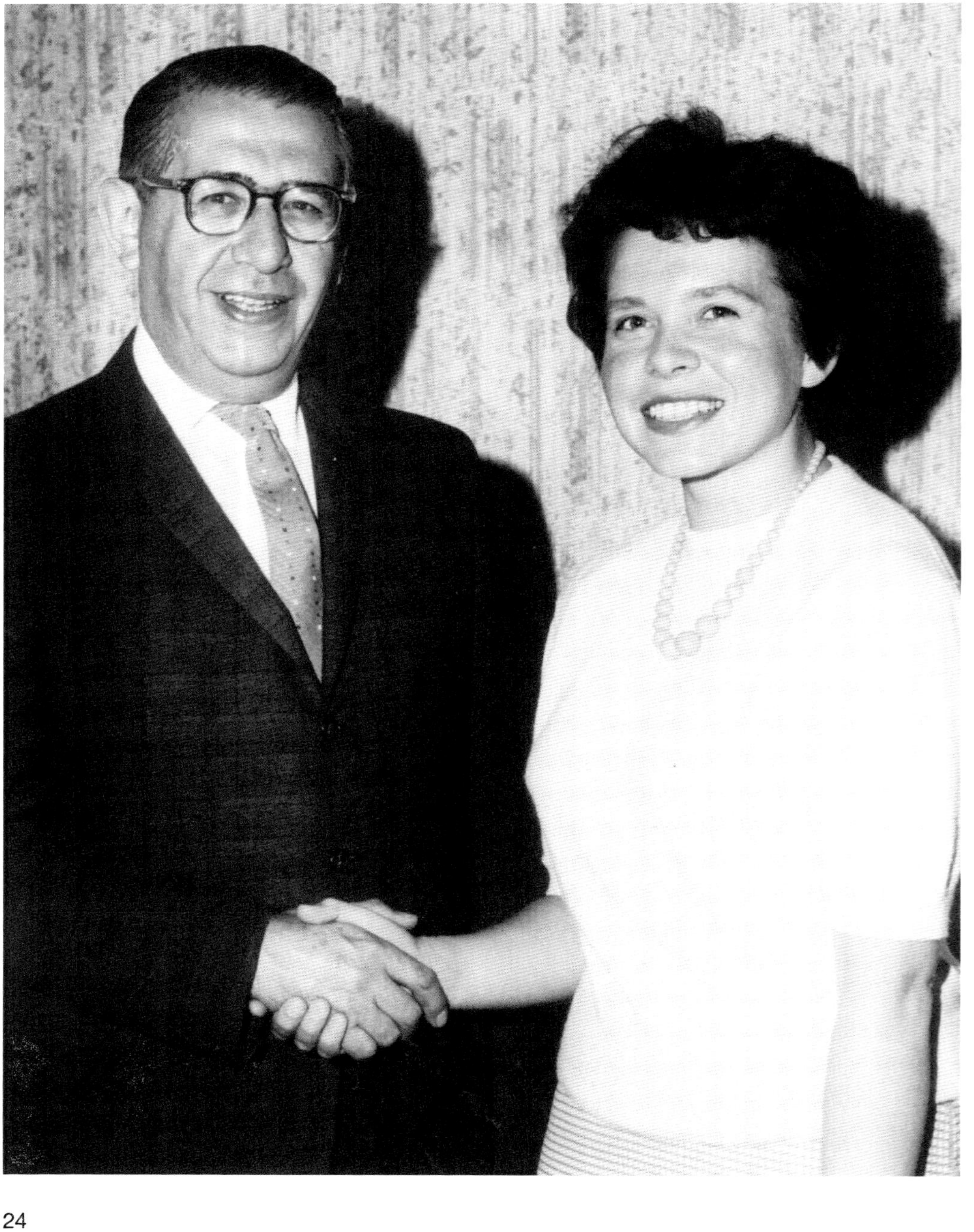

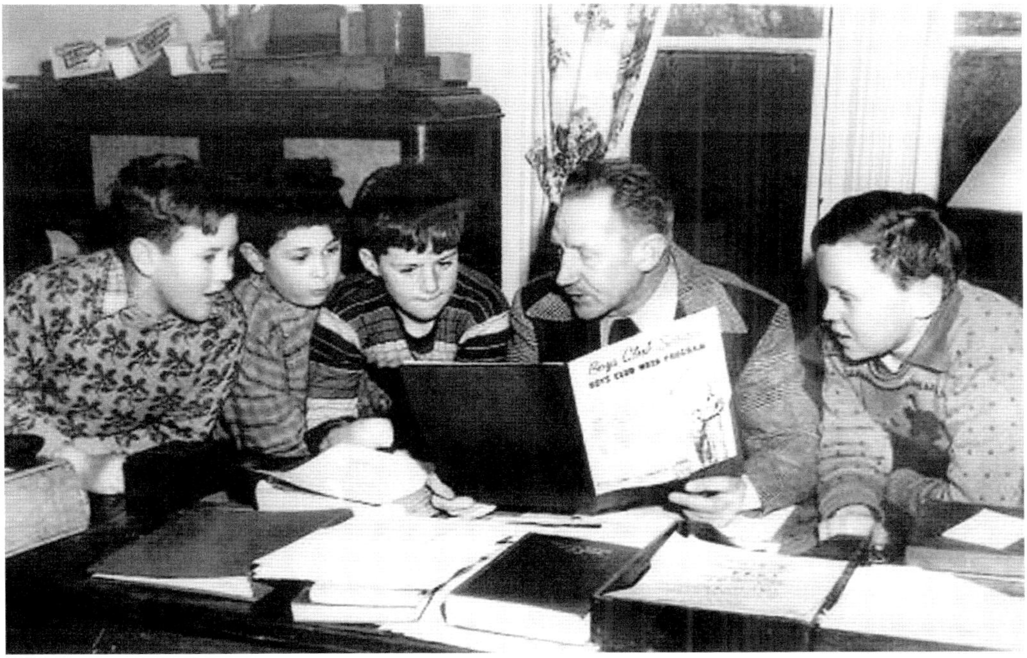

Boys Club Legend

In 1939, police chief Michael Vanore and a group of local businessmen asked Henry Milnes to start a Boys Club for local youth. Milnes and his wife, Esther, took on the job, using the large Adam Hopper home and barn to house numerous sports and recreational activities. In the attic was a radio club run by Bell Labs scientist Roger Carlton. Milnes also developed a summer camp for the boys in Kinnelon, New Jersey, on land donated by Carl Carlson. The boys called the fatherly leader "Pop" Milnes. He led the Boys Club until his death in 1952. Milnes School was named in his honor. (Above, courtesy of the Fair Lawn High School Athletic Hall of Fame; below, courtesy of Cadmus House Museum.)

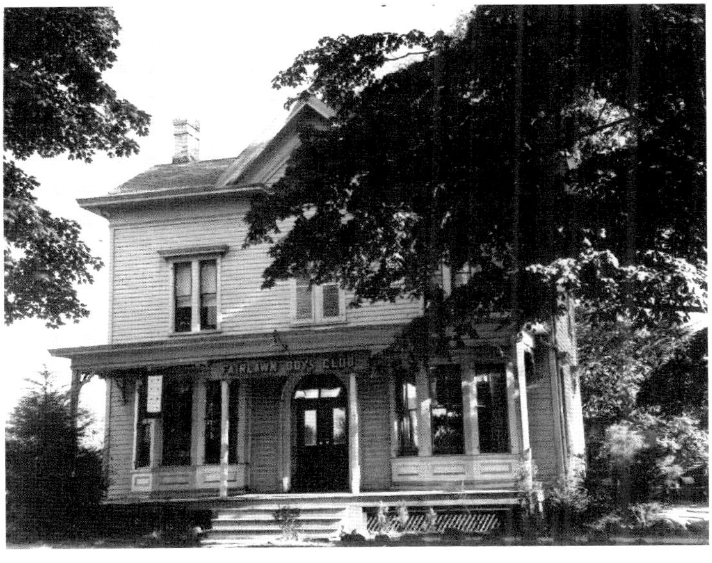

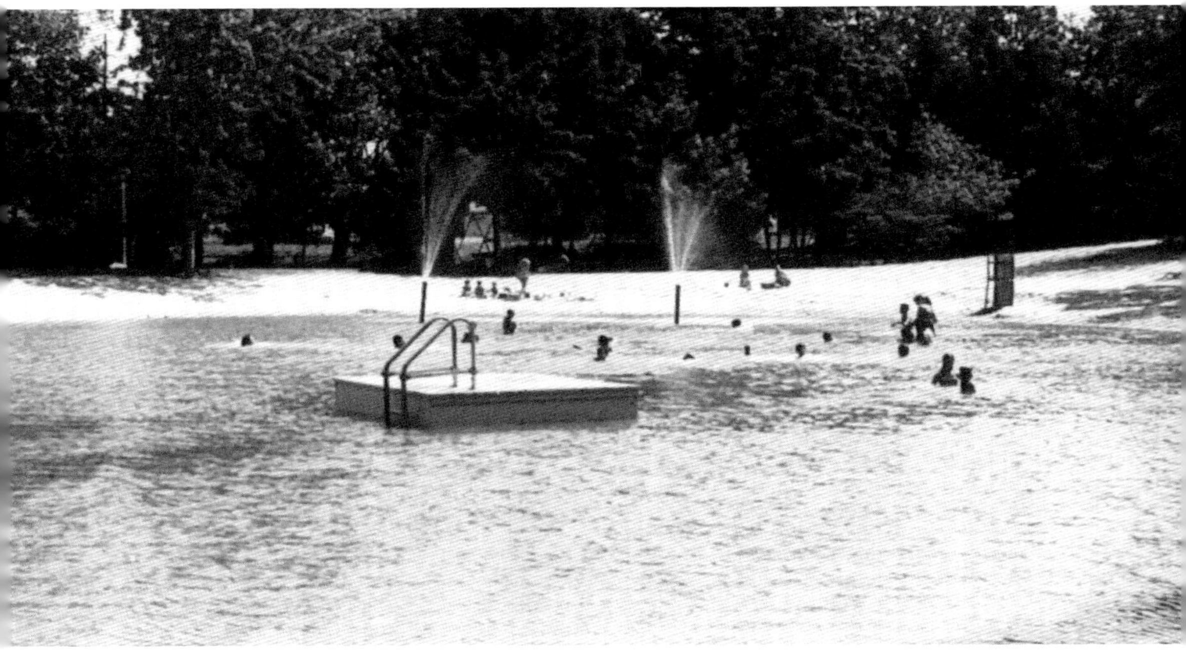

Walsh Pool Advocate

Helda Walsh was a director of the Boys Club and was active in the Columbia Heights Association. She persuaded the borough to allocate the land around Snyder's Pond for a neighborhood swimming pool and led the Columbia Terrace Pool Association in developing and running the pool. It was named in her honor in 1962. The pool has now been drained to provide for a skateboard or other recreational facility. (Courtesy of CH.)

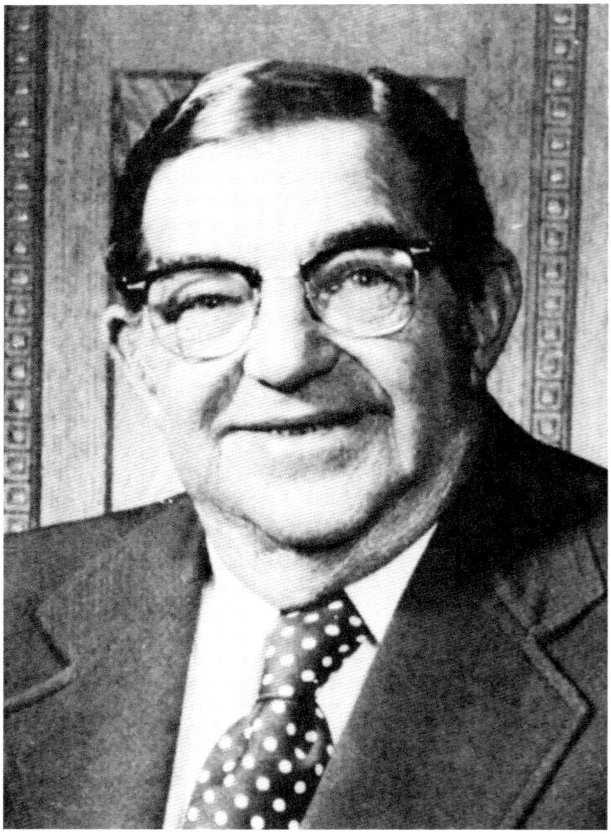

Opportunity Center Founder

John Gottlieb was a founder of the Opportunity Center and led the fund drive to provide a facility to teach skills to adults with mental and physical challenges so they may develop their full potentials. Gottlieb served on the holiday celebrations committee and was chairman of Fair Lawn's 40th and 50th anniversary celebrations. He was elected councilman and became a deputy mayor.

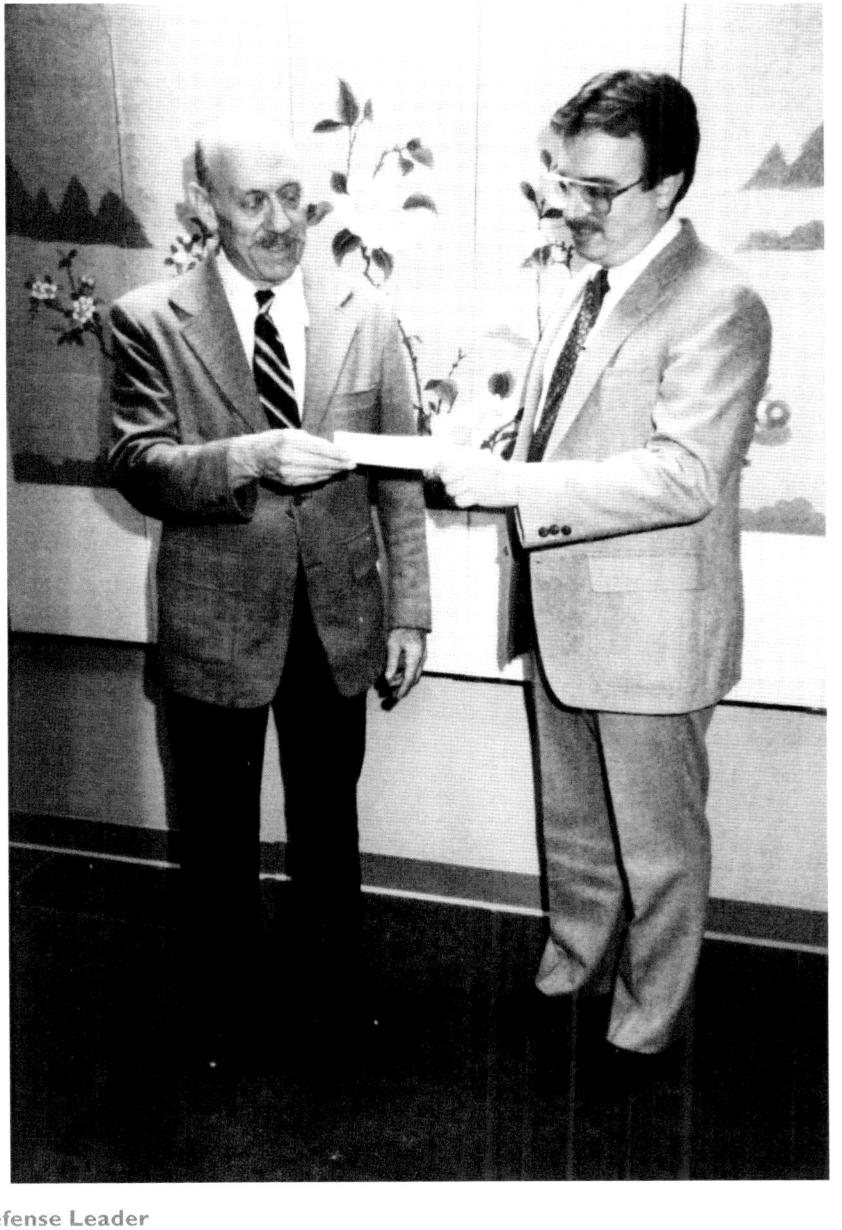

Civil Defense Leader

Carl Koenig served as director of Fair Lawn's civil defense and disaster control (CD-DC) organization for more than 20 years, starting in 1952. Under his direction, the focus of the CD-DC moved from planning for possible enemy attack to preparation for natural and other disasters. He served as the volunteer county CD-DC coordinator and as consultant and staff engineer for the board that developed the civil defense survival plan for the tri-state metropolitan area. He then became project director in charge of developing the civil defense plan for the state. One of the leaders in preserving the historic Cadmus House, "Colonel" Koenig was a longtime president of the group that developed the house into the borough museum. He was responsible for securing collections and opening the museum to the public. This photograph shows Koenig, left, accepting a grant from Ike Herman of Lea & Perrins. (Courtesy of CH.)

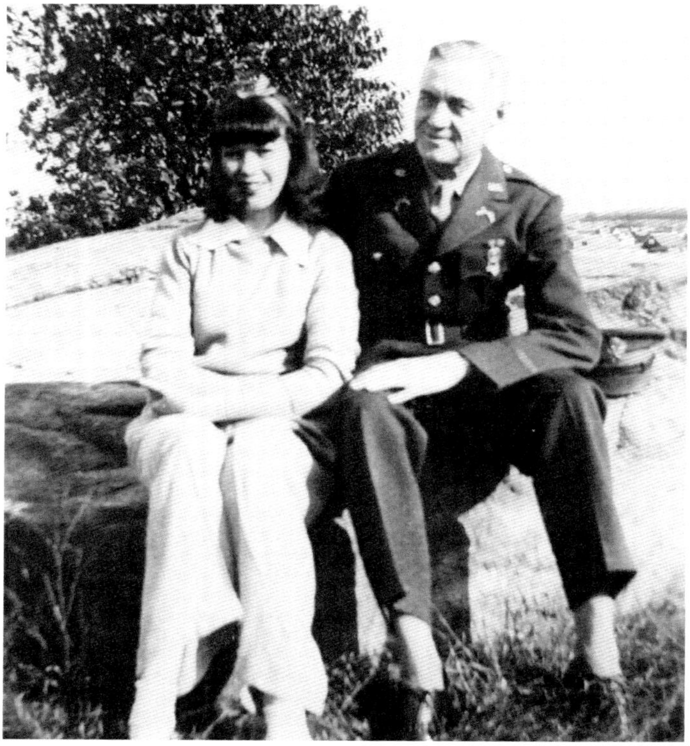

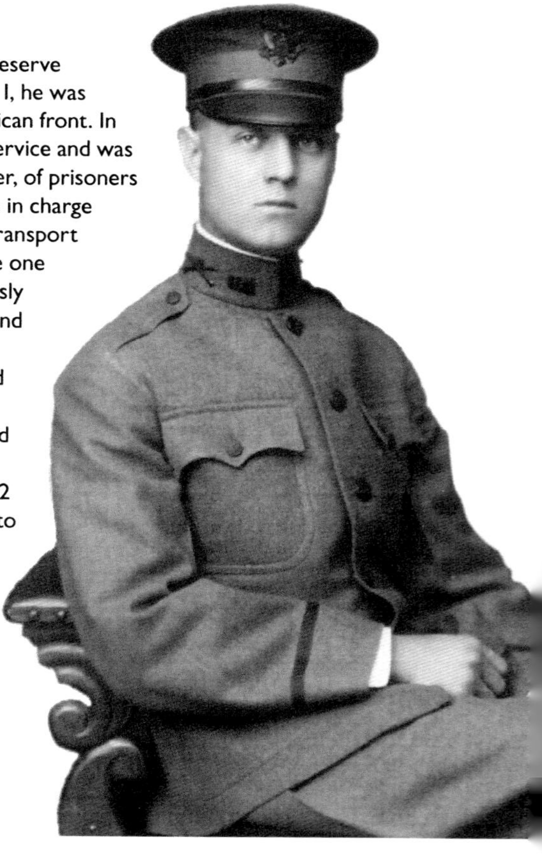

War Brides

Floyd Lyle, known as Pete to his friends, was an Army Reserve officer who served in both World Wars. In World War I, he was a temporary captain as adjutant to a general at the Mexican front. In 1942, by then a lieutenant colonel, he volunteered for service and was put in charge of troops going by ship to England and, later, of prisoners coming to the United States from North Africa. He was in charge of more transports across the Atlantic than any other transport commander. Still in the service, he reported to his office one day in January 1946 and found the desk officer suspiciously glad to see him. He was hastily sent to embark for England to be in charge of the first contingent of British war brides—some with infants—coming to America, aboard the SS *Argentina*. The last-minute assignment was due to the fact that the officer who was slated to do the job had shown up intoxicated. Colonel Lyle was responsible for the welfare of 452 brides, 171 infants and children, and 12 newspapermen and photographers on a stormy voyage to New York. He later called it "the diaper run." He gave a heartwarming welcoming speech to the brides, saying, "We are cousins, not in blood and language alone, but in a heritage of freedom and democracy." At right, Lyle is pictured in World War I; above, he is on leave with his daughter during World War II.

A Different War Story

In 1968 in Vietnam, Capt. James Storozuk was an American advisor to a Vietnamese patrol living off the land for a two-week training period. On the 13th day, Storozuk decided to march his half-starved patrol on the shortest route to base camp and food—down Highway 14, called "a street without joy"—instead of avoiding contact in the jungle. Soon, the point man jumped up and down excitedly as if the enemy were coming. Instead, a huge bull elephant was lumbering toward them—possibly a rogue. The men were lacking enough firepower to stop an elephant, but Storozuk hoped to stun or scare the beast with smoke grenades. The plan was for Storozuk to fire when the elephant reached a point 75 yards away. At that time, the patrol would split and escape by circling around the animal. Instead, the elephant suddenly veered into the jungle. The troops ran past the beast as it was crashing into the trees and made it to the base camp safely. Storozuk says that he was lucky, like all the servicemen who survived. He knows many of the war stories of "the lucky ones" from Fair Lawn and regrets that they could not be told here.

Jim Storozuk served 18 months in Vietnam with several groups, including the 5th Special Forces. He made 15 parachute jumps to qualify for the Master Parachutist badge. He has been a Fair Lawn resident since 1942 and served on the board of ethics, as chair of the local veterans council, and as coeditor of *Fair Lawn's 50th Anniversary Journal*.

In 2004, Storozuk, along with Harvey Mayer, assembled the names of all the veterans from Fair Lawn who had been killed in wars. They put those 47 names on two memorials they designed, one at the municipal building and one at Memorial Park, pictured at right. They also created paver walks at the borough hall with the names and ranks of Fair Lawn veterans. (Top, courtesy of Jim Storozuk.)

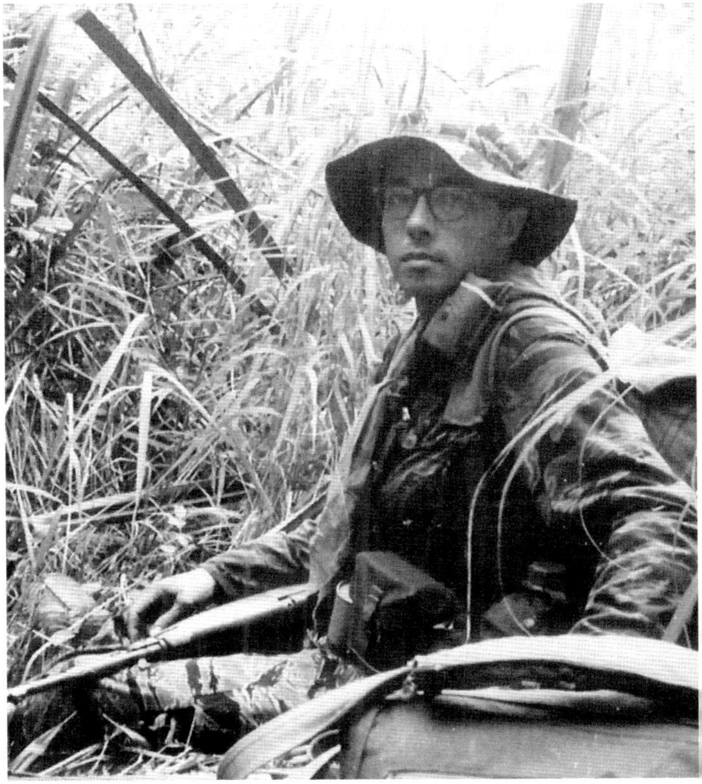

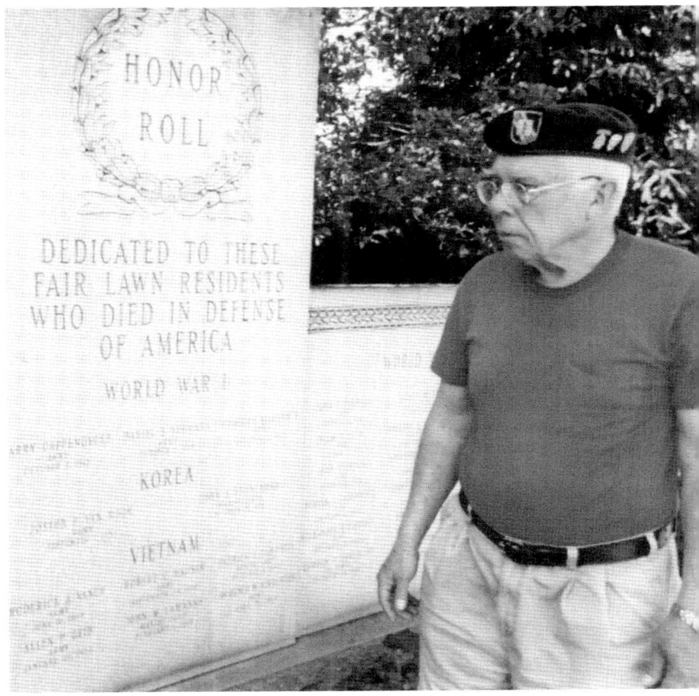

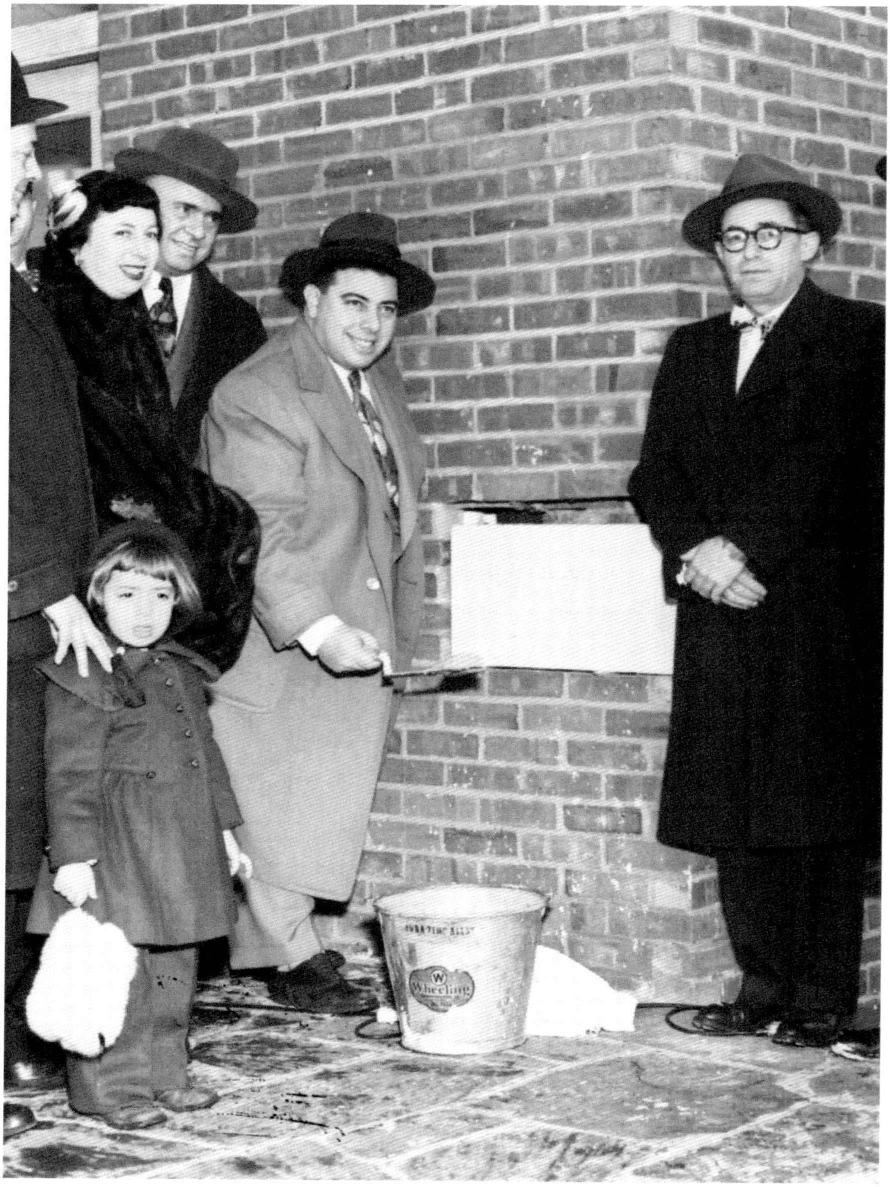

A Leading Couple

Marge and Julian Bornstein were a dynamic couple who were deeply involved in borough affairs. Both worked for the establishment of the Fair Lawn Jewish Center, the borough's first synagogue. Julian was a founding member and a president of the center. Marge was described as a leading light at the start of the center. Both Bornsteins were also interested in civic affairs. Julian joined the Nonpartisan League and was elected to a three-year term as councilman, starting in 1953. Marge served on the board of education for 12 years and was its president during a period of school expansion. The Bornsteins were also active in several Jewish organizations including the Jewish Federation of North Jersey, of which Julian Bornstein served as president. The Cadmus House photograph shows Julian Bornstein laying the cornerstone of the Jewish Center with Marge at his side.

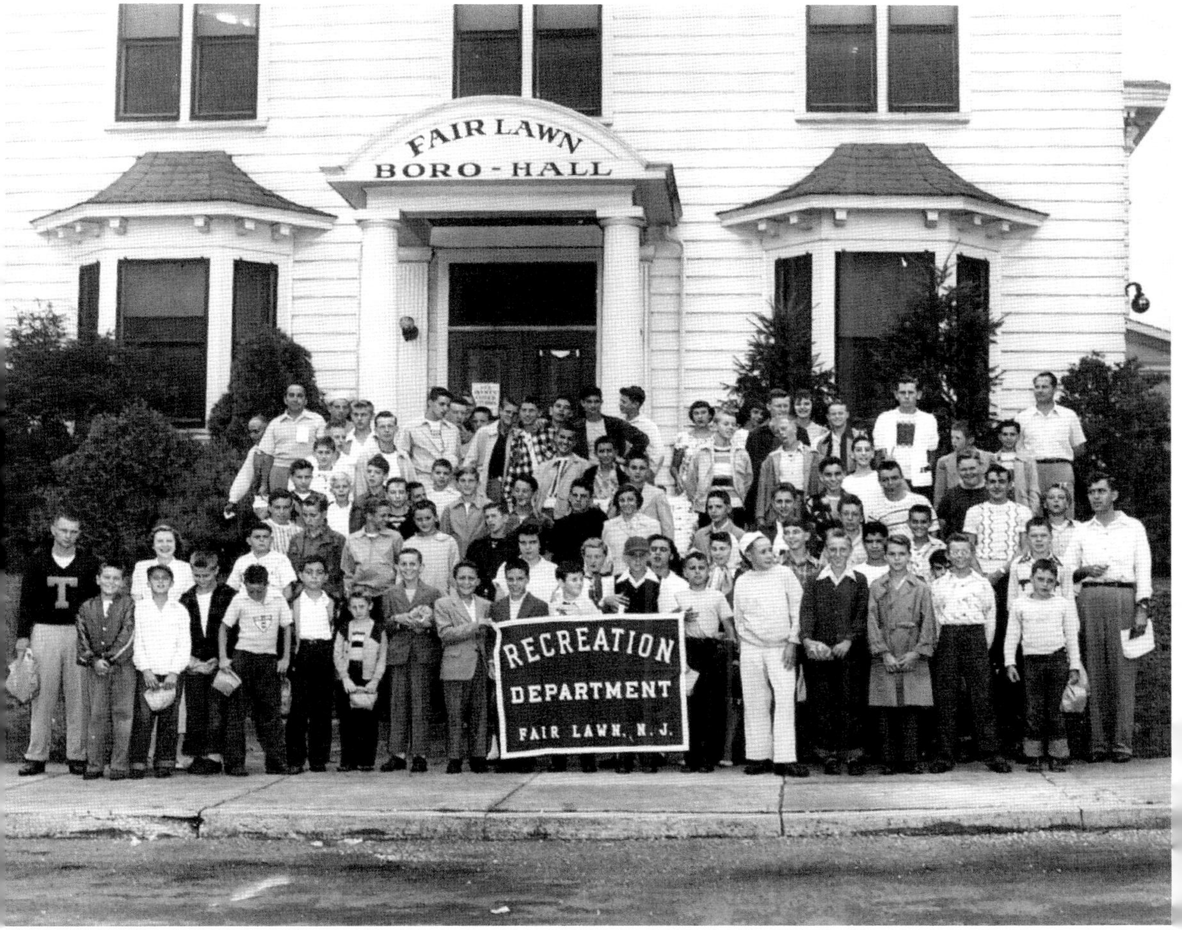

Recreation Program Founder

Monte Weed came to Fair Lawn as recreation director in 1948 and developed the local recreation program into one of the most comprehensive in the nation. He increased the number of playgrounds from 4 to 14 and instituted activities for all age groups, from toddlers to seniors, ranging from table tennis to art and theater. In 1951, Weed inaugurated the Fair Lawn Little League baseball program, of which he was commissioner. The first team sponsors were the Veterans of Foreign Wars, the Police Benevolent Association, Sun Photo, and Strehl's Pharmacy. The field was at Memorial Park, which saw its first home run by Charlie Hochkeppel. Weed had a national reputation in his field, receiving several awards from the National Recreation Association for outstanding contribution and devoted service to public recreation and parks. He served as president of the New Jersey State Recreation Association. His lifelong experience with youth included service as a teacher and a Scout executive. Weed turned down a post with the National Recreation Association because he did not want to leave Fair Lawn, the town he loved. He was proud of all "his kids" who had come through the program he founded, Fair Lawn All-Sports Association, such as Olympic sprinter Dr. Dave Sime and Los Angeles Dodger relief pitcher Ron Perranoski. Monte Weed is shown at the extreme right of the photograph.

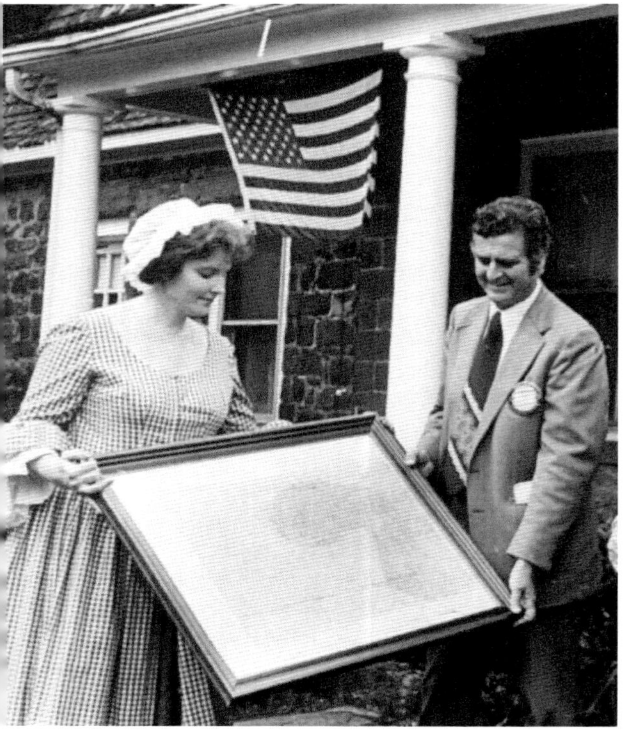

Savior of the Garretson House

Lois Horowitz was the leader of the campaign to save the Garretson House (below) and its farm buildings from demolition. She tirelessly organized fundraising events until there was sufficient money for a down payment for a mortgage. She founded the Garretson Forge and Farm organization and served as its president. The group persuaded Bergen County to complete the purchase of the buildings and worked to restore them. Horowitz also founded the local 4-H Club, which raised funds to save the house. With Boy Scout Troop No. 240, the club set up the summerlong 50th Anniversary Farm in 1974 and grew the ingredients for a giant anniversary cake. At left, Horowitz is showing the original deed to the property to Rotarian Dante Lozzi. (Below, courtesy of Laurence Koplik.)

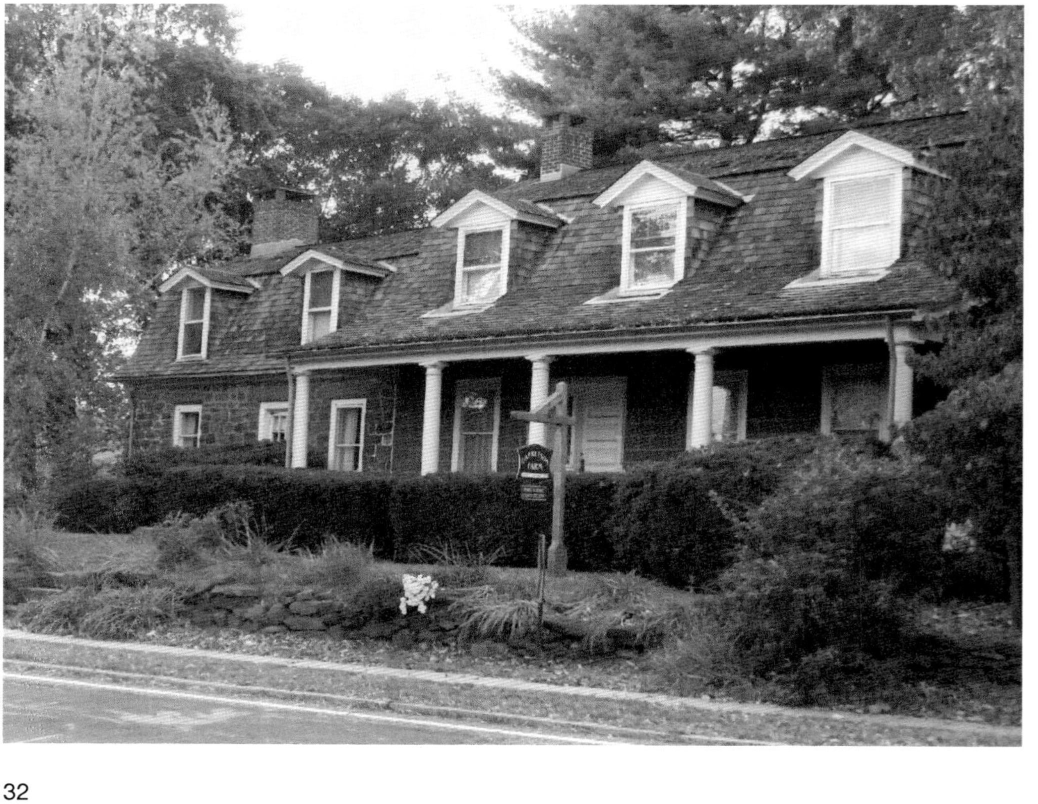

Workshop for the Developmentally Disabled

The energetic executive director Nadine Kaiser currently runs the Opportunity Center. The center was founded in 1965 by parents and civic organizations dedicated to improving the lives of adults with mental and physical challenges. In those days, society offered few services to adults with mental and physical challenges after graduation from high school. These young adults usually languished at home, regressing in their development, as anxious parents searched in vain for suitable daytime programs. To address this important social need, the Opportunity Center first opened its doors in a small, borrowed space. In 1975, it moved into a large house at 13–19 Fair Lawn Avenue. This private, nonprofit center is open all year with the goal of providing a life-enriching day program for 25 to 35 clients with a broad range of disabilities including autism, mental disabilities, Down syndrome, and cerebral palsy. The center is a sheltered workshop for developmentally disabled young adults aged 21 and older. It offers vocational work, cooking classes, activities of daily living, and exercise. The center seeks to enhance the lives of its clients by encouraging their development as individuals, improving their self-esteem, and enriching their lives through recreation, vocational activities, social interaction, educational programs, and day trips. The Opportunity Center provides a supportive and friendly environment with opportunities for its participants to feel useful, needed, and wanted. With the support of a dedicated and caring staff, along with volunteers, parents, directors, and friends, the clients are able to grow and learn and become more productive and independent members of their families and their communities. The center receives some funding from municipal and county grants, but it is primarily funded by private donations from individuals and charitable organizations, especially the Fair Lawn Lions Club. The photograph shows Nadine Kaiser (second from the left) with several clients and the volunteer performing group, the Agape Road Show, led by Cornell Christianson (third from the left, seated).

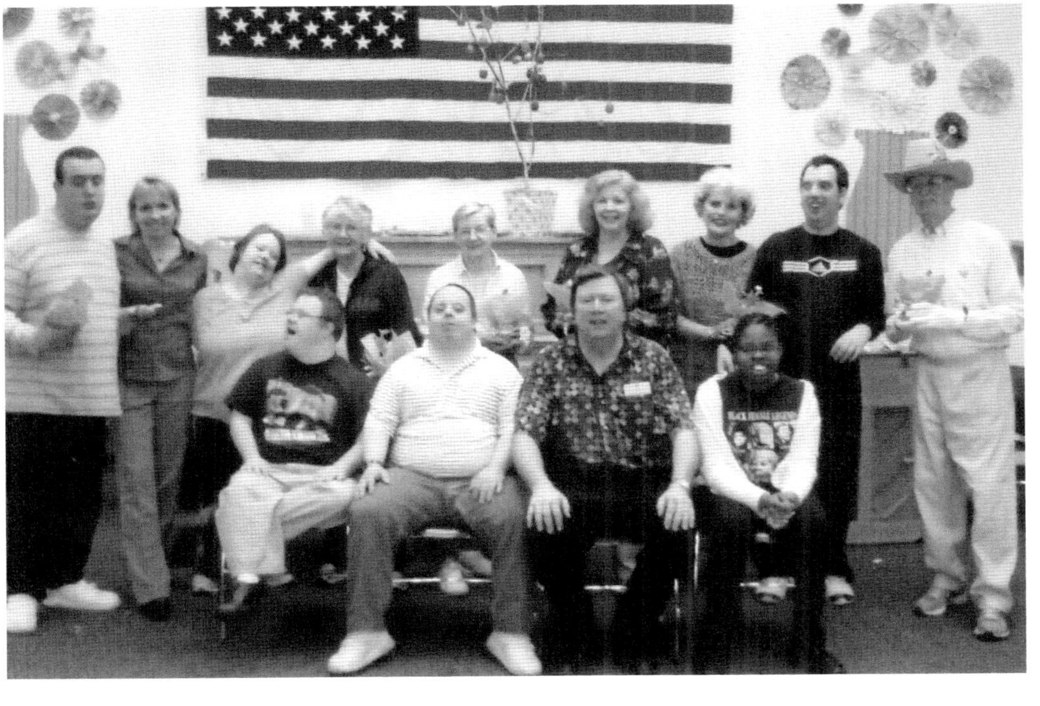

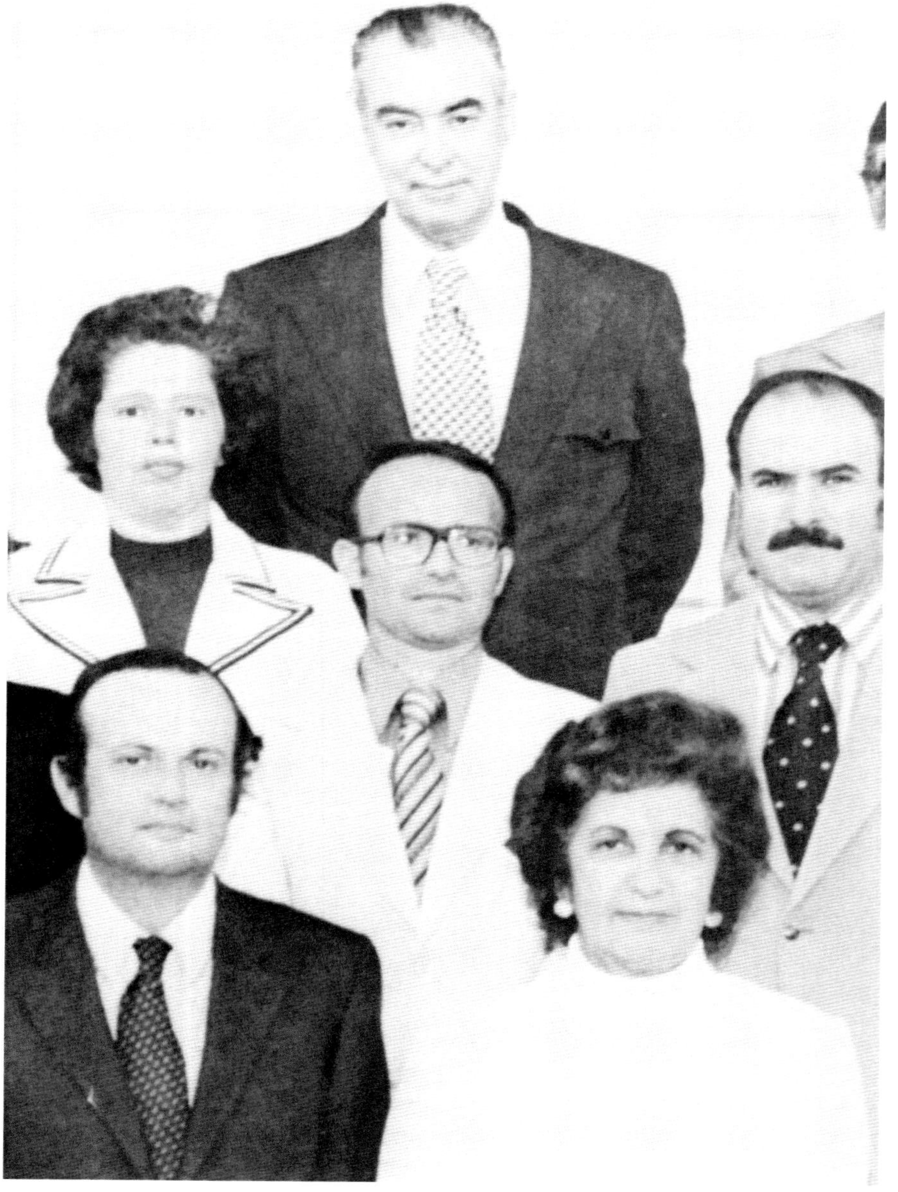

A Civic Leader

Diane Blumberg had a wide variety of civic interests and was actively involved in many organizations. She served many years on the boards of several of these groups, including the advisory council of the community school, the League of Women Voters, and the drug abuse council. She was the president of the league and the local chapter of ORT America and was chair of the drug abuse council. She served as a trustee on the boards of several Jewish organizations, including the Jewish Federation of North Jersey. Blumberg was elected to the board of education and served for several years. She is in the lower right in the photograph with other members of the drug abuse council, including, clockwise from lower left, Harold Hoffman, Selma Lash, John Cosgrove Sr., Richard Colton, and Irving Gerber.

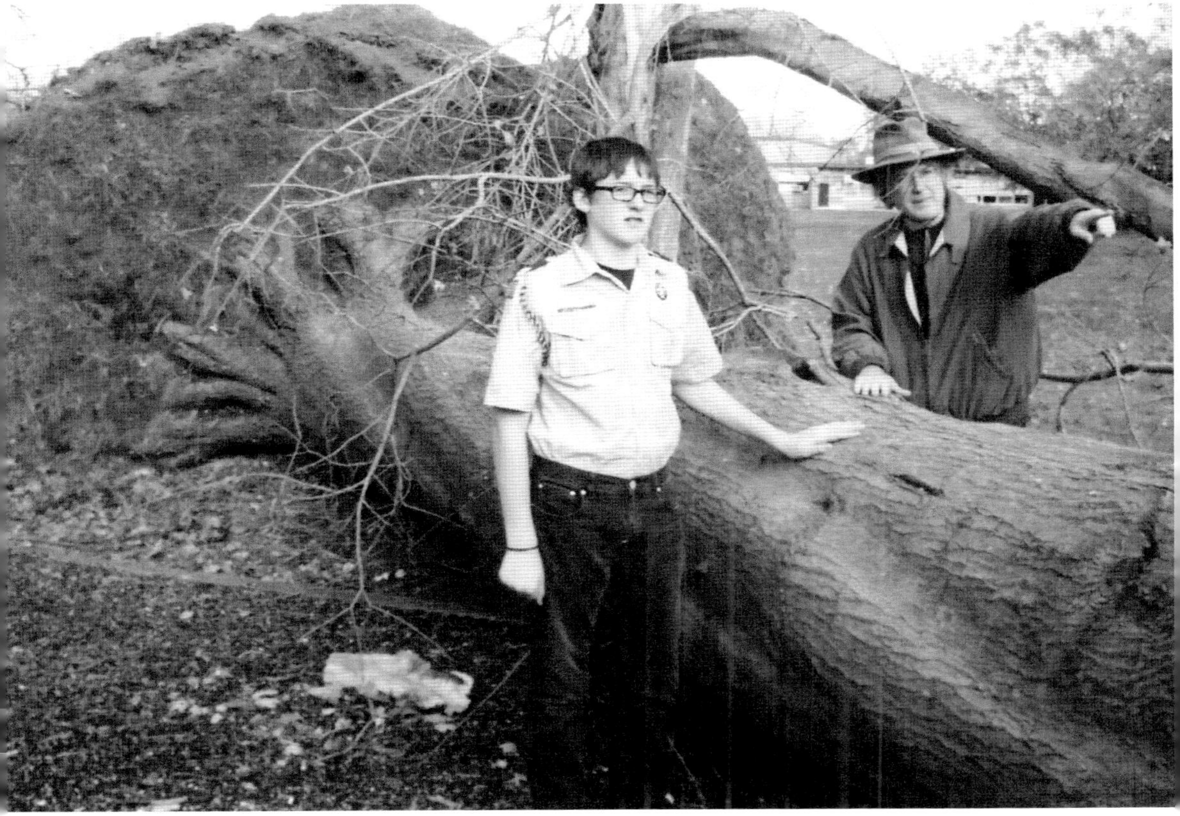

The Tree Expert and the Scout

Tree expert Stephen Taylor (right) shows Boy Scout Robby Glassett a gigantic red oak, which is New Jersey's state tree. It was knocked down behind Edison School by the biggest super storm ever to hit Fair Lawn—Hurricane Sandy, which struck on October 29, 2012, with winds over 75 miles per hour. Taylor is advising Glassett on his Eagle Scout project, which will create signs for the rarest trees in Fair Lawn, including one for a sassafras, European beech, metasequoia redwood, female ginkgo, walnut, American larch, and a rare American elm, one of the few survivors of the Dutch elm disease fungus that killed all the elms in America in the 1960s. Robby Glassett was chosen to represent his Fair Lawn High School's sophomore class at the leadership conference in Washington, DC.

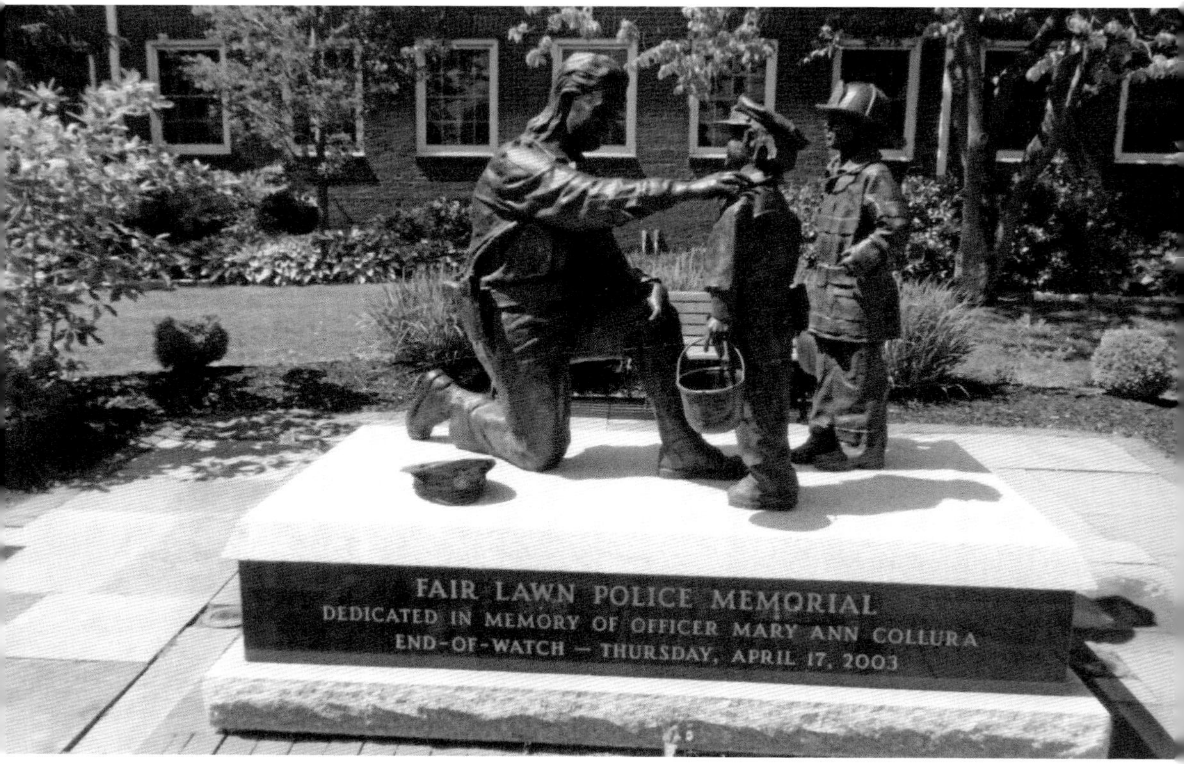

Police Officer Mary Ann Collura

Ofc. Mary Ann Collura was fatally shot by a suspect she was trying to arrest on April 17, 2003. A vehicle speeding through Clifton was seen by a police officer there. He tried to stop the vehicle and then chased it through several cities. When it reached Fair Lawn, it crashed on the front lawn of a church. Officer Collura arrived at the scene to help the other police officers who had been on the chase. A suspect got out of the crashed vehicle and ran to the rear parking lot. A Clifton police officer tackled him but the suspect pulled out a gun and fired four times at Collura, which killed her. The suspect then shot the Clifton officer twice and fled in Collura's police car. He managed to reach Florida where he was shot and killed by police officers. At age 43, Officer Collura was an 18-year veteran of the Fair Lawn Police Department. A graduate of Fair Lawn High School, she was a lifelong resident of Fair Lawn. She was Fair Lawn's first female police officer, which was her life's dream. Officer Collura was a certified New Jersey Police Training Commission instructor and had served as one of the department's firearms officers and armorer. Officer Collura received numerous awards, including a departmental Meritorious Service Award and the Hackensack University Medical Center EMS Excellence Award for saving a life with a defibrillator. She received numerous commendation letters from the community for her prompt, courteous, and thoughtful service. It was Officer Collura's suggestion that the elementary schoolchildren be given glowing light sticks to wear at night when trick-or-treating to make them more obvious to motorists. Her project has been repeated in Fair Lawn every year since and has become a countywide program funded by Bergen County. A statue of Officer Collura honoring her memory stands in front of borough hall; the statue depicts her talking to children dressed in costumes for Halloween.

CHAPTER THREE

The Government Leaders

While Fair Lawn was still part of Saddle River Township, some area residents were active in government. Henry A. Hopper served as a township committeeman and went on to be a freeholder. His son, Isaac Hopper, was the township assessor for many years and, later, served as county collector.

When the borough was founded in 1924, the mayor-council form of government was established. Elections were held, and Robert A. Smith was chosen as the first mayor, followed by Nicholas A. Kuiken. Several succeeding mayors went on to serve as freeholders or in the state legislature. Notable among these were Richard Vander Plaat, the longest-serving mayor, and Robert Gordon, who rose to be a state senator. Others, such as John J. Cosgrove, had long service volunteering in community affairs before becoming mayor.

Kay Lyle was the first woman to be elected to the council, and "Flossie" Dobrow was the first female mayor. Some public servants were not in politics. Morris Dobrin was a noted municipal magistrate, and Stuart Brotman was an advisor to four presidential administrations.

The Melon King

Henry A. Hopper owned farms on both sides of Small Lots Road, present-day Fair Lawn Avenue. The farm was reputed to be the finest in the county and was famous for its expanse of melons, giving Hopper the title of "the Melon King." He was also active in civic affairs, serving as township committeeman, Bergen County sheriff, and freeholder and as representative to the state legislature. Henry was the grandson of Peter H. Hopper who settled in Fair Lawn in 1766. The younger Hopper built a large house in the Italianate style on his farm. The farm was later sold to William Croucher, and the house stood until 1989 when it was demolished to make room for an interchange at Route 208. (Illustration from *History of Bergen and Passaic Counties, New Jersey* by Woodford Clayton.)

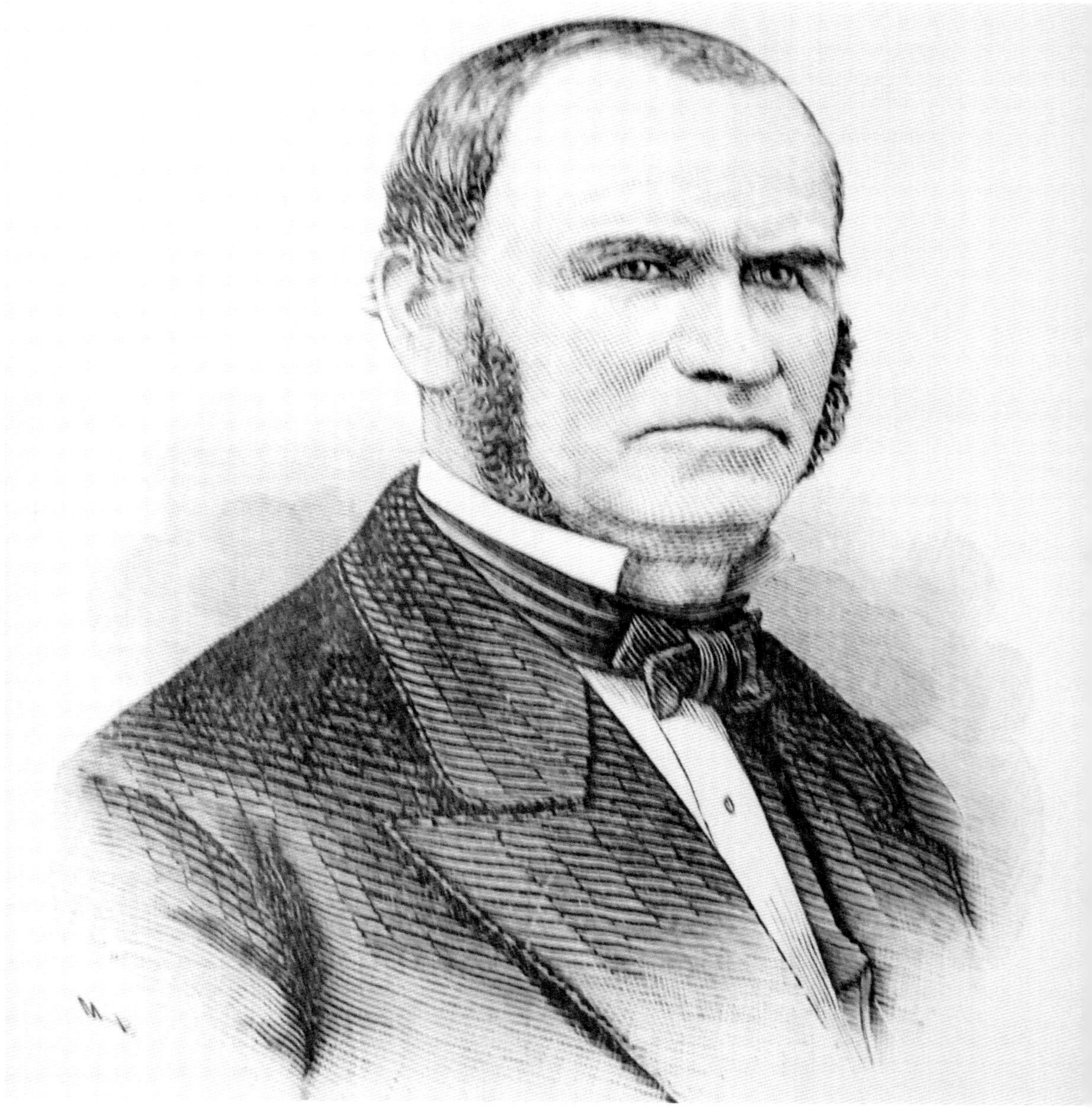

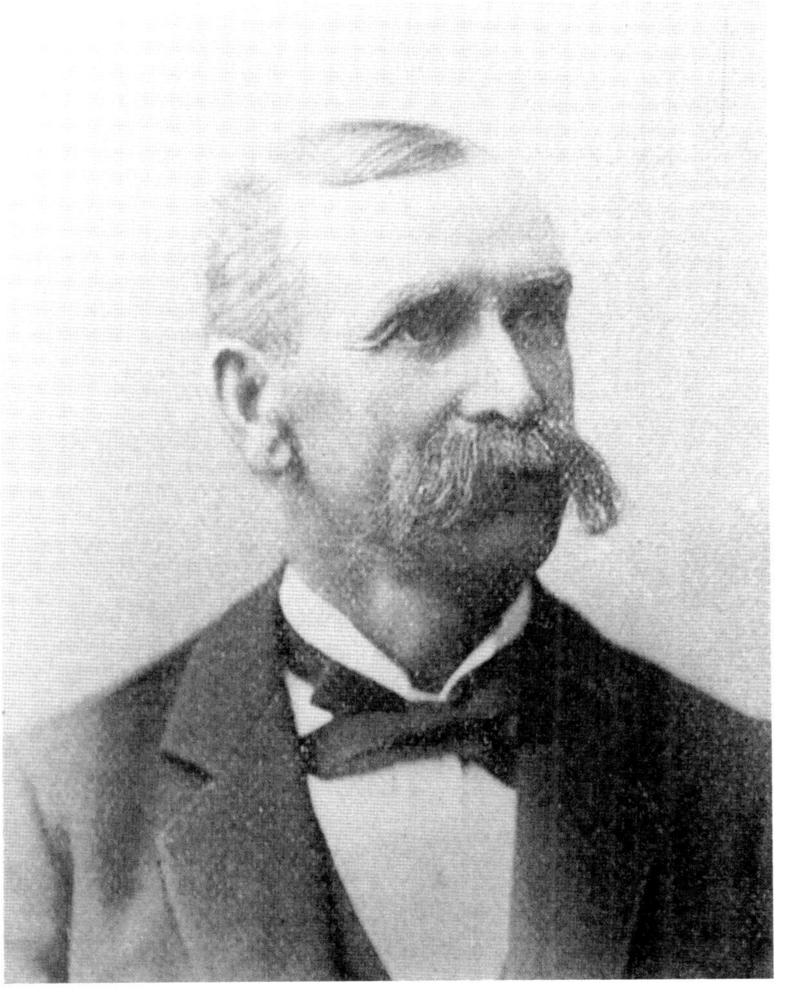

A Compassionate Man

Isaac A. Hopper, a son of Henry A. Hopper, followed the family tradition of public service. Starting in 1875, he served as assessor of Saddle River Township for 42 years. He was elected sheriff of Bergen County in 1881 and county collector in 1892. During his four-year term, he worked to improve public roads. He liked to boast that he was the only living man who served in public office for 62 successive years.

As a young man, Hopper enlisted in Company E of the 22d New Jersey Volunteers and served in four Civil War battles, including Gettysburg. He married Maria Hopper and had one child who died young.

When Alice Sisco, a three-year-old Black child from the Dunkerhook Road neighborhood, became parentless, the Hoppers took her in and raised her. The child's father had been found dead by the railroad. People said a train killed him, but some evidence indicated that he had been murdered and dragged there. Her mother never recovered from the tragedy and was sent to Greystone Asylum. Alice apparently became a treasured member of the Hopper family; when Henry Hopper died in 1927, he left her $3,000, a ring, and his diamond stud.

Isaac Hopper built a large Victorian-style house on Fair Lawn Avenue, near the corner of today's Plaza Road. After his death, the developers of Radburn bought the house and 20-acre farm. The house was used for Radburn's nursery school and other activities and was known as "the Children's House." (Illustration from *Genealogical History of Hudson and Bergen Counties, New Jersey* edited by Cornelius B. Harvey.)

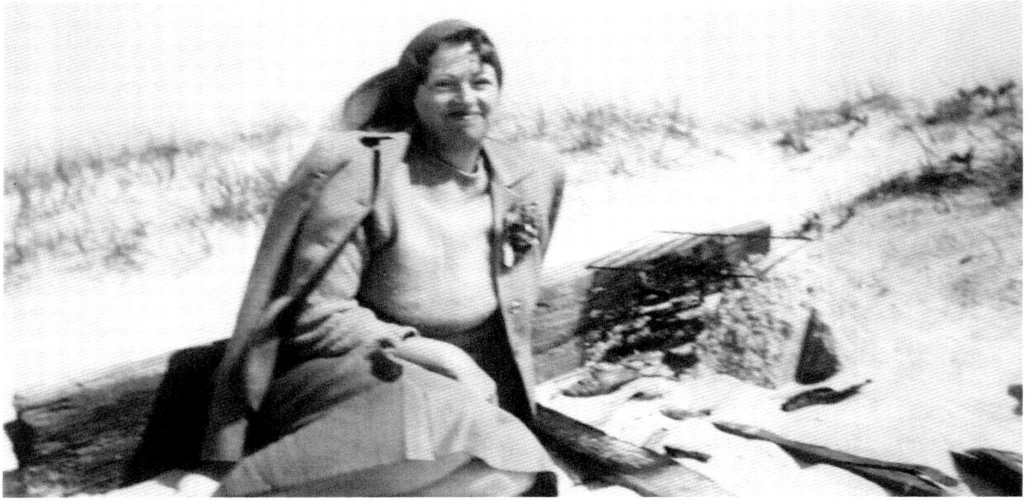

The First Councilwoman

In 1937, Kathryn "Kay" Lyle wrote to the New Jersey State League of Women Voters seeking information on how to be a more intelligent voter. The league responded by asking her to form a Fair Lawn chapter of the organization. She accepted and became the Fair Lawn league's first president. In 1939, she was appointed to the borough's first planning board and served as its member secretary for nine years. During World War II, Kay served on the local rationing board and worked on a committee to furnish the day room for the troops encamped in Radburn. Kathryn Lewis Lyle, pictured at left in the bottom image, was elected Fair Lawn's first woman member of the borough council where she worked for the establishment of the council-manager form of government. She later served as secretary of the group that worked to develop Memorial Pool, and she was a member of the library board.

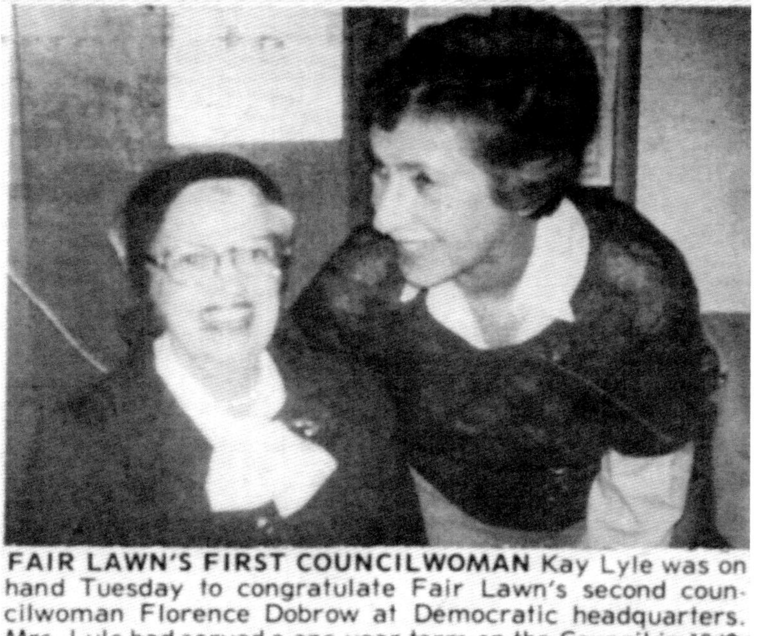

FAIR LAWN'S FIRST COUNCILWOMAN Kay Lyle was on hand Tuesday to congratulate Fair Lawn's second councilwoman Florence Dobrow at Democratic headquarters. Mrs. Lyle had served a one-year term on the Council in 1948.

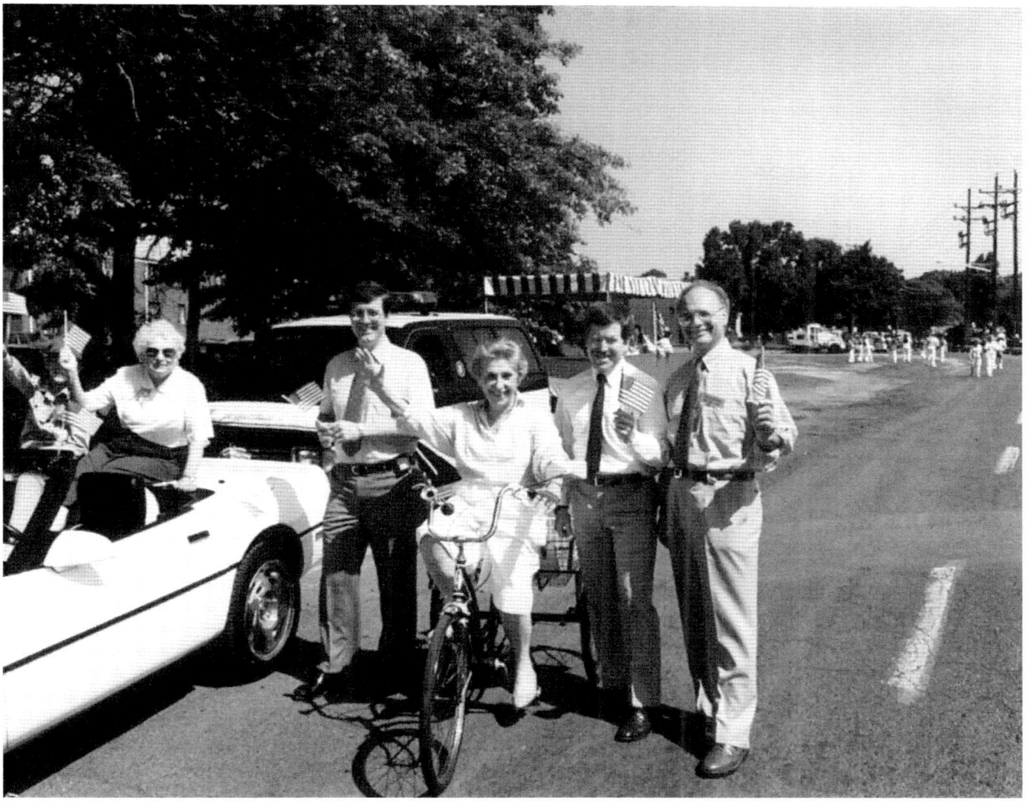

The First Woman Mayor
Florence "Flossie" Dobrow (seated on the tricycle) was chosen as the first woman mayor of Fair Lawn by her fellow council members in 1981. She had the distinction of being elected to the council for 27 years, the longest-serving woman in New Jersey. Her proudest accomplishment was the building of the senior center, for which she had worked tirelessly. The borough's seniors were so appreciative of this that they were partly responsible for Flossie's high votes in election after election. Dobrow's interest in government came from her involvement in the League of Women Voters. In her long service on the council, she secured funding for the Columbia Heights athletic field, later named in her honor; was a founder of the garden club; and formed "Flossie's posse" to help beautify the town. In recognition of her service, the New Jersey League of Municipalities made her a member of the Elected Officials Hall of Fame.

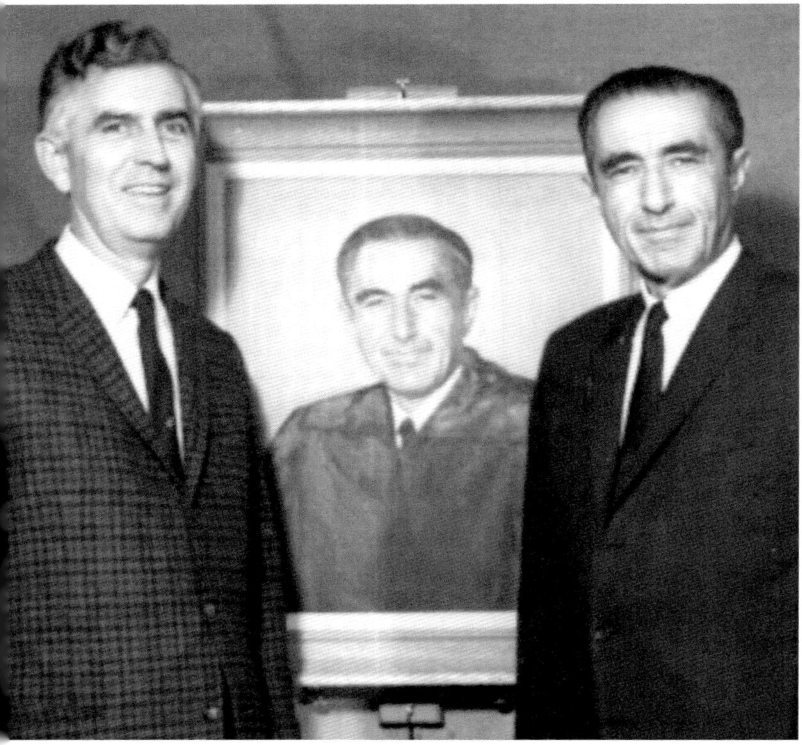

A Civic-minded Judge
Morris Dobrin served as magistrate of the municipal court for many years and was known for his empathetic manner in dealing with cases. Also involved in community affairs, he led the fundraising drive for construction of the Memorial Pool, worked for the borough's recreation program, and was a founder of the chamber of commerce. At left, Monte Weed is presenting Judge Dobrin (right) with a portrait of himself.

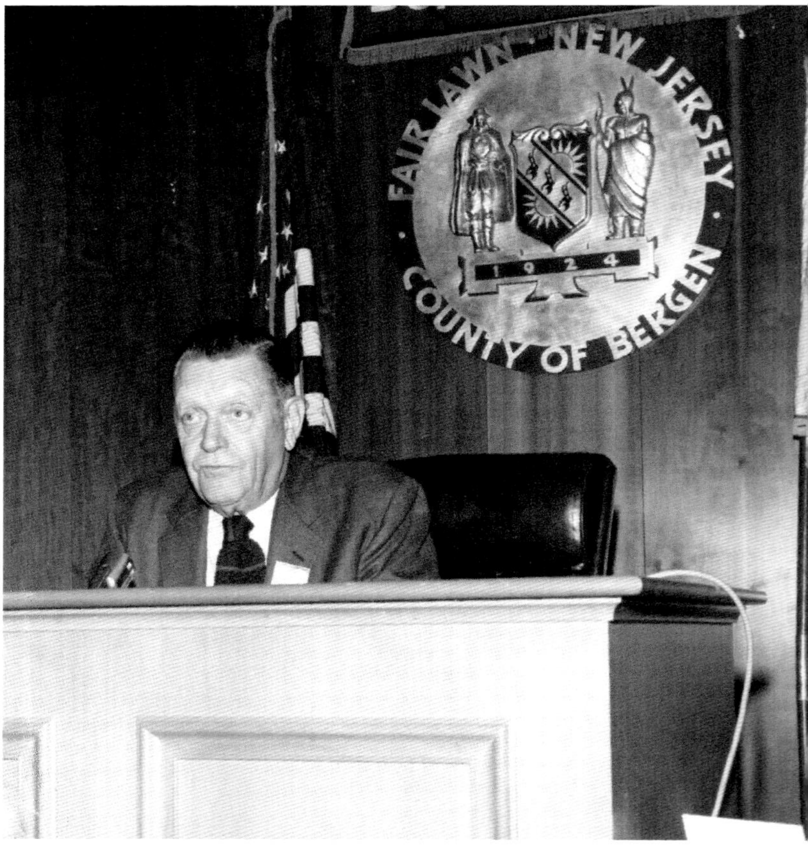

Mayor and Freeholder
John K. Pollitt was elected to the first governing body to be formed under the new nonpartisan council-manager form of government in April 1948 and was chosen by his fellow councilmen as mayor, a position he held for four years. He went on to serve on the Bergen County Board of Chosen Freeholders for 10 years and was chosen freeholder director for one term.

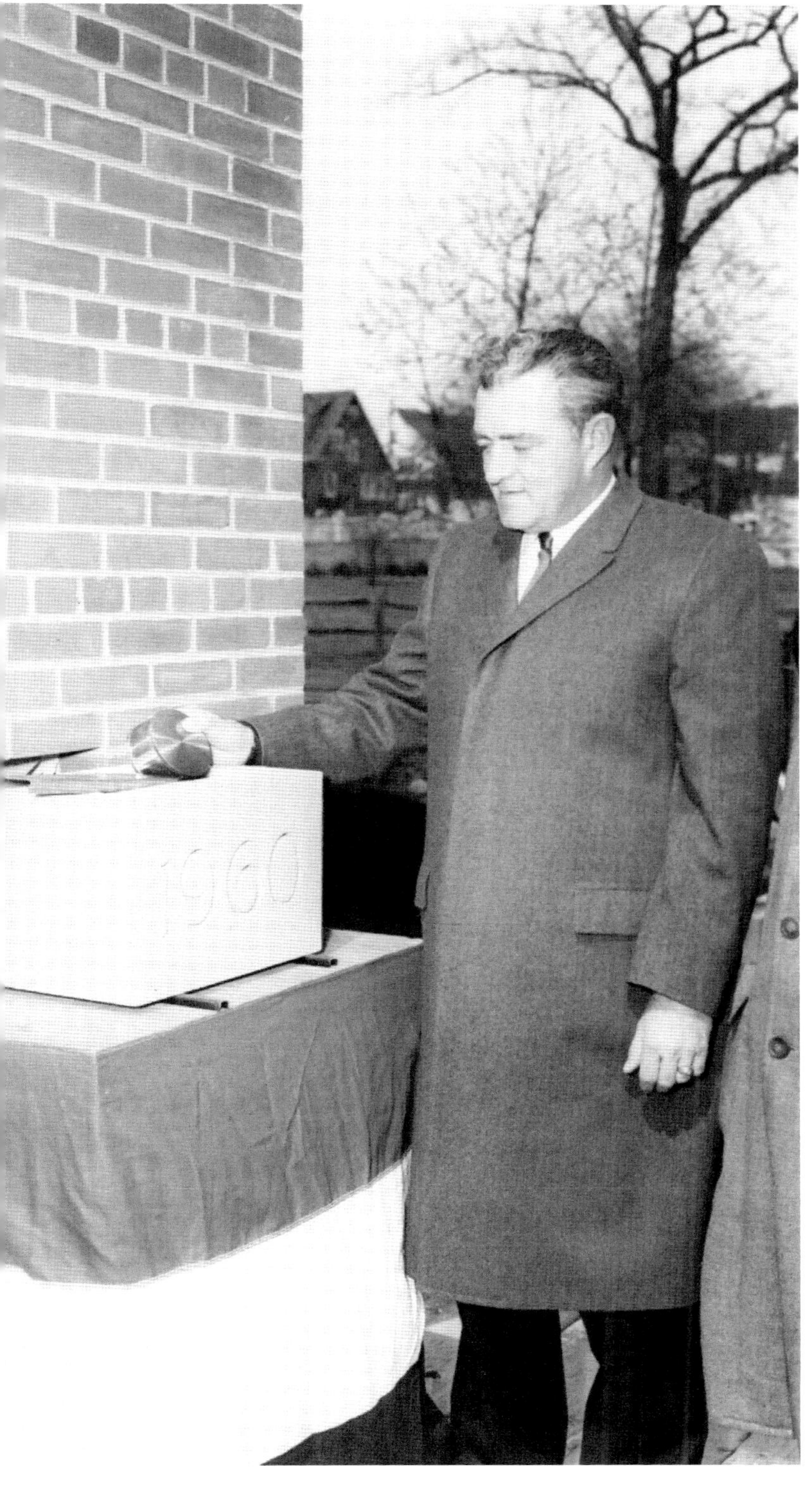

The Longest-Serving Mayor
Richard "Dick" Vander Plaat was a 16-year member of the borough council and the longest-serving Fair Lawn mayor, holding that office from 1958 through 1968. He was elected to the New Jersey Assembly, serving from 1964 until 1971, when he was appointed to the waterfront commission, which is now the Port Authority of New York and New Jersey. Vander Plaat also worked for the care and rights of handicapped children. His grandfather, who came from Holland, founded the family funeral business. Dick Vander Plaat was the third generation to carry on the business when he built the funeral home in Fair Lawn. This photograph shows Mayor Vander Plaat placing an item in the cornerstone of the new borough hall in 1960. (Courtesy of the Cadmus House Museum.)

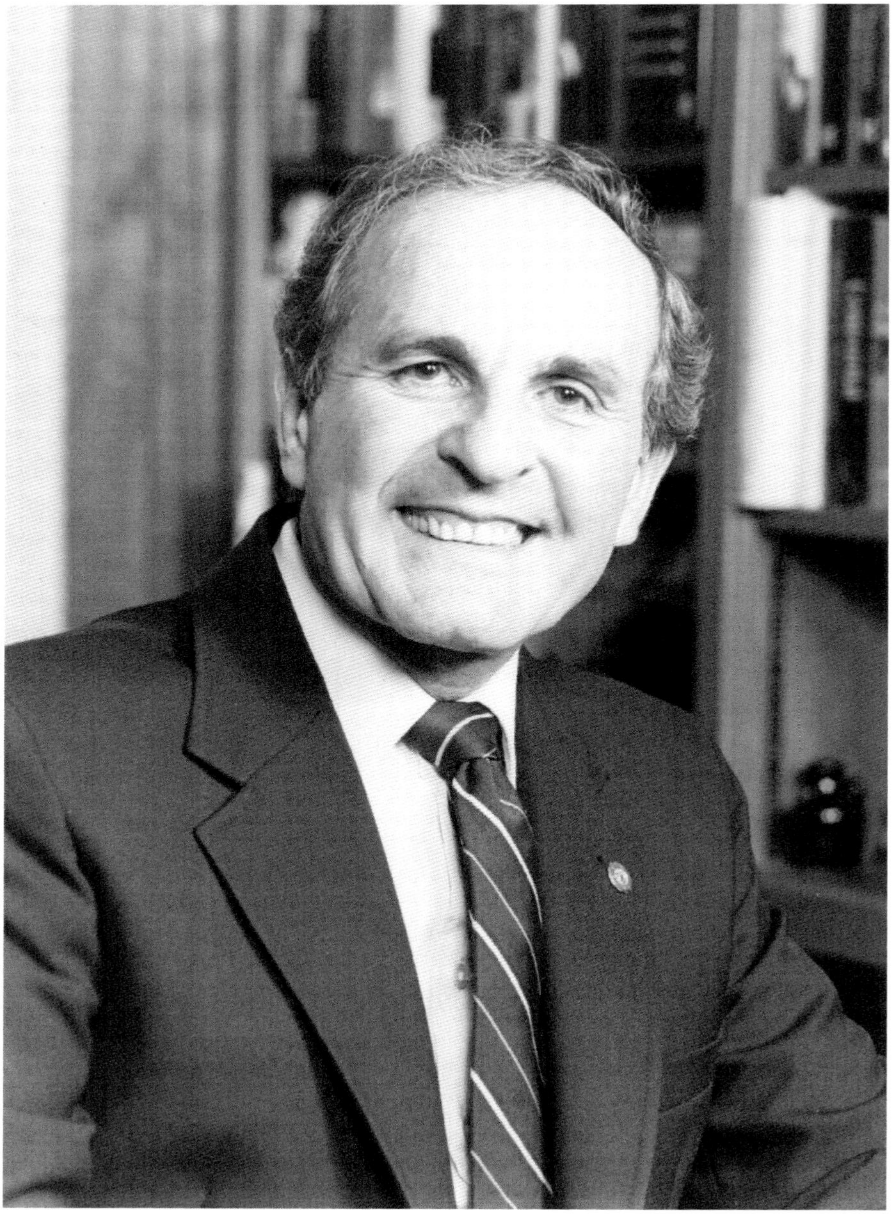

An Assemblyman and Preservationist
Nicholas R. Felice served on the borough council from 1967 to 1975 and was chosen mayor for the 1972–1973 term. He was elected to the state assembly in 1981, rising to become speaker pro tempore from 1996 until his retirement in 2001. Nick Felice founded the local senior citizens advisory committee and served on the Fair Lawn Planning Board and the youth advisory committee. He had a keen interest in historic preservation, working to secure donations to buy the Garretson family's house and farm buildings. He also was a founding trustee of the group that worked to save the historic Cadmus House from demolition and secured grants from the state to move it to its present site and to restore it. He remained a trustee of Cadmus House Board for more than 20 years. (Courtesy of Nick Felice.)

Freeholder and Numismatist

David Ganz served on the borough council for eight years, starting in 1998, and was chosen as mayor by his colleagues for seven of those years. He served on the Bergen County Board of Chosen Freeholders, starting in 2003, and was later selected as freeholder chairman by his colleagues. Ganz is a noted expert on coins and currency and has published several books of the subject. He promulgated the idea for the 50-state quarters series. Philip N. Diehl, former director of the US Mint, said, "The lion's share of the credit for making the 50 State Quarters Program a reality goes to David." Ganz has testified several times before the subcommittee on consumer affairs and other subcommittees of the House Committee of Financial Services. (Courtesy of David Ganz.)

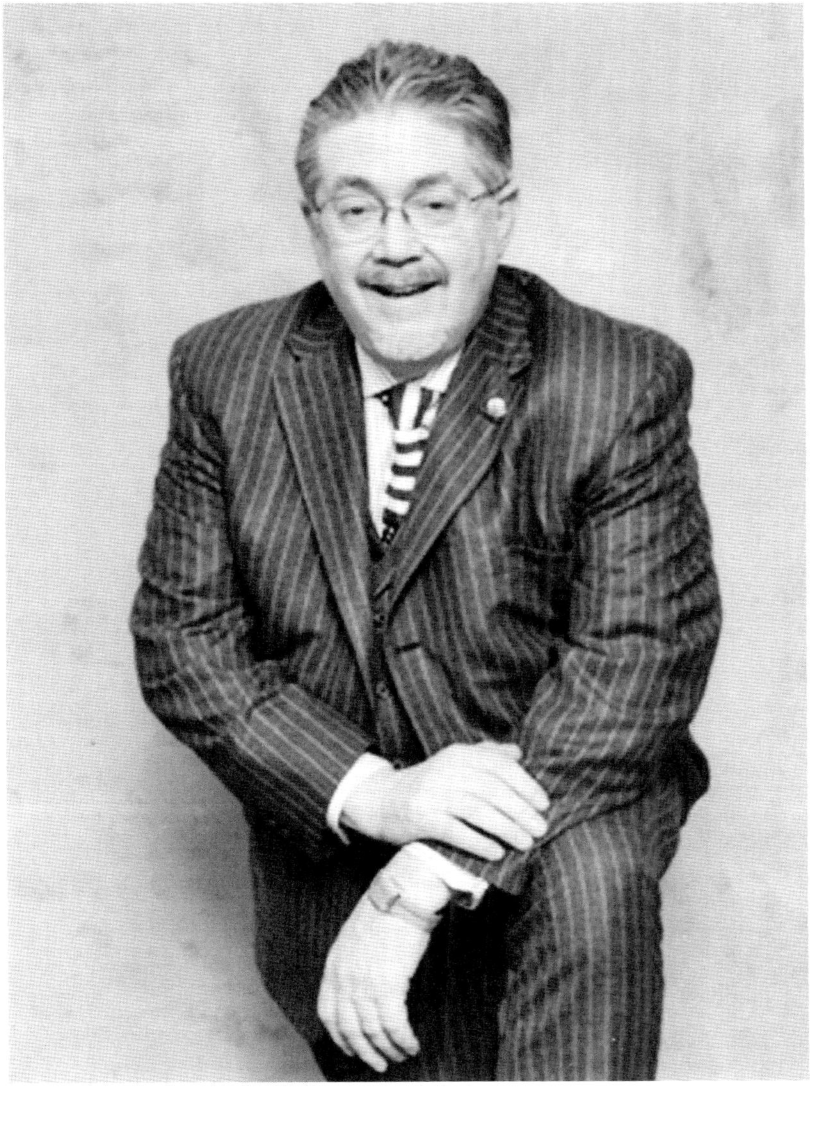

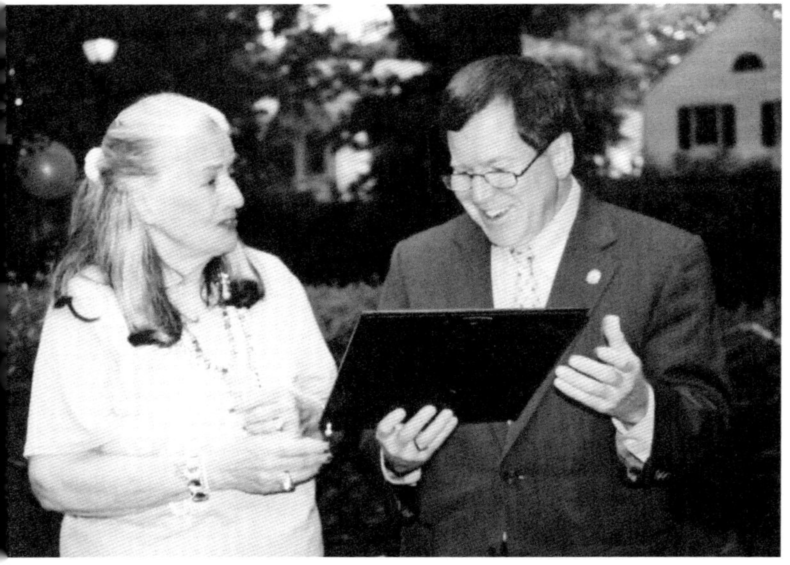

Fair Lawn Native Legislator

Robert M. Gordon is a New Jersey state senator, representing the 38th Legislative District. He has served in the New Jersey General Assembly, on the borough council, and as mayor of Fair Lawn. In addition to being a state senator, Gordon is a US Homeland Security consultant. He is shown presenting a Senate Citation to Fritzie Christianson for her outstanding community service, which includes teaching theater to young people.

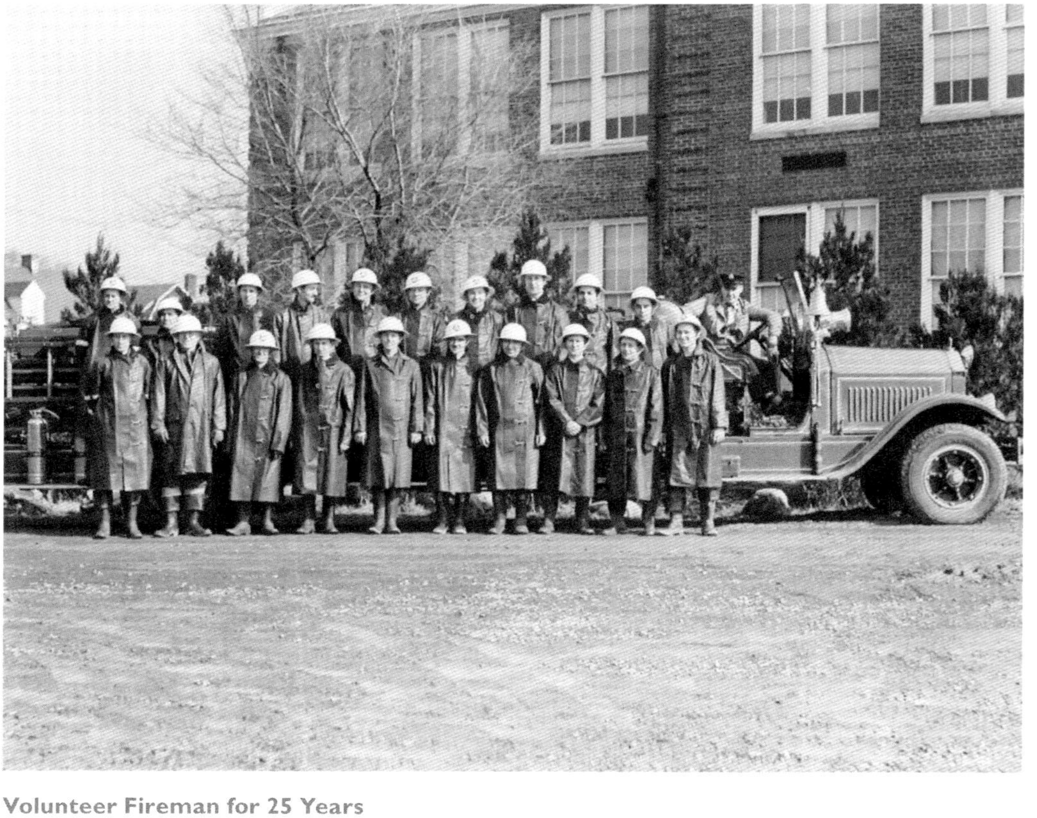

Volunteer Fireman for 25 Years

John A. Cosgrove is in the driver's seat as Fair Lawn fire chief in this 1964 photograph. He also served on the zoning board of adjustment, the Opportunity Center Board, the borough council, and the drug abuse council. All who knew him said he was a good and kind man. (Courtesy of John J. Cosgrove.)

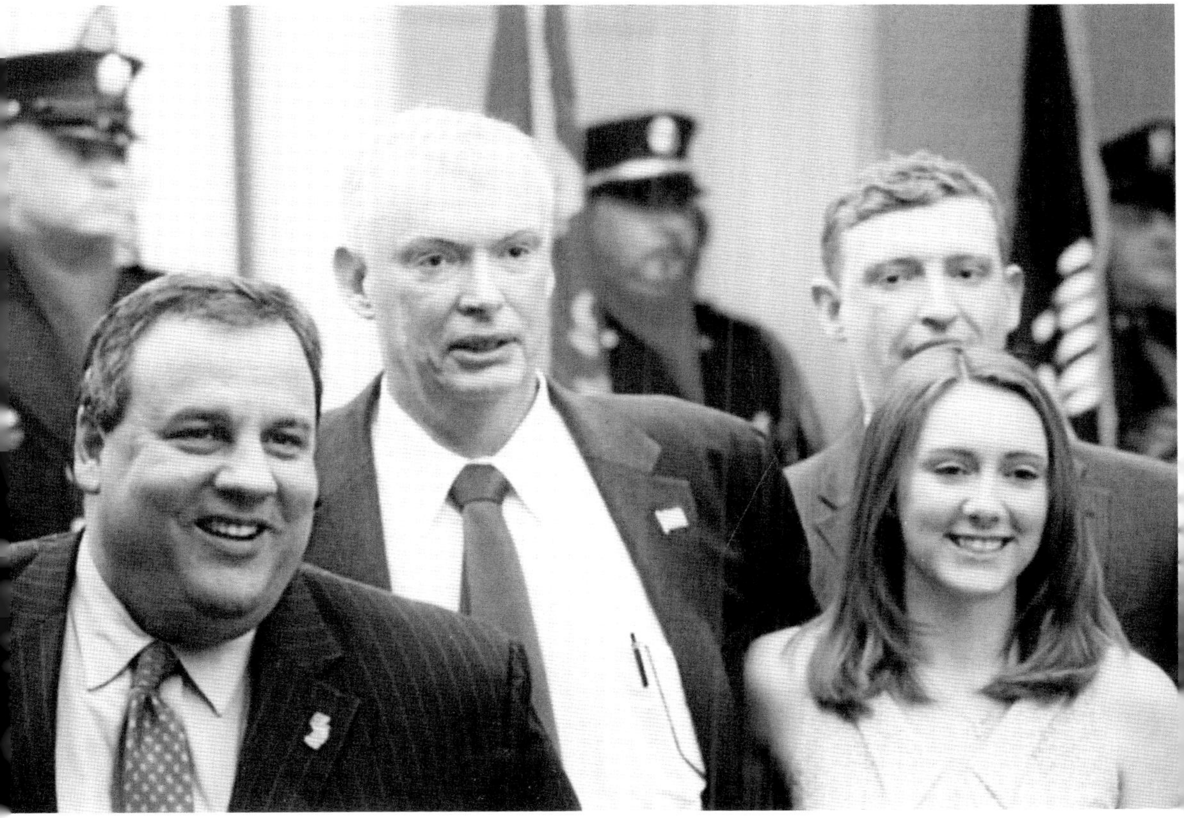

Mr. Fair Lawn

A lifelong resident of Fair Lawn, John J. Cosgrove has dedicated his life to helping others. An active volunteer fireman for many years, he has held every office in the Fair Lawn Fire Department and was fire chief in 1997. He was awarded the fire department Valor Award, the Citation Star for Bravery, and the VFW Valor Award for his heroic actions in the rescue of an unconscious man from a house fire. In 1999, Cosgrove served as chairman of Fair Lawn's 75th anniversary celebration and has been named three times the Bergen County Volunteer of the Year. The Fair Lawn Chamber of Commerce honored him in 2007 as the Fair Lawn Person of the Year.

As chairman of the Fair Lawn Community Center Committee, Cosgrove oversaw the design and construction of the center for which he was honored with the dedication of the John J. Cosgrove Gymnasium. He has been very active in sports, volunteering to coach baseball, street hockey, and lacrosse. He founded the Fair Lawn Lacrosse Club and the Fair Lawn Touchdown Club, serving as president of both. He has been on the boards of directors for the Fair Lawn Athletic Hall of Fame, the Fair Lawn Football Association, and the Fair Lawn High School Parents Committee for Athletics. Cosgrove has done extensive volunteer civic work, serving on the boards of directors for the Bergen Regional Medical Center Foundation, Fair Lawn Old-Timers, Fair Lawn Chamber of Commerce, St. Catherine's Fathers Guild, and the New Jersey Business Network.

John Cosgrove was elected to the Fair Lawn Borough Council in 2011 and served as the mayor of Fair Lawn. He has been working in the storage and handling business for 33 years and is active in the Material Handling Equipment Distributors Association. In 2005, he founded Atlantic Handling Systems, located in Fair Lawn, and serves as its president. Cosgrove (center) is shown with New Jersey governor Chris Christie and Cosgrove's daughter Kerryann. (Courtesy of John J. Cosgrove.)

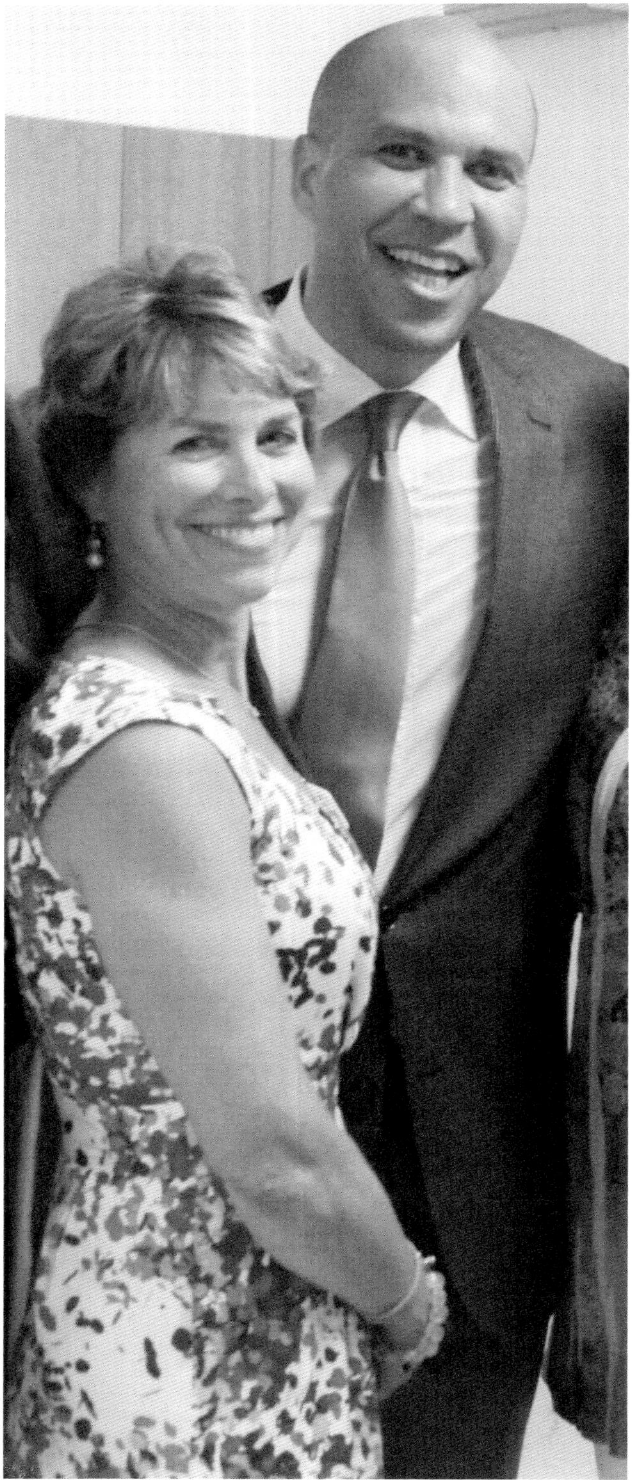

Marathon Runner and Mayor

Lisa Swain almost always wins the races in her age group, whether it is the 5K, 10K, sprint triathlon, or marathon. And when she does team triathlons with her husband, they usually win. Shown in this photograph with Newark mayor Cory Booker, Swain has extensive experience in government, fundraising, and event management. Currently a councilwoman for the borough, she was the fourth female mayor of Fair Lawn and was also deputy mayor. Her accomplishments include negotiating labor contracts with the police department, starting the Green Team, serving on the planning board, bringing the first development with solar panels into the borough, and overseeing a $46-million budget. As manager of community campaigns and events for Save the Children, Swain was responsible for raising $750,000 through national and local events, volunteer activities, and individual contributions. (Courtesy of Lisa Swain.)

CHAPTER FOUR

The Artists, Authors, and Entertainers

A representative group of artists and entertainers who lived in Fair Lawn would include actress Millie Perkins, best known for her role as Anne Frank in *The Diary of Anne Frank*. But her most exciting moment may have been when she got to kiss Elvis as his girlfriend in *Wild in the Country*. Lee Meredith played the sexy blonde bombshell Ulla in the original 1968 film version of *The Producers* with Zero Mostel and Gene Wilder.

Bob Dietch's Kiddie Zoo is remembered with nostalgia by all the children—and their parents—who spent happy days there.

Tony Trischka is a nationally known banjo player who is considered America's best picker. Great jazz artists include Keith "Red" Mitchell and Gordon "Whitey" Mitchell. Fair Lawn has two actors who have been seen on Broadway. Donna Vivino had leading roles in *Wicked* and *Les Misérables*. Trevor Braun has had leads in *Billy Elliot*, *The Little Mermaid*, and *Beauty and the Beast*. Larry Hochman had five Tony Award nominations for Best Orchestrations and finally won for *The Book of Mormon*.

Peter "Ace" Andrews directed and produced the CBS soap opera series *Guiding Light* for 16 years. His wife, Chris Andrews, was a fashion model in her twenties and again in her seventies when she won a national modeling contest for seniors. Barry Edelstein is a leading director of Shakespearean plays and is now artistic director of the Old Globe Theatre. Authors from Fair Lawn include Vivian Carlin and Dr. Albert Rosen. Some unusual artists who create Halloween monsters are John Bernabeo and 11-year-old Michael Kwasnik. Sam Glassett has the distinction of winning national awards in both high school band percussion and the game Pokémon.

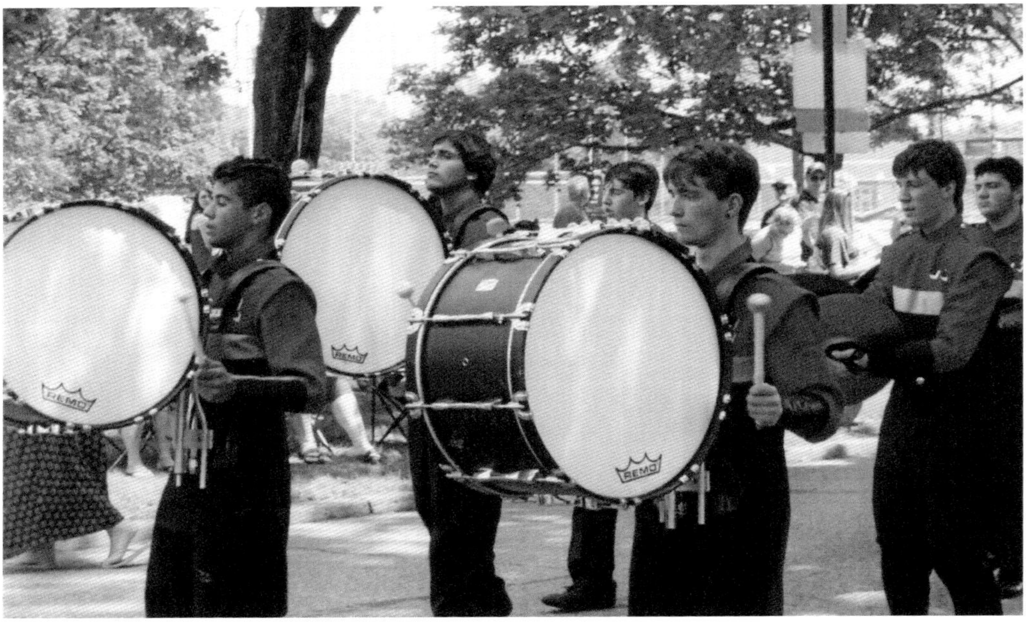

Creator of the High School Band

L. Barry Tedesco joined the Fair Lawn High School faculty as the music teacher when the school opened in 1943. He started and trained the marching band and its color guard, the majorettes, and the cheerleaders, and he led the band until his retirement. Barry Tedesco also found time to direct the Fair Lawn Choral Society, which was established in 1946. It had almost 50 members by 1950. Tedesco later served on the board of education. But he is most remembered for the marching band, which performed at all the high school football games. Pictured below are the first band, color guard, and majorettes in 1944; above is the drum section in 2013. (Courtesy of Bob Glassett.)

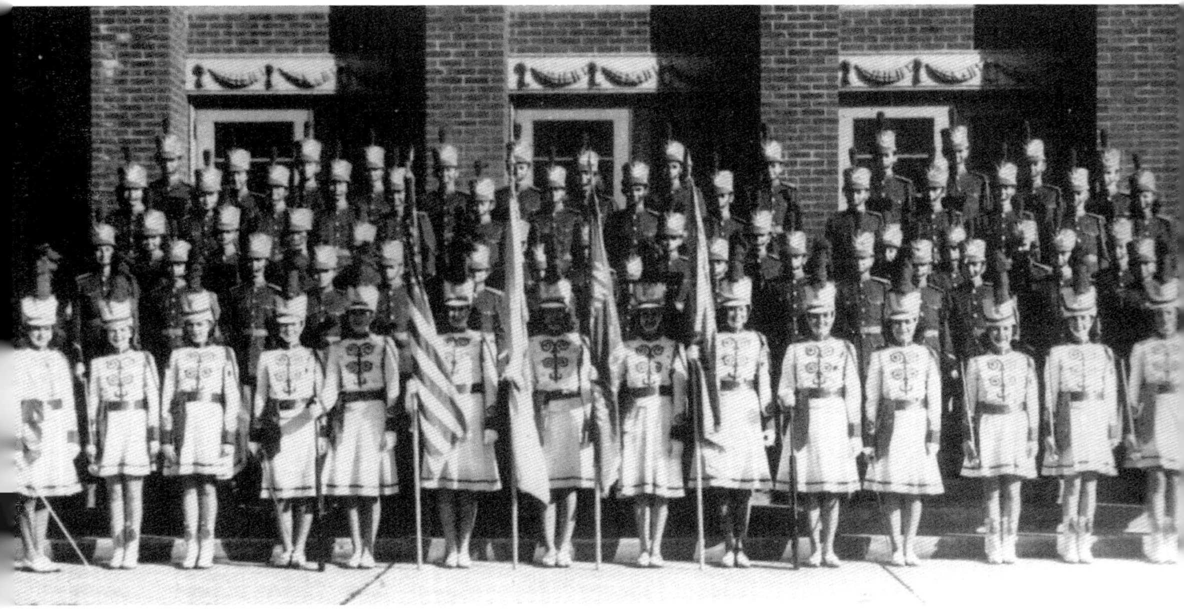

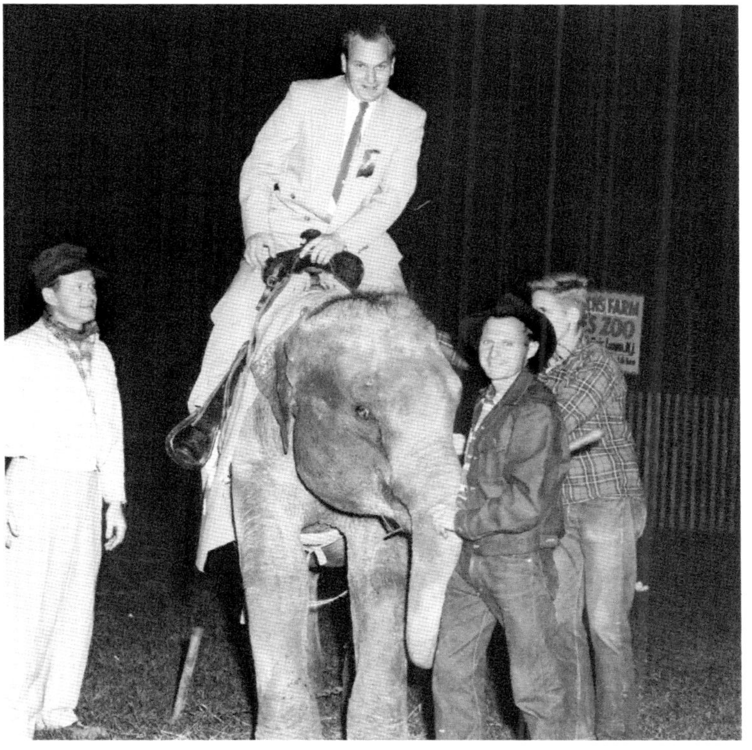

Dietch's Kiddie Zoo

Bob Dietch started his wildly popular Kiddie Zoo almost by accident. He had a 10-acre farm on Saddle River Road, and he occasionally rented out his barnyard animals for children's parties. He was asked if he could break a pair of llamas so kids could ride them, and he took the plunge. This was followed by other projects, and then animal dealers asked him to board their wildlife. For one dealer, he boarded a 1,200-pound hippo. Soon, he had many animals in his barn for storage or training, but some customers reneged on their deals, and Dietch was left with an odd assortment of beasts. So in 1951, he started Dietch's Kiddie Zoo. The place grew fast. Dietch was joined by Van Walsh who had bought an 1895 locomotive, flatcars, and a caboose. He built a narrow-gauge railroad around the property and charged a small fee for rides. Another entrepreneur, Kasmir Ulaky brought in kiddie rides—a caterpillar, boats, cars, and a small carousel with miniature fire engines for seats. Ulaky hosted birthday parties with cake and ice cream. Another concessionaire had a food stand. There were also pony, elephant, and camel rides. Business boomed. Dietch helped it along by publicizing events, such as a lost penguin and his "One-Hump Jiffy Camel Washer," a gadget he improvised to shower his camel. His animals appeared on early television shows such as those of Ed Sullivan, Arthur Godfrey, and Captain Kangaroo. The assortment of animals was diverse: at one time or another, the zoo had baby elephants, bears, bison, zebras, ocelots, seals, horses, cows, parrots, a peacock, foxes, and a lion that woke neighbors with its roaring at night. A petting zoo held sheep, goats, pigs, and various barnyard fowl. Some of the old Ringling Bros. circus wagons were stored in the back of Dietch's property, along with giraffes, a hippopotamus, and an okapi. Once a year, the wagons and animals were taken to Madison Square Garden for a show. In the late 1960s, the zoo was closed, and Bob Dietch had a florist business on the property. Developers were interested in the tract and proposed various projects. Finally, a subdivision for homes on what are now Geiger Place and Christine Court was approved. The tennis courts and Young Israel were built later on the front of the property. Pictured above, Doug Kuiken is riding on an elephant, and Bob Dietch is wearing the hat on the right. (Courtesy of Doug Kuiken.)

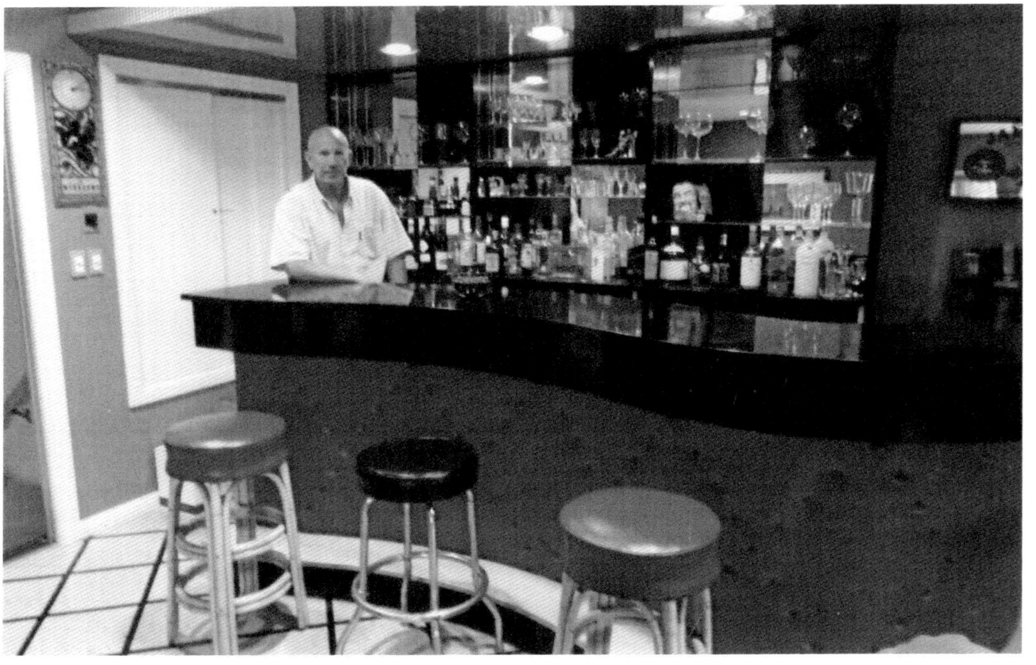

Milton Berle's Mother, Sarah Berlinger

Milton Berle was a famous comedian and television star, known to millions of viewers as "Uncle Miltie" and "Mr. Television" during the 1950s. In 1953, he built and owned a house in Fair Lawn for his mother, Sarah Berlinger. The house is currently owned by Edward Schwartz, who is shown behind the bar that Berle had built. Milton's mother was a very aggressive stage mother who took six-year-old Milton to do work as an extra in 1914 and, later, in supporting roles at movie studios in Fort Lee, New Jersey, including the first-ever feature-length comedy, *Tillie's Punctured Romance*, which starred Charlie Chaplin. As a child actor, Milton made more than 50 silent films in Hollywood and New Jersey while performing kid acts on the vaudeville circuit.

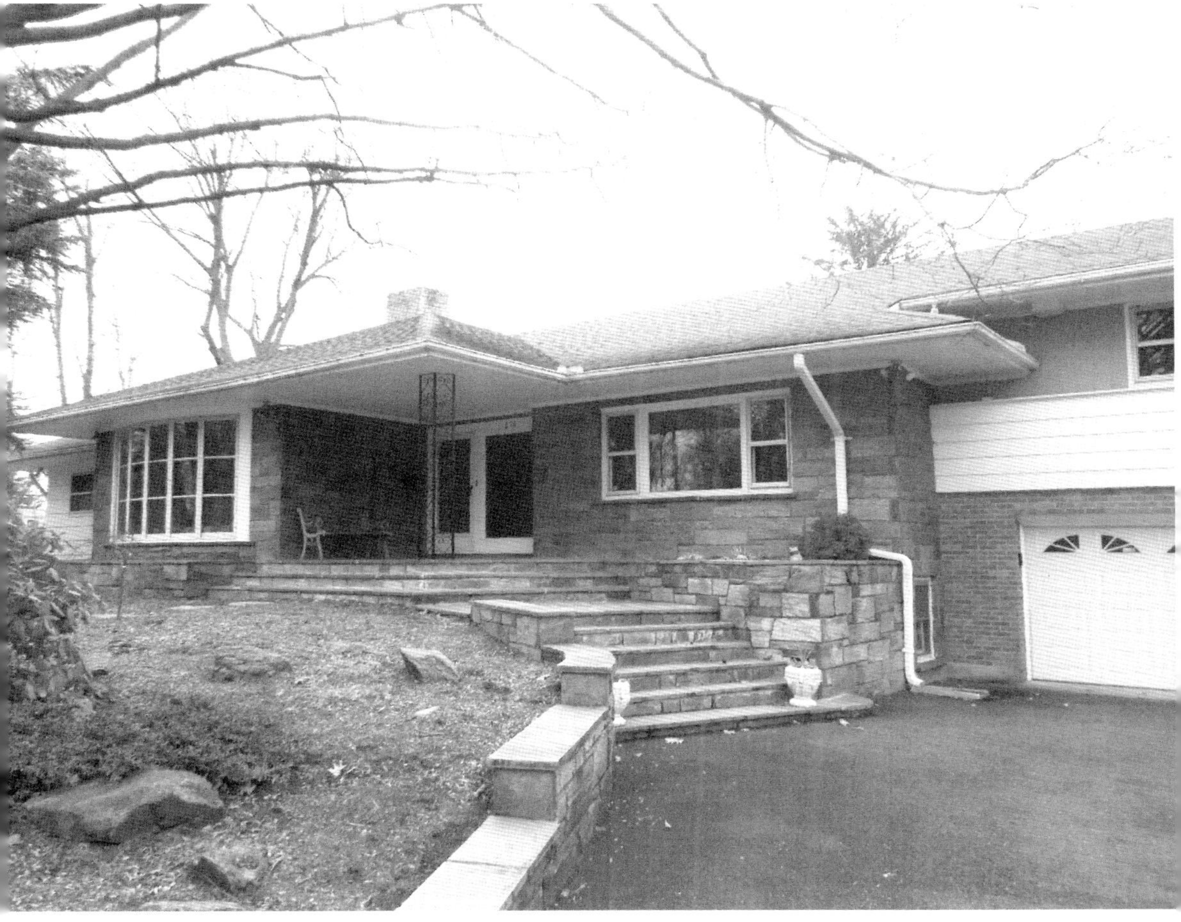

The House that Berle Built
Milton Berle and his family would come out from New York City on weekends and visit his mother at the house he built for her in Fair Lawn. The swimming pool and tennis courts are still there. In the winter, with no leaves on the trees, the family could see from their picture window the "Old Mill" across the street. At the time, Berle starred in the hit NBC television series *Texaco Star Theater*. The show was so popular that many people are said to have bought television sets just to watch "Uncle Miltie". So valuable was Berle to NBC that the network signed him, in 1951, to a "lifetime contract," which paid him $100,000 annually whether he performed or not. The show was the single most popular comedy/variety series of television's earliest years and earned the comedian one of the industry's first Emmy Awards.

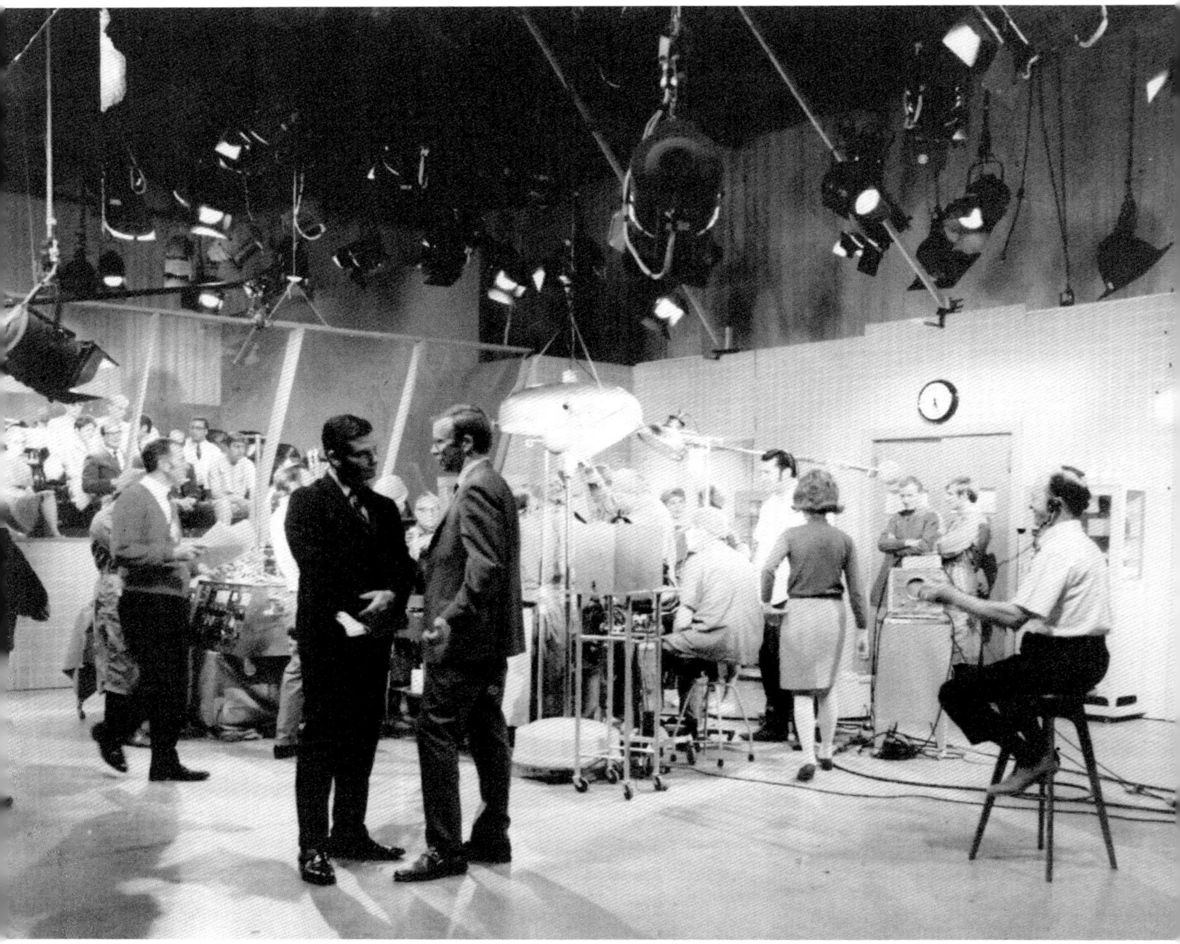

Director-Producer of *Guiding Light*

When Peter "Ace" Andrews began work on the CBS soap opera series *Guiding Light* in 1957, the show was live and in black and white. He went on to see it taped and in color as he directed and produced the daily show for 16 years. It was a show about doctors, as seen in the above photograph showing a surgical operation scene. Ace is in the center speaking to a man (in a black coat) who was with the sponsor Proctor & Gamble. Ace has been married for many years to Chris Andrews and is a lifelong resident of Fair Lawn. (Courtesy of Peter Andrews.)

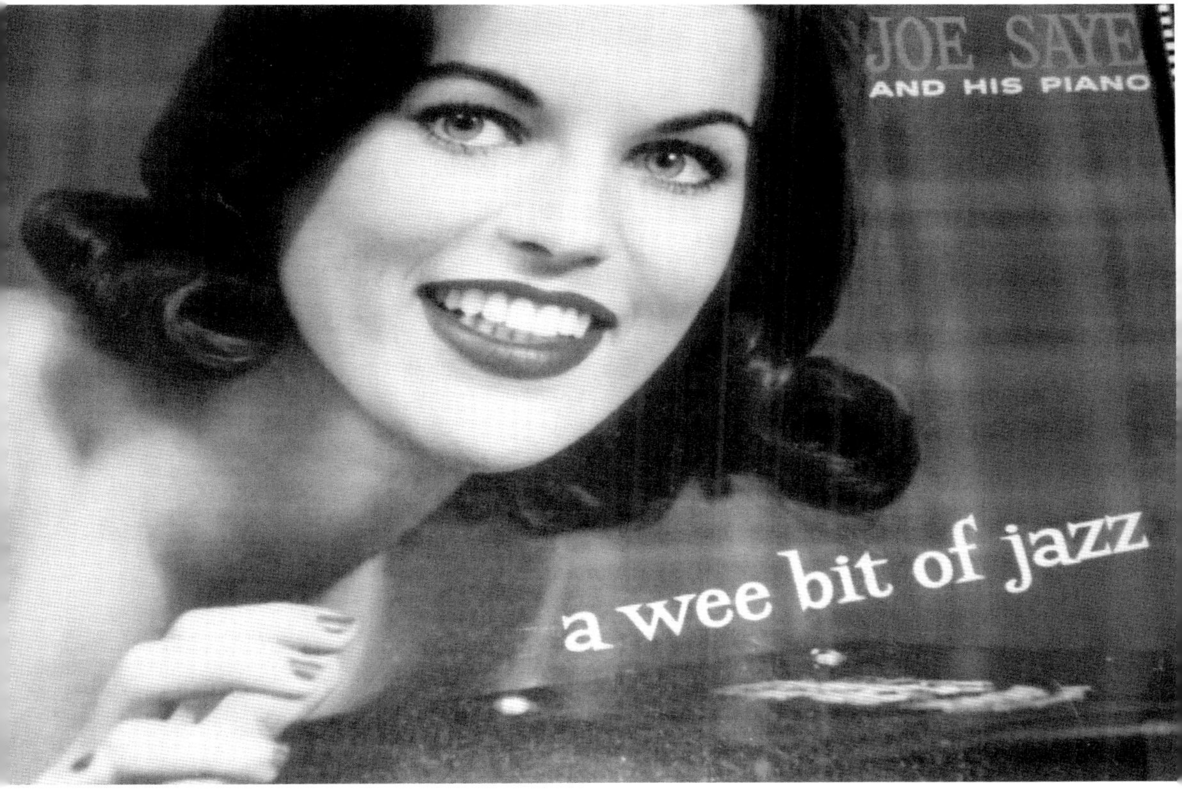

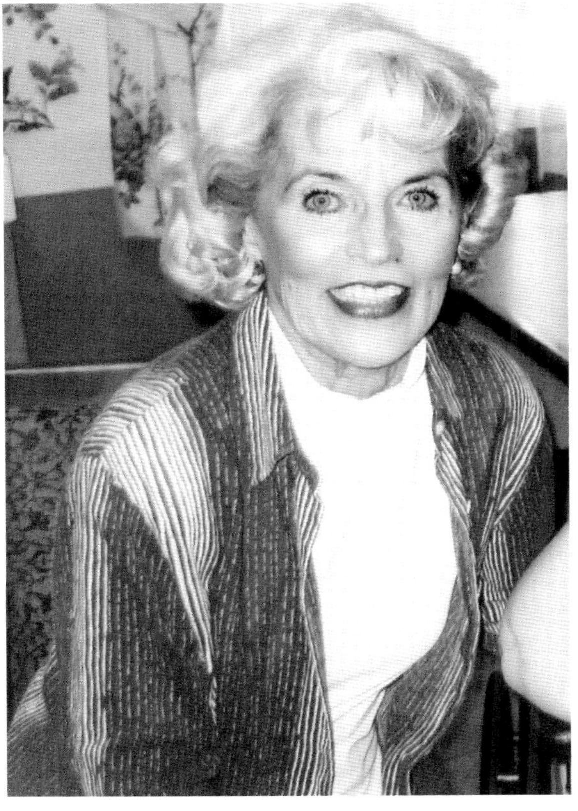

Fashion Model Young and Old

Chris Andrews was a fashion model (above) in New York City at age 23, doing print and runway modeling. Then, at age 73, she won a national modeling contest sponsored by AARP for people over 50 (left), beating 14,000 entries. But Chris Perkins Andrews considers her greatest achievement to be raising her four beautiful daughters in Fair Lawn and being married for 40 years to Ace Andrews, the director-producer of *Guiding Light*. Her sister, Millie Perkins, became a movie star. Both of them were fashion models in New York when approached to go to Hollywood to be actresses. Millie went, but Chris decided it was not for her; she wanted a family. (Courtesy of Chris Andrews.)

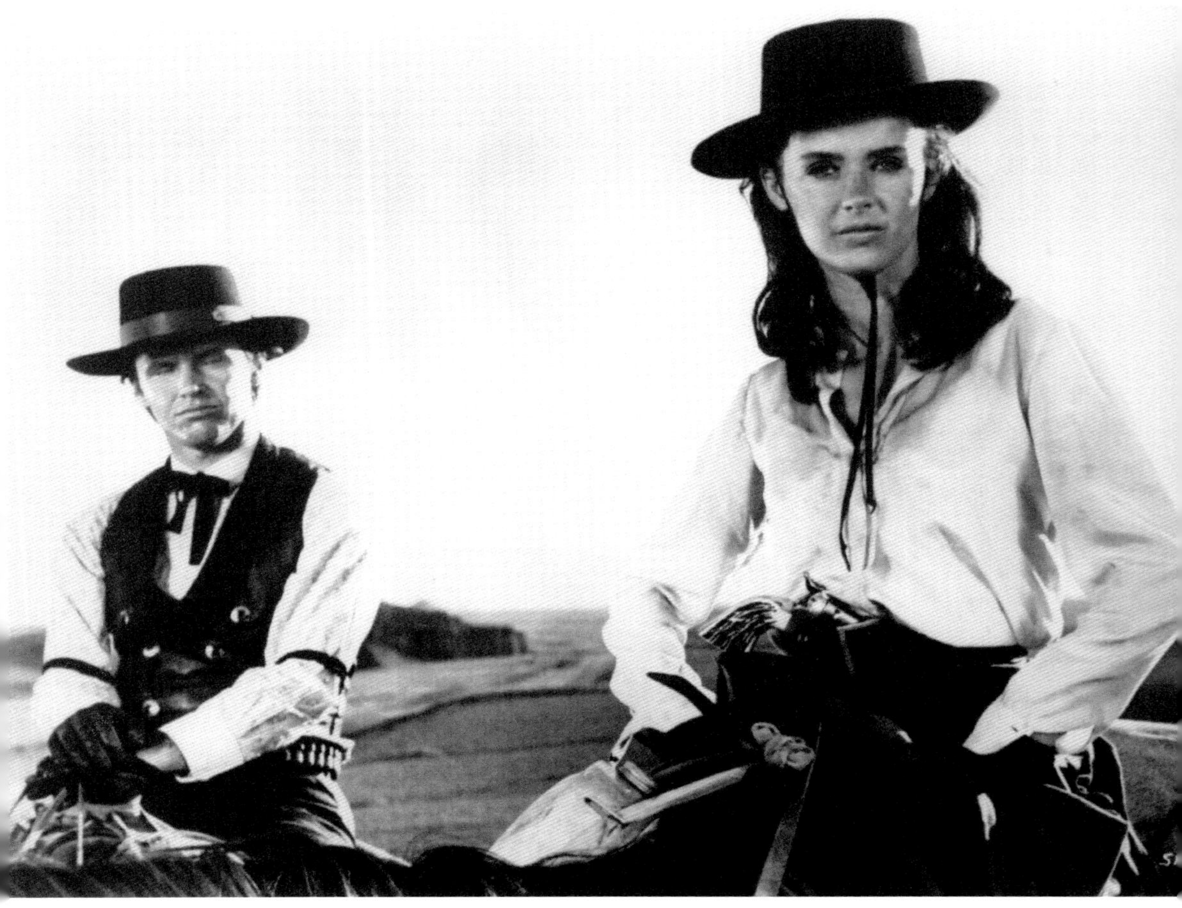

Actress Millie Perkins

In 1964, Millie Perkins was the female lead in Jack Nicholson's inaugural film productions *The Shooting* and *Ride in the Whirlwind*. After graduating from Fair Lawn High School, she worked as a receptionist in New York when a photographer discovered her, and she became an international cover girl. When director George Stevens saw her magazine covers in 1958, he flew her to Hollywood for a screen test and cast her as Anne Frank in his film *The Diary of Anne Frank*. Perkins received excellent reviews and was placed under contract to 20th Century Fox. (Courtesy of Millie Perkins.)

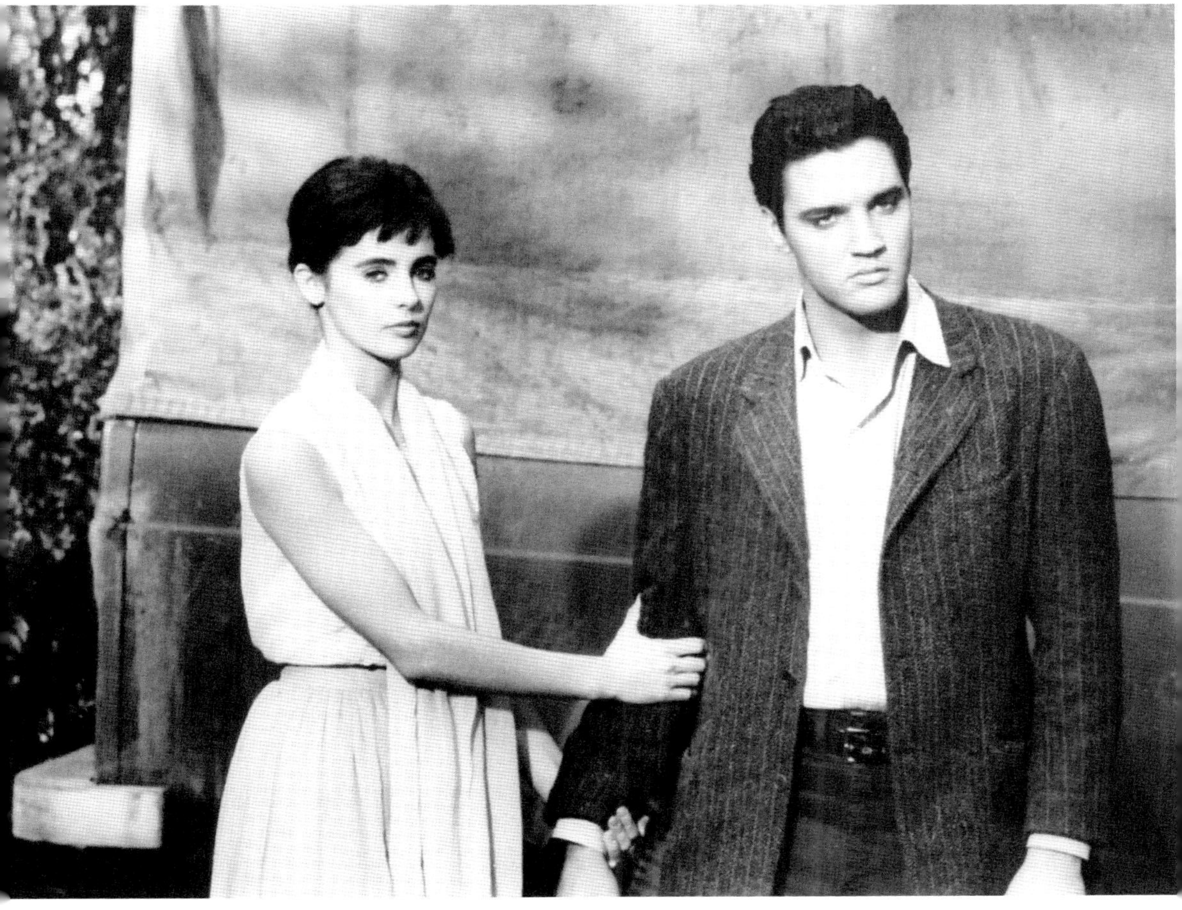

Actress Who Kissed Elvis

In 1961, Millie Perkins played the girlfriend of Elvis Presley and got to kiss him in *Wild in the Country* when he was at the height of his career. Perkins had many other film roles, such as Jon Voight's ex-wife in *Table for Five*, Charlie Sheen's mother in the 1987 movie *Wall Street*, and the bereft Jewish mother in John Grisham's *The Chamber*. She played Annie Potts's grandmother in the television series *Any Day Now* and Elvis's mother in the ABC series *Elvis the Early Years*. In all, she appeared in 24 films and more than 35 television shows. (Courtesy of Millie Perkins.)

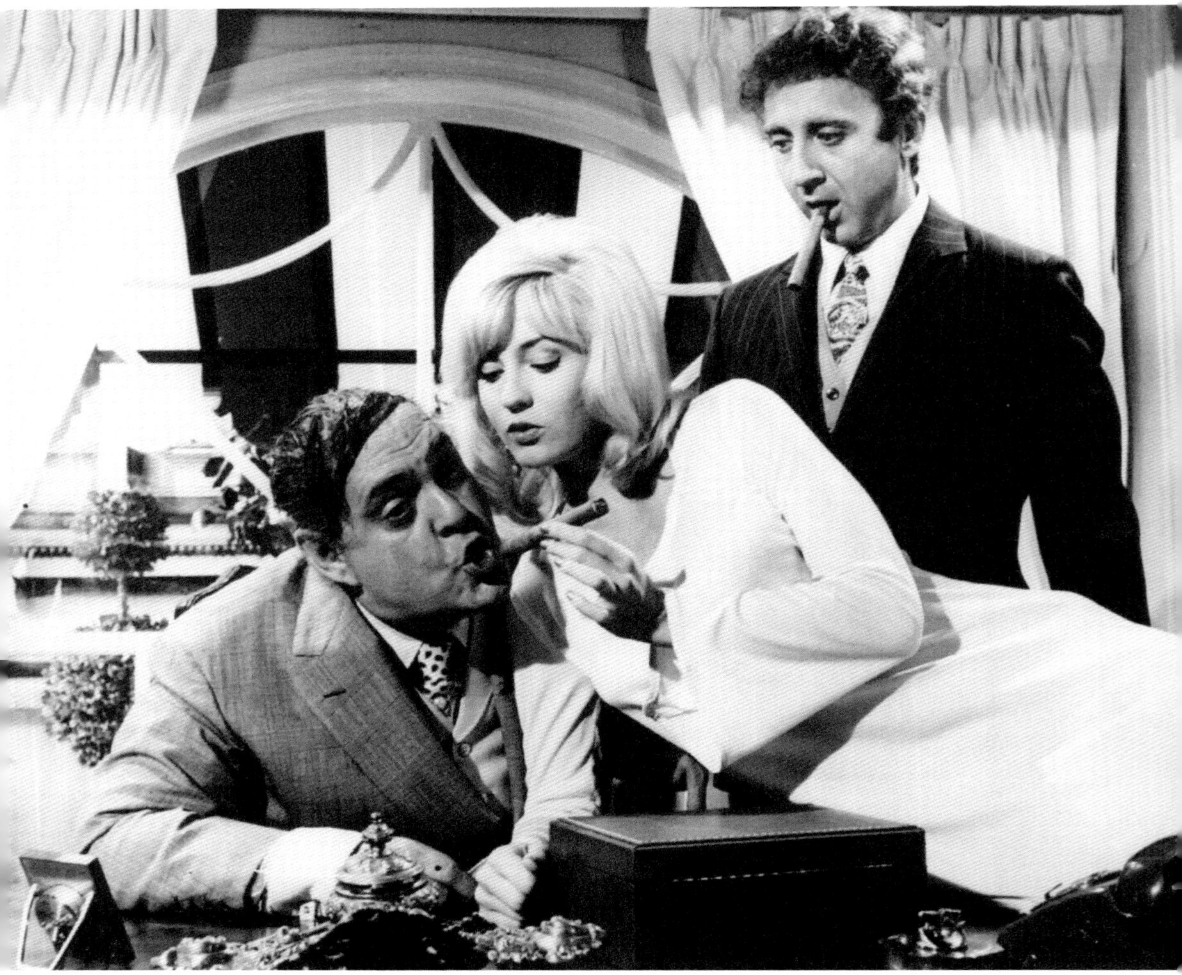

Blonde Bombshell in *The Producers*
Lee Meredith is shown above playing the ditzy, blonde Scandinavian secretary and the object of Zero Mostel's fantasies in the original 1968 film version of *The Producers*, also starring Gene Wilder. In 1972, she appeared in the original Broadway production of *The Sunshine Boys* followed by the film version with Walter Matthau and George Burns. Other Broadway credits included the comedies *A Teaspoon Every Four Hours* (1969), *Once in a Lifetime* (1978), and *Musical Chairs* (1980). She has appeared on several television programs, including the game show *Match Game*, which airs on the Game Show Network. (Courtesy of Lee Meredith.)

The Miller Lite Beer Girl

For 18 years, in the 1970s and 1980s, Lee Meredith was the "Doll" opposite tough guy Mickey Spillane in the Miller Lite All-Star campaign. Her Charmane character in *As the World Turns* brought prime-time humor to a daytime soap. Her career spanned dozens of television and film appearances with the likes of Jackie Gleason, Barbra Streisand, and Omar Sharif. She appeared with Stacy Keach in the Mickey Spillane movie *Murder Me, Murder You.* Her name was Judith Lee Sauls when she attended Fair Lawn High School. (Courtesy of Lee Meredith.)

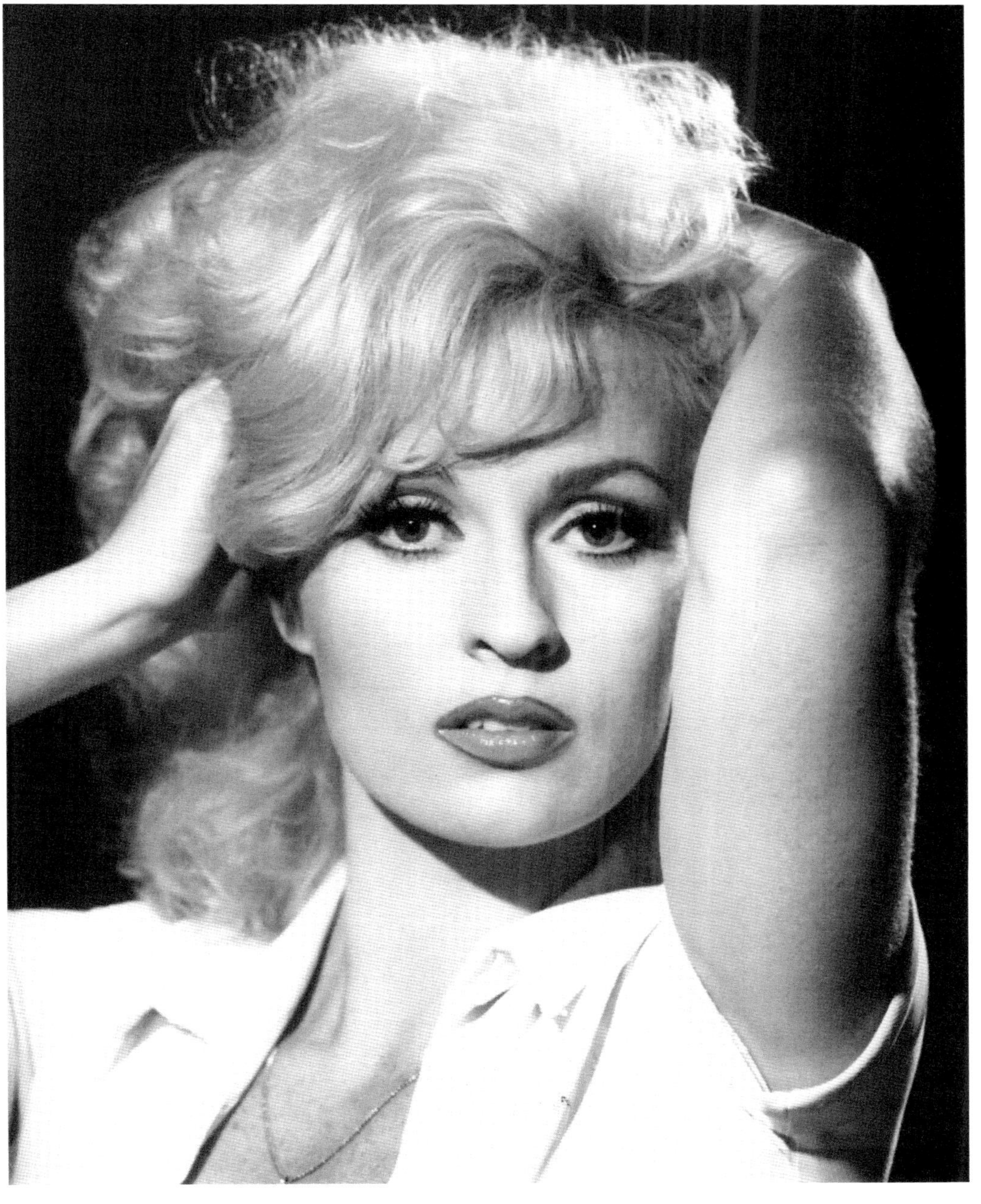

Jazz Bassist Red Mitchell

Keith Moore Mitchell, known as "Red" for his light-auburn hair, was a renowned jazz bassist who also composed music and lyrics. Red grew up in Fair Lawn and entertained his friends with his original "boogie-woogie" piano pieces. He soon turned to the bass as a solo instrument and, by 1948, was playing with a jazz trio in New York. He played with Woody Herman's big band and performed with such greats as Billie Holiday, André Previn, and Ornette Coleman. In 1968, he tuned his bass in fifths as other stringed instruments were tuned. This made possible a much greater range of notes, chords, and dynamics, and soon, other jazz bassists adopted this way of tuning. In 1968, Red Mitchell moved to Stockholm where he performed, composed, and wrote poetic song lyrics, for which he won two Swedish Grammys. Jim Hall, jazz guitarist in whose trio Red performed said that he "played the most gorgeous melodic solos of anybody on any instrument." (Courtesy of Allan Zolnekoff.)

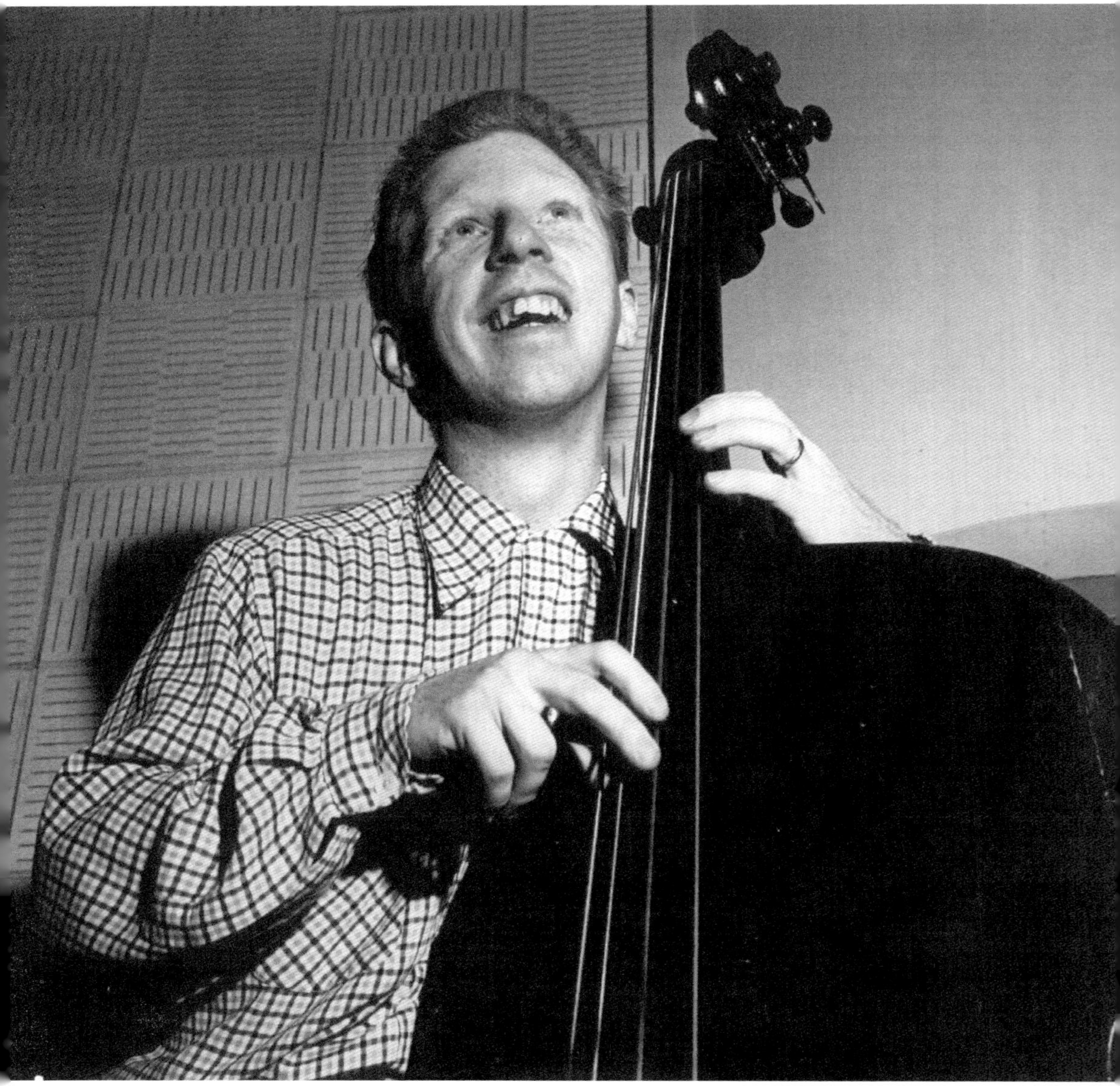

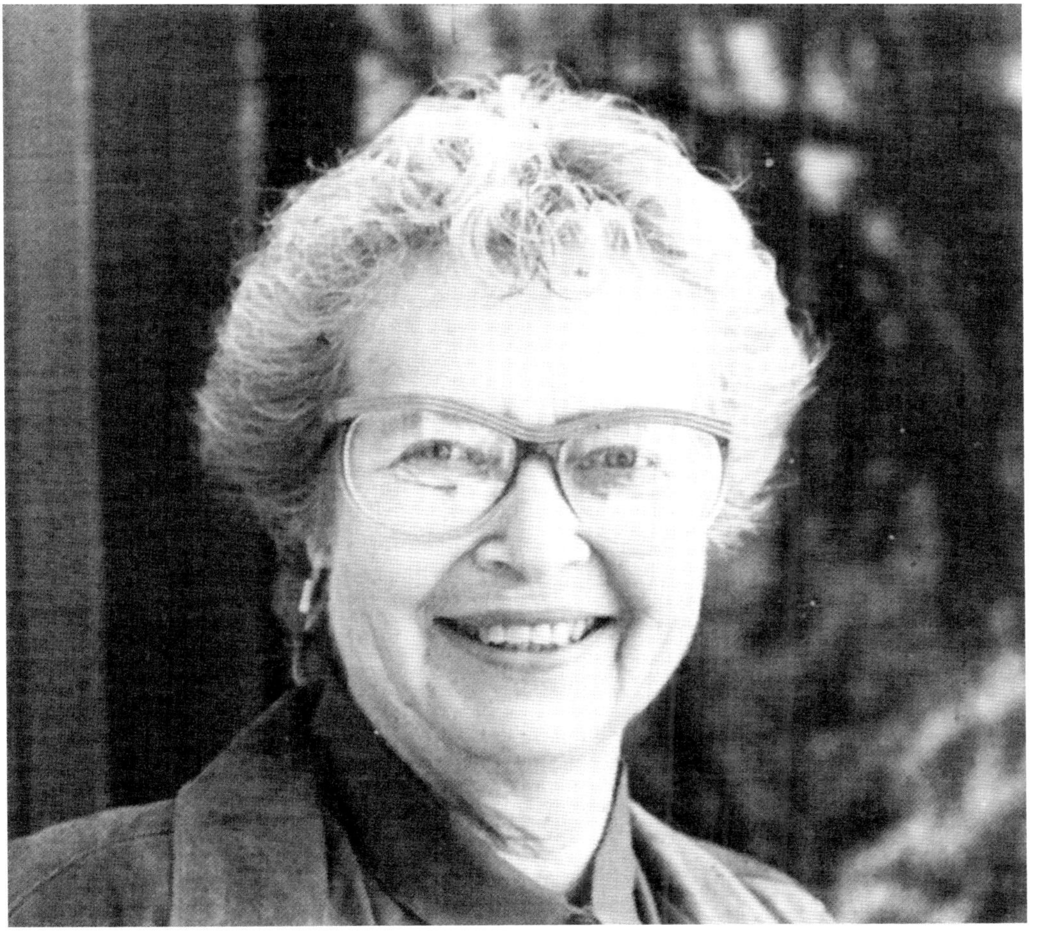

Activist and Author

Vivian Carlin was a dynamo. Soon after she moved to Fair Lawn, she joined the League of Women Voters, served on its board, and later was elected its president. Very involved in local affairs, she ran for borough council. When she lost, she worked for bipartisan candidates. Relocating to Princeton, she worked to establish housing for seniors there. She worked as a specialist and supervisor for the New Jersey Division on Aging and was a delegate to the White House Conference on Aging. After getting her doctorate in gerontology, she authored or coauthored four books on choices for living accommodations for the elderly.

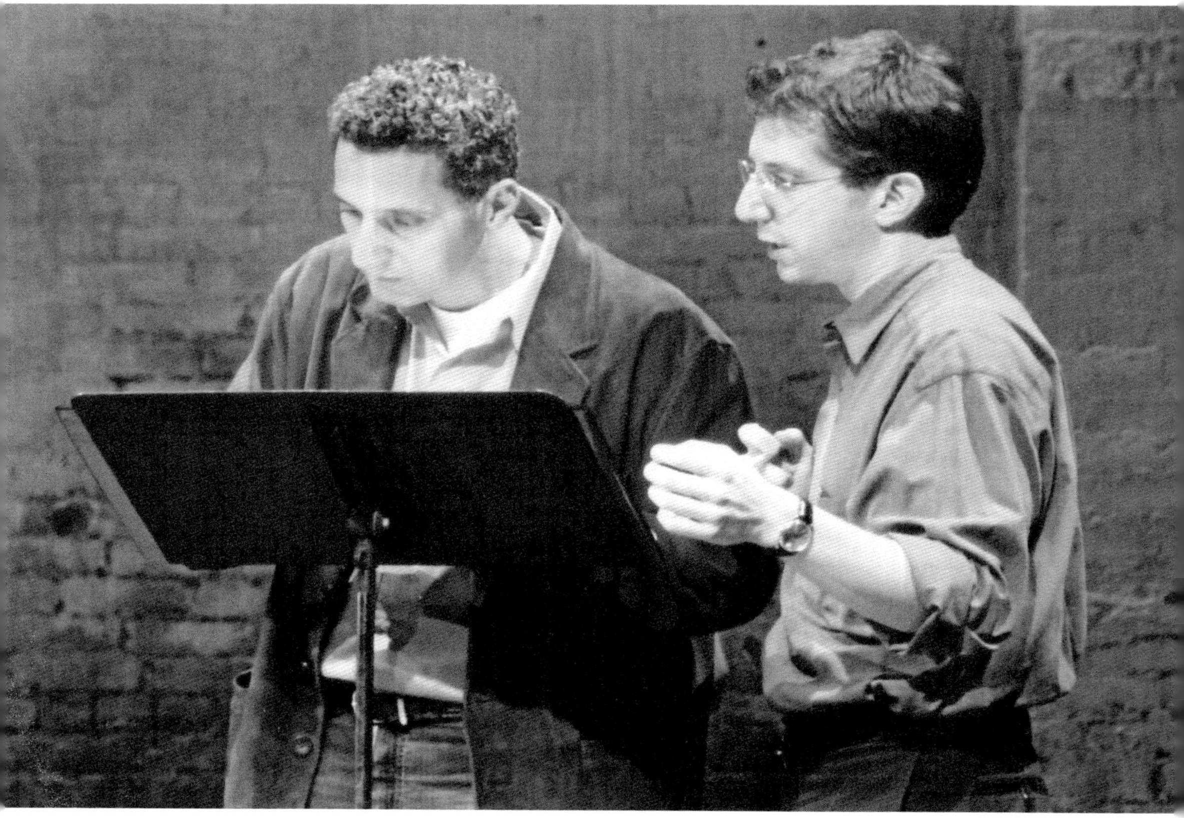

Shakespeare Expert

Barry Edelstein (right) is a theater director, producer, and writer. He is pictured directing actor John Turturro, who starred in *Barton Fink* and *O Brother, Where Art Thou?* Barry worked at the Public Theater in New York where he oversaw the company's annual summer Shakespeare productions in New York's Central Park. He has directed more than half of Shakespeare's plays, two Steve Martin plays, and Arthur Miller's *All My Sons*, which won the Lucille Lortel Award for Best Revival. His book *Thinking Shakespeare* was called "a must read for actors" by *New York Magazine*. In October 2012, he was appointed as artistic director of the Old Globe Theatre in San Diego. Edelstein grew up in Fair Lawn and went to Fair Lawn High.

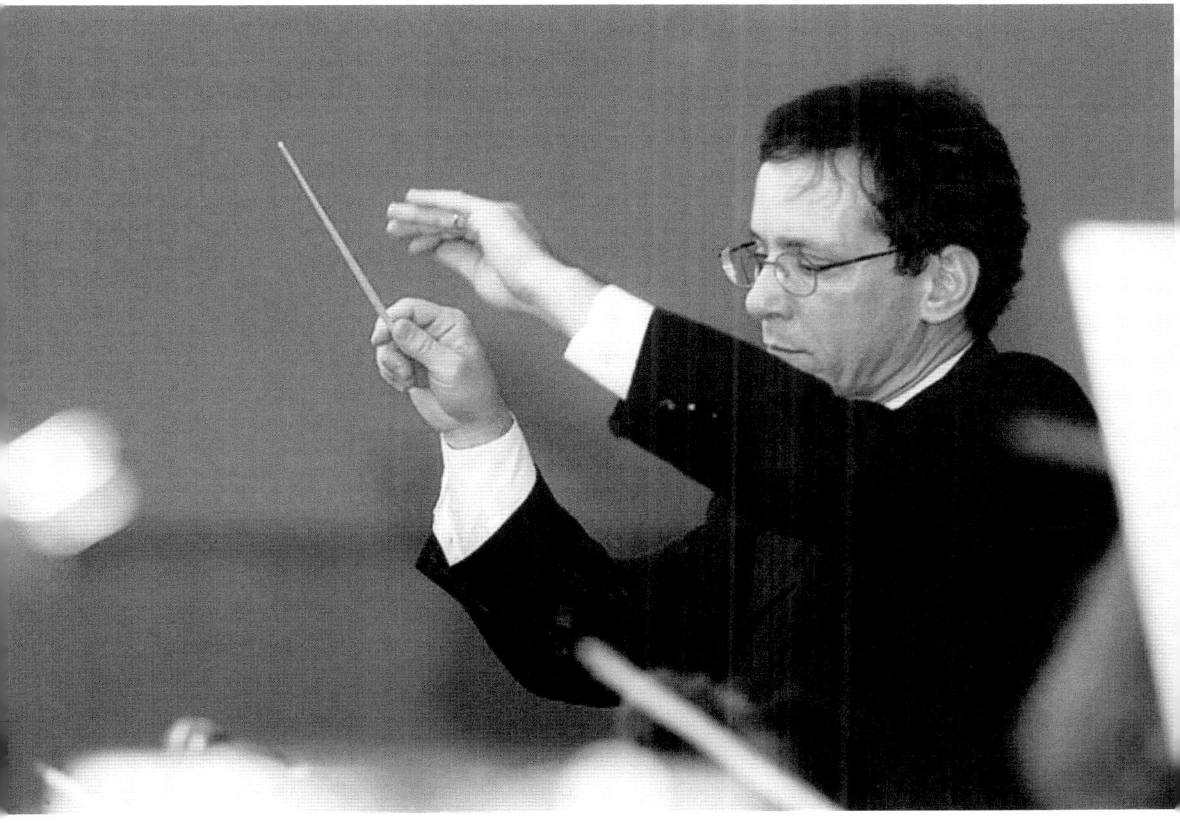

Five Tony Nominations and One Win

Larry Hochman won the 2011 Tony Award for Best Orchestrations for The *Book of Mormon*. He had four other Tony nominations for best orchestrations for *The Scottsboro Boys*, *Spamalot*, *Fiddler on the Roof*, and *A Class Act*. Hochman did the orchestrations for 13 other Broadway shows, including additional orchestrations for *Shrek*, *The Little Mermaid*, and *The Music Man* (Revival). He has won four Emmy Awards for his original music on the television series *Wonder Pets!* He also has done orchestrations for 18 films including Disney's *Lady and the Tramp II*, *Once Upon a Mattress*, and *Dead of Winter*. Hochman has lived in Fair Lawn for most of his life. (Courtesy of Larry Hochman.)

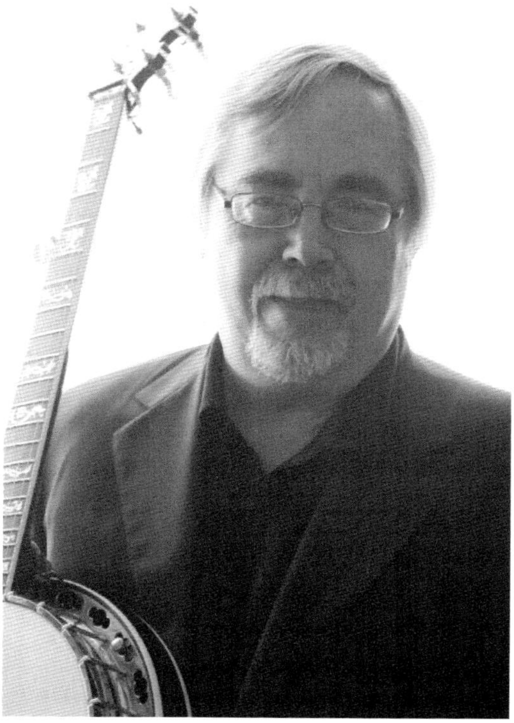

Banjo Player Extraordinaire

Tony Trischka has been deemed "the most influential banjo player of the latter part of the 20th century." His avant-garde styling has had a strong influence on generations of progressive bluegrass players. The *New York Times* called him "the godfather of what's sometimes called new acoustic music." He is also considered a top teacher and has put out videos and books about banjo playing. Trischka has performed at the Kennedy Center and Avery Fisher Hall as well as many international venues, and he has appeared on radio and television. He was named Banjo Player of the Year and has won many other awards. The musician is a longtime resident of Fair Lawn. (Photograph by permission of Tony Trischka.)

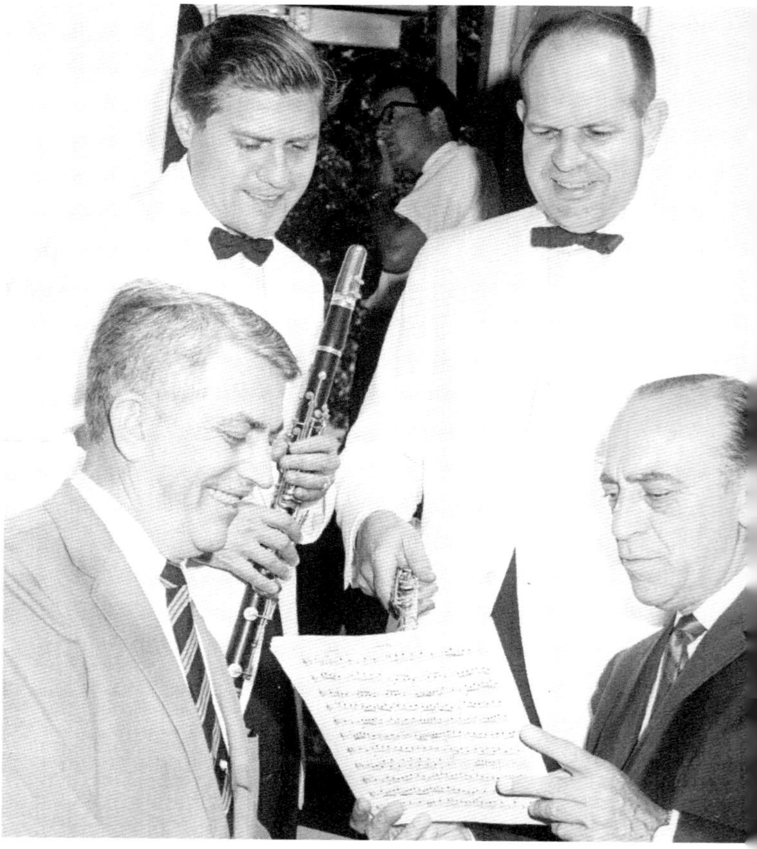

Concert Organizer

Isadore Freeman was a professional musician who organized the Summer Festival of Music and worked for the construction of the band shell, which bears his name. The free evening concerts range from big band and jazz to classical music. Freeman, pictured at the lower left, also organized chamber music concerts held at the Fair Lawn Library.

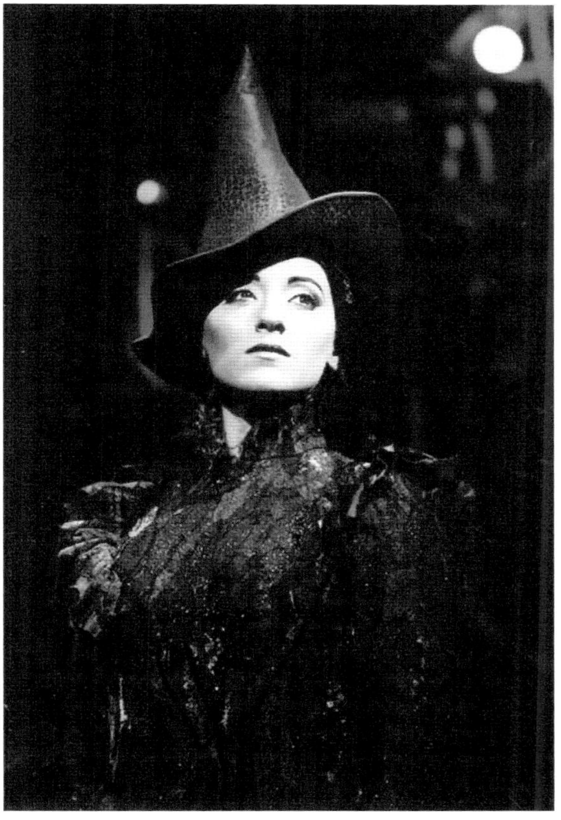

Broadway Star of *Wicked*
Donna Vivino starred for two years as Elphaba in the First National Tour of *Wicked* and has also performed the role on Broadway. Other Broadway credits include *Hairspray*, *Martin Short: Fame Becomes Me*, and *Saturday Night Fever*. In 1987, Donna originated the role of Young Cosette in Broadway's *Les Miserables*. She also originated the role of Enid Hoopes in all of the pre-Broadway workshops of *Legally Blonde* but was unable to do the show because of scheduling conflicts with the Martin Short production. Film and television credits include *A Gifted Man*, *The Sopranos*, *Everyday People*, *Married to It*, and *All My Children*. Like many of the artists featured in this section, Donna was a product of Fair Lawn Schools. (Both, courtesy of Donna Vivino.)

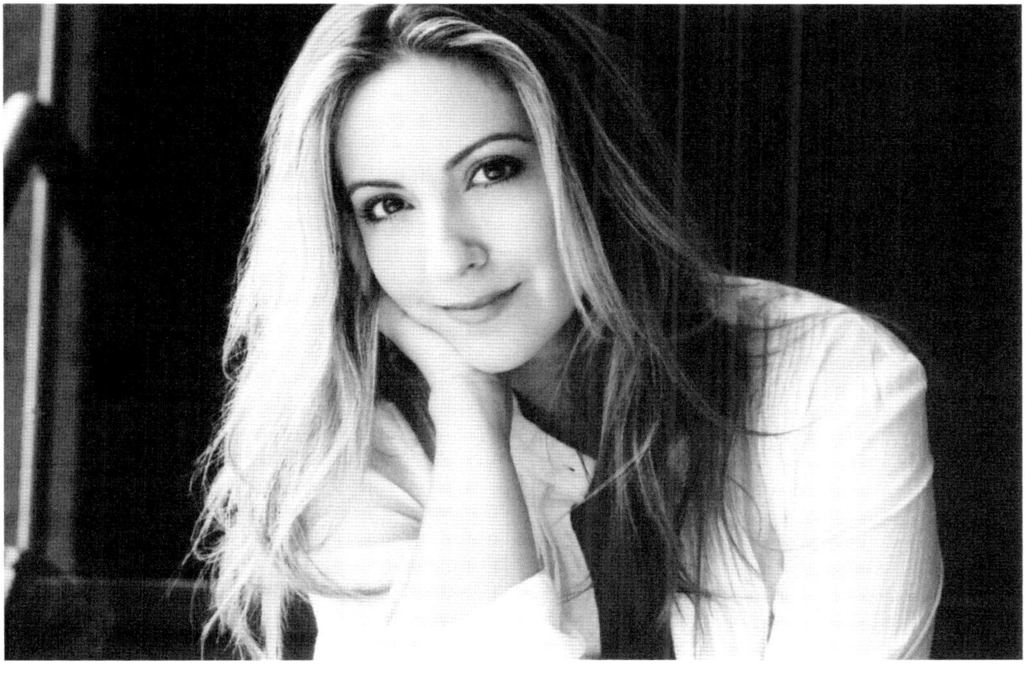

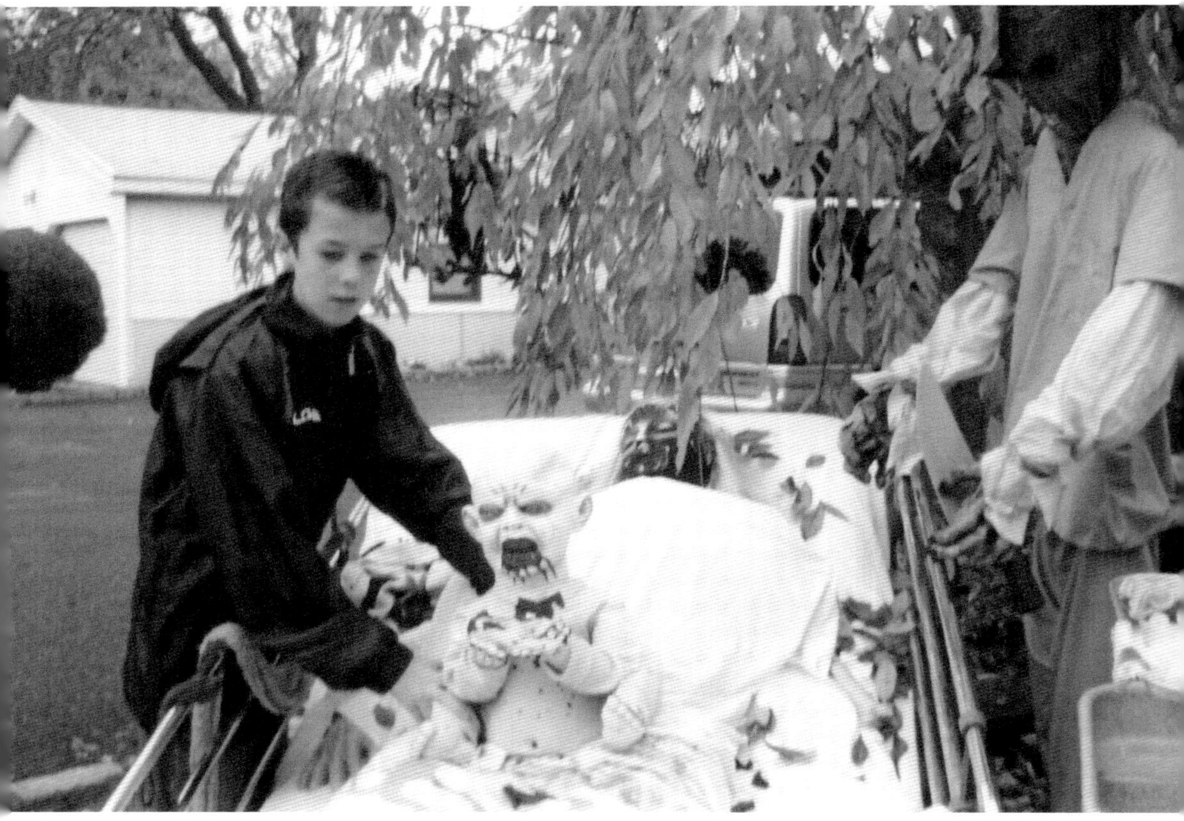

Eleven-Year-Old Monster Creator

Michael Kwasnik has been crafting monsters by hand for three Halloweens. A relative who works as a hairdresser gives him mannequin heads that hold wigs, Michael carves and paints the heads to look like those that belong to monsters. His mother, who teaches at a dance studio, gives him old costumes and clothes for the bodies. After seeing other handmade Halloween monster houses, Michael said, "I thought it would be pretty cool to do my own house." He is a sixth-grader at Thomas Jefferson Middle School and believes monster making is a chance to work with tools and make something. His haunting display was a winner in the *Patch* contest "Scariest Halloween Houses in Fair Lawn."

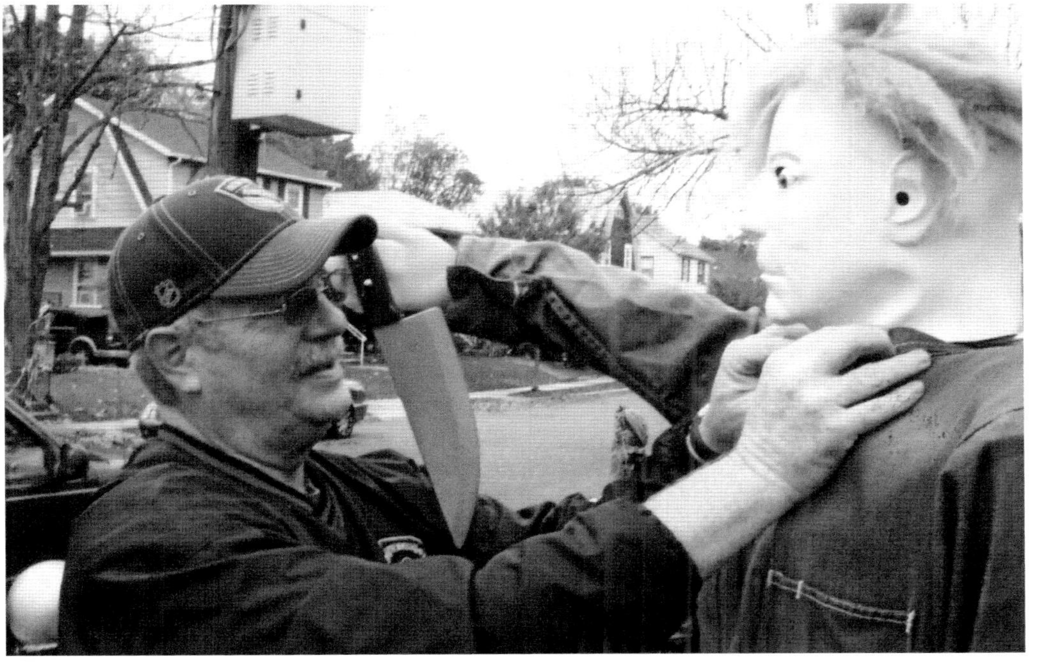

Artist-Engineer of Monsters

For Halloween 2013, resident John Bernabeo displayed 23 monsters that he built using PVC pipe and chicken wire. He also uses his electrical and plumbing skills to place motion sensors on a number of the monsters, rigging them to jump out at the trick-or-treaters as they walk by on the sidewalk. Also activated by sensors are sounds of monsters and thunder and the flashing of lightning. Children who reach the front door can sit on a replica electric chair that vibrates when they sit down while a light flashes above their heads. An animated group of witches stirs a cauldron of brew, and a mad scientist carves up a blood-spurting body on an examining table. Bernabeo began making monsters in 1995 and has been adding new ones each year.

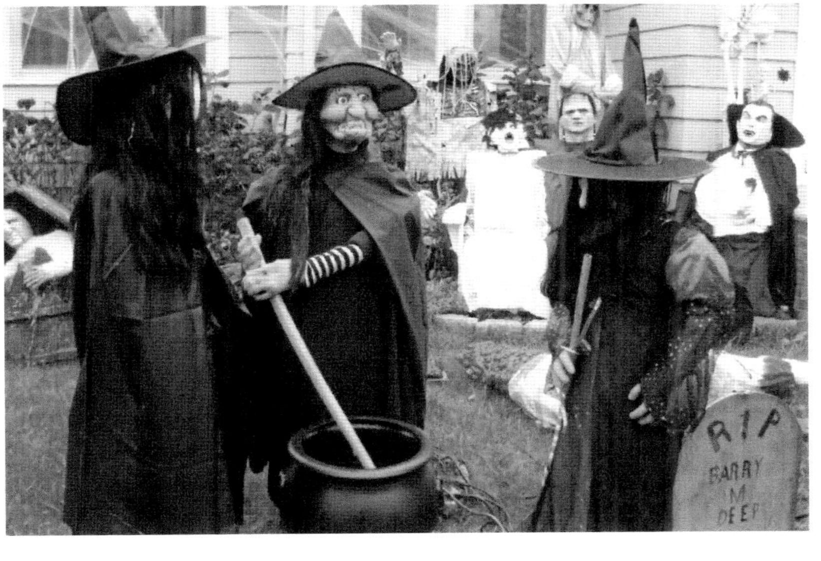

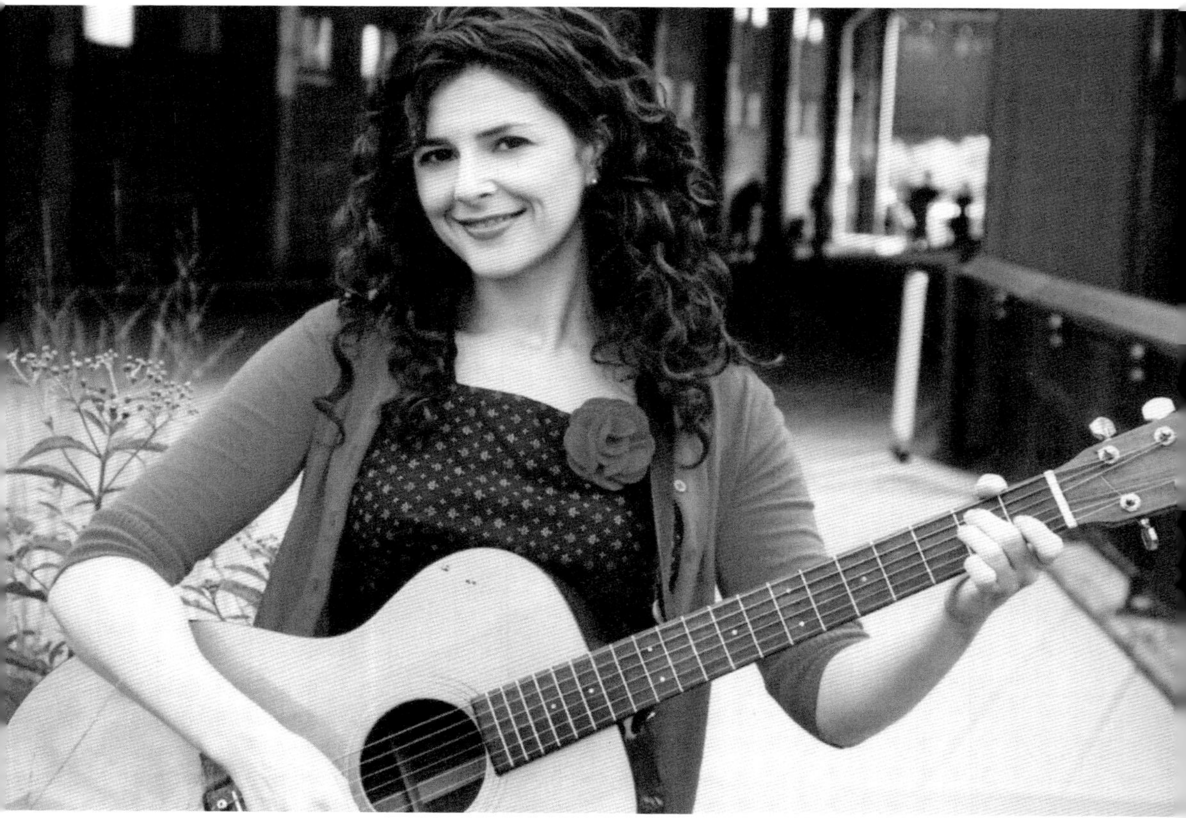

PBS Star for Children's Entertainment

Meredith LeVande is the creator of *Monkey Monkey Music*. Her videos are broadcast multiple times each day on 100 public television stations in 70 markets on iconic shows such as *Sesame Street* and *Curious George*. In the videos, she sings and plays the guitar, which has made her nationally famous with a following and popularity that the really popular children's entertainers have. LeVande was raised in the borough and went to Fair Lawn High School. Her experience with children comes from entertaining at more than 600 birthday parties, which allowed her to hone her performance. Her music resonates with children because it encourages them to get up, dance, and sing along to the upbeat songs. (Courtesy of Meredith LeVande.)

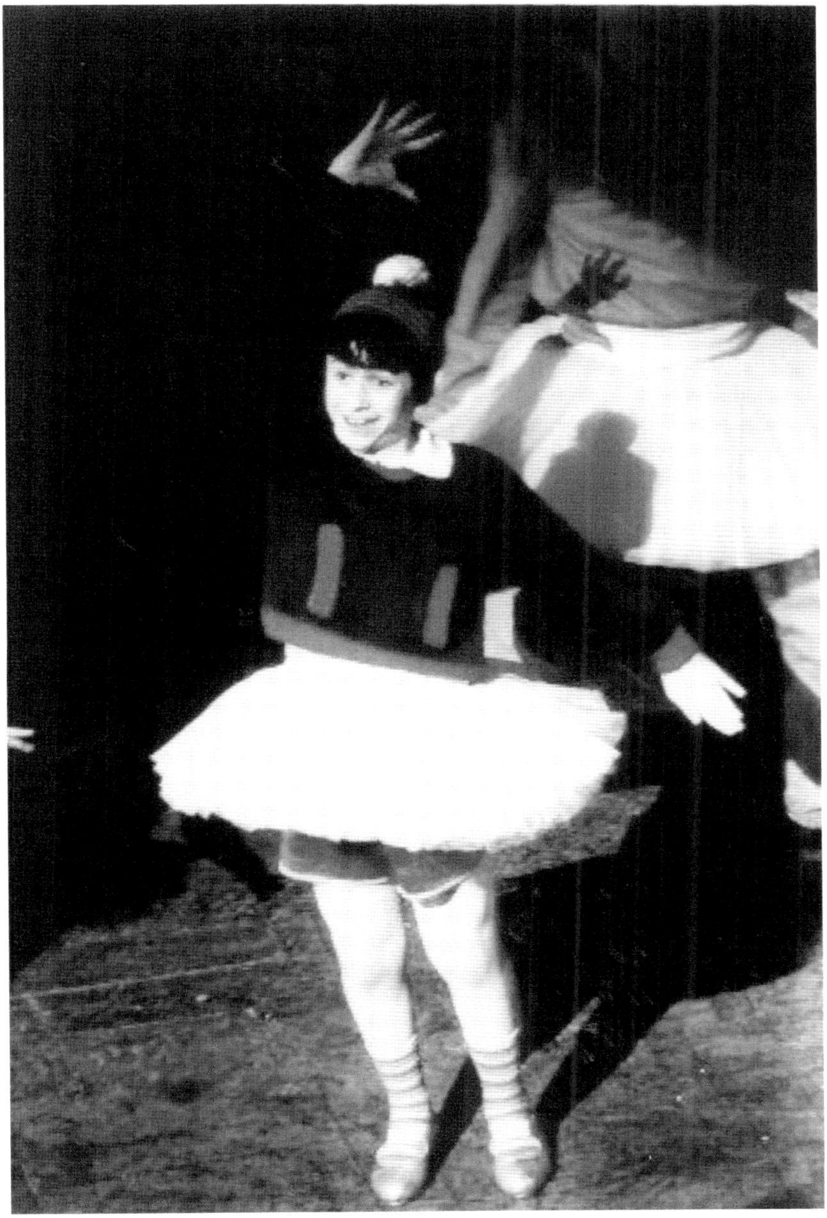

Performer in Broadway Musicals

Trevor Braun made his Broadway debut at age seven when he appeared as Chip in the musical comedy *Beauty and the Beast*. He went on to perform for a year as Flounder in *The Little Mermaid*, hence his nickname "Fish & Chips." His most famous role (shown above) was as one of the boys in the Tony Award–winning show *Billy Elliot: The Musical*. He is a member of the Broadway Kids, which is a concert group based in New York. The group consists of a rotating company of children, aged 8 to 16, who have performed in at least one Broadway, off-Broadway, or major national touring production. Braun has appeared in the television show *Curb Your Enthusiasm*. He also performs in Fair Lawn High School musicals. (Courtesy of Trevor Braun.)

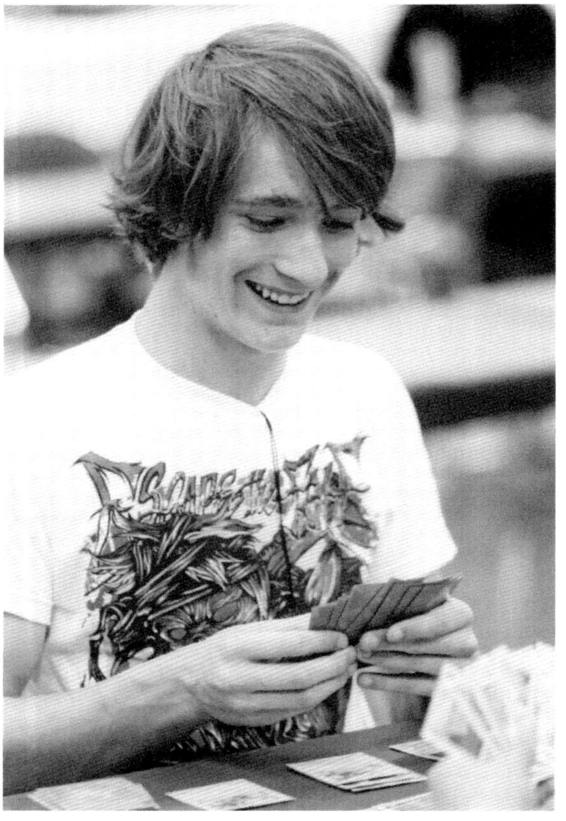

Pokémon and Marching Band Champion

Sam Glassett not only plays drums for the national championship–winning percussion section of the Fair Lawn High School marching band, but he was also the third-place winner at the Pokémon TCG National Championship in Indianapolis in 2010. For his third-place victory, Glassett was awarded a $1,500 scholarship, a Nintendo DS, and a free trip to the World Championships in Kona, Hawaii. There, he finished 16th in the world. Pokémon, which means "pocket monsters," began as an animated television show in Japan. The cartoon creatures were an instant hit leading to video games and trading cards. The company behind Pokémon created a game that utilizes the trading cards and then organized tournaments of these games. The game involves the strategy of warfare and each card has one of 60 characters. The game is compared to chess because players have to think several moves in advance. The game also requires good social skills because in order to win, a player has to trade information and share with the opposing players. North Jersey has the most Pokémon tournaments in America and the most players who are ranked in the top 10 nationally. Glassett began playing the game at age nine when he played against members of his family. Glassett also loves to play the drums. His percussion group of the Fair Lawn High School marching band three times won the championship at the US National Marching Band Championship. The band itself finished in the top five overall in 2010 through 2012. Since the USSBA National Championships format was introduced in 2006, Fair Lawn has been the only school to represent Bergen County as an open class band. Glassett will attend college at Rutgers University School of Engineering where he plans to major in astrophysics and mechanical/aerospace engineering; he wants to be a rocket scientist. He will not be performing with the band but will still compete in Pokémon. (Courtesy of Bob Glassett.)

70

CHAPTER FIVE

The Athletes

For such a small town, Fair Lawn High School has had a disproportionate number of students who went on to be professional and Olympic athletes. Probably the best known is Hubie Brown, who is currently the lead commentator for NBA basketball games on ESPN and ABC. Ron Perranoski was one of professional baseball's best relief pitchers when he played for the Los Angeles Dodgers and then the Minnesota Twins in the 1960s. In the 1950s, Tom Acker was both a starter and relief pitcher for the Cincinnati Redlegs and held Hall of Famers Ernie Banks, Roy Campanella, Eddie Mathews, Bill Mazeroski, and Pee Wee Reese to a collective .190 batting average. Hank Goin played baseball for the St. Louis Cardinals, Philadelphia Phillies, and the Washington Senators in the 1960s.

Bruce Jankowski is most famous for his dramatic over-the-shoulder catch that allowed Ohio State to beat rival Michigan, a photograph of which made the cover of *Sports Illustrated*. Professional baseball player Zack Smithlin set franchise records in hits, runs, and stolen bases for the New Jersey Jackals. John Schmunk played professional lacrosse in the North American Lacrosse League and is considered to be the greatest lacrosse goalie in Rutgers University history. Jack Van Olden was a professional speed skater who won the Madison Square Garden Silver Skates.

Dr. Dave Sime was a sprinter who won a silver medal in the 100-meter dash at the 1960 Summer Olympics in Rome. Track Hurdler Barbara Jacobs Jordan is a Senior Olympic medalist and has won numerous national championships in Masters Track and Field. A nationally ranked fencer, Steven Griffiths made the US Olympic team as an alternate in 1984. As coach of the Stanford women's tennis team, Frank Brennan won an astounding 10 NCAA titles including a record six in a row. Wrestling coach Frank Bennett was inducted into the National Wrestling Hall of Fame. The gymnasium at Fair Lawn High School is named for him. Virgil Sasso coached baseball teams at Fair Lawn High School to three state titles in the 1940s. The football stadium is named in his honor.

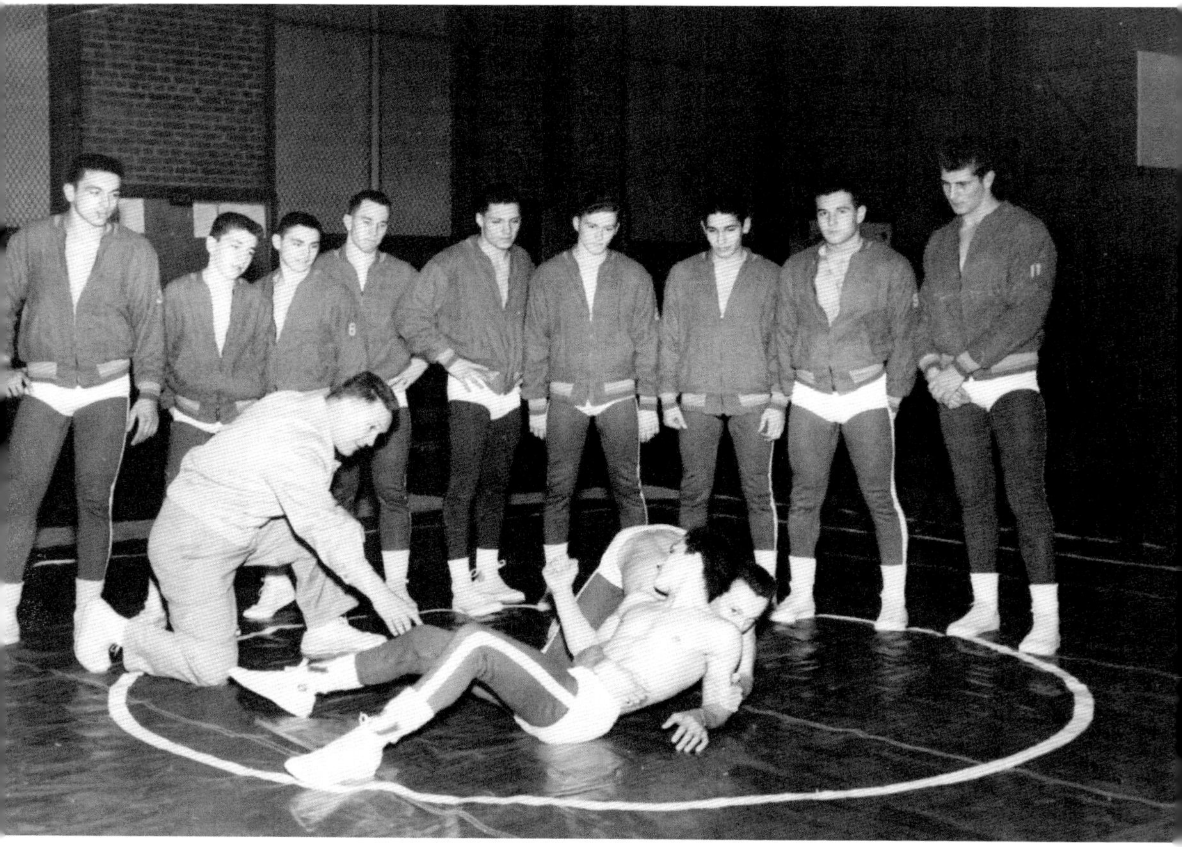

Greatest Wrestling Coach

Frank Bennett was a wrestling coach who was inducted into the National Wrestling Hall of Fame. The gymnasium at Fair Lawn High School is named for him. He introduced wrestling at Fair Lawn High School and, from 1953 to 1958, his teams compiled a record of 52-5 including two undefeated seasons. When he retired from coaching, Bennett became one of the most outstanding college wrestling officials in New Jersey and three times officiated at the state finals. He was inducted into the Bergen County Hall of Fame in 1996. Bennett was instrumental in getting wrestling programs established in East Paterson, Glen Rock, Ridgewood, and Woodridge. (Courtesy of George Bennett.)

Also a Great Football Coach

Frank Bennett was equally, if not more, famous for being the football coach at Fair Lawn High School from 1945 to 1960 with a record of 71-55-6 (.563), five league titles, and a co-state championship. His 16 seasons at the football helm are the most of any coach in Fair Lawn High School history. He was one of the organizers of the Fair Lawn All Sports Association. Players Bennett coached include three in this book: Cincinnati Reds pitcher Tom Acker, Los Angeles Dodger pitcher Ron Perranoski, and Olympic sprinter Dr. David Sime. A Fair Lawn resident, Bennett spent summers as a lifeguard at the Radburn pool. (Courtesy of George Bennett.)

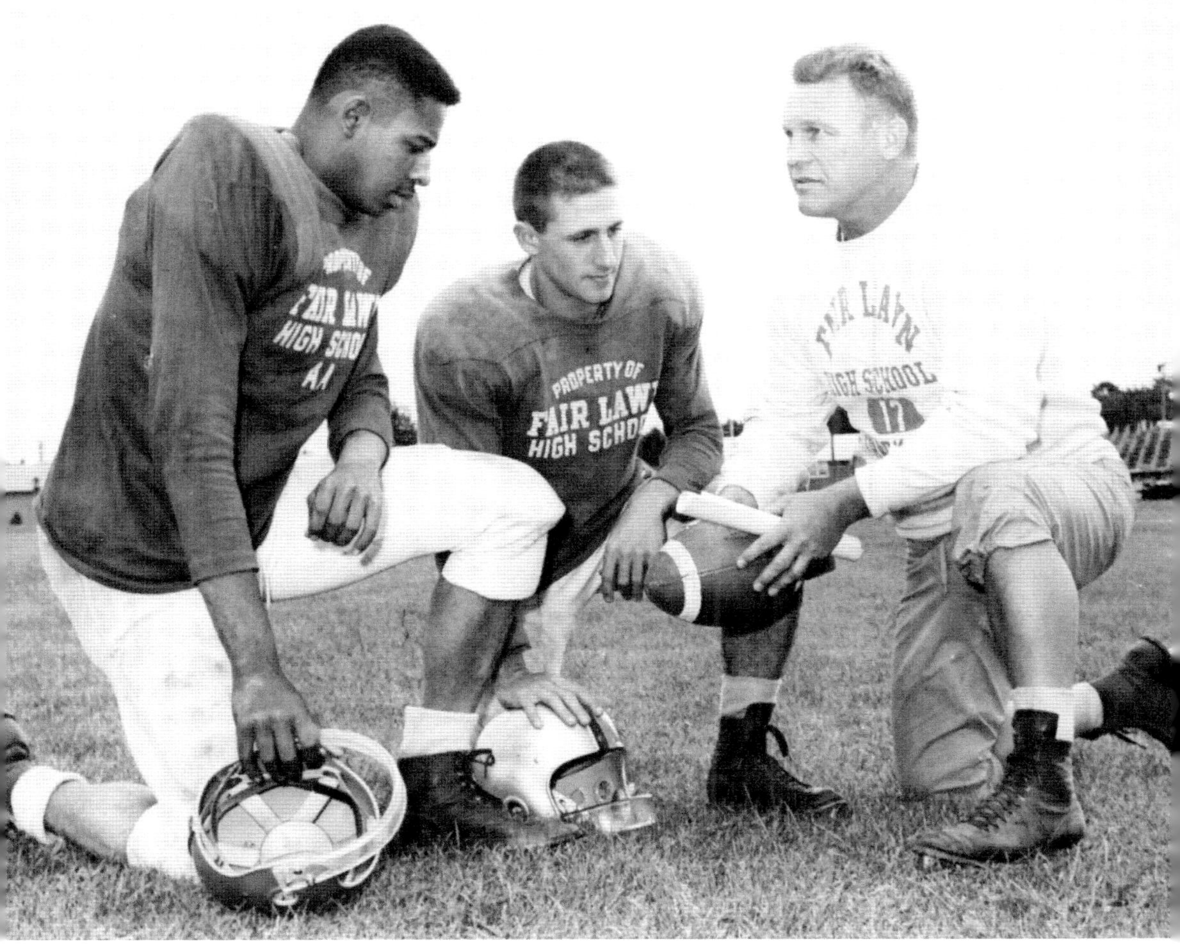

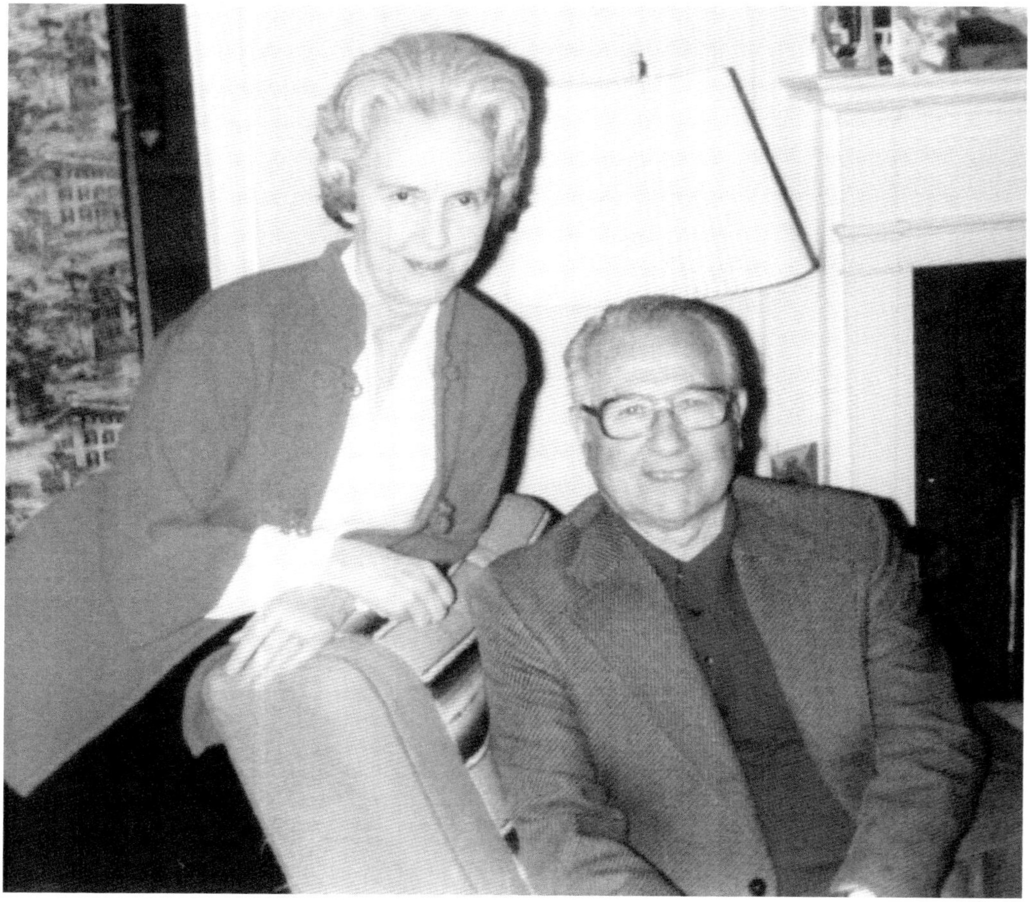

Football Stadium

Virgil Sasso was the athletic director at Fair Lawn High School from 1944 to 1978 and was honored when the football stadium was named Sasso Field. He taught biology at the high school and, in his later years, was the vice principal of Fair Lawn High School. He coached the most successful era of baseball in Fair Lawn history. The 1946, 1947, and 1948 teams won their league and state titles.

Among Coach Sasso's team members was star pitcher Dave Acker, who went on to professional baseball as a pitcher for the Cincinnati Redlegs. Sasso's star hitter was Dr. Dave Sime who hit in 23 consecutive games and had a batting average of .525. Sime went on to win a silver medal in the 100-meter dash at the 1960 Summer Olympics in Rome.

Another great baseball era for Coach Sasso was the in the 1950s when the team won league and state titles every year from 1954 through 1958. In 1954, Ron Perranoski pitched 57 scoreless innings and 10 shutouts. Perranoski went on to become one of professional baseball's best relief pitchers when he played for the Los Angeles Dodgers and then the Minnesota Twins. Hank Goin played for the 1954–1956 teams and became a professional baseball player with the St. Louis Cardinals, Philadelphia Phillies, and the Washington Senators. Bobby Muller pitched for Coach Sasso from 1956 to 1958, earning three league and one state title. Muller went on to become a scout for Major League Baseball teams.

Sasso served as director of the New Jersey National Council of Secondary School Athletic Directors (NCSSAD) and was elected to the NCSSAD Hall of Fame as well as the West Chester Football Hall of Fame. He was also one of the organizers of the Fair Lawn All Sports Association. He is shown with his wife, Edna. (Courtesy of Fritzie Christianson.)

Olympic Sprinter, Multitalented Athlete

Dr. Dave Sime was a sprinter who won a silver medal in the 100-meter dash at the 1960 Summer Olympics in Rome. He held several sprint world records in the 1950s and is considered to be one of the fastest humans of all time. He was favored to win three gold medals at the 1956 Olympics and was on the cover of *Sports Illustrated* in July of that year. However, he aggravated a groin injury and was unable to run in the games. At age 13, Sime won a silver medal in skating at Madison Square Garden. At Fair Lawn High School, he was All-State in football and baseball. Playing for Coach Virgil Sasso, he had a batting average of .525 his senior year, which earned him a $50,000 offer to play for the New York Giants. Instead, he took a baseball scholarship to Duke University. At a baseball game, the Duke track coach was impressed by Sime's speed and asked the baseball coach if he could try Sime in a track meet. In the first time he ever competed in track, he ran the 100 yard dash in 9.6 seconds, missing the world record by only .3 seconds. Still to this day, Sime has the Duke school records for the 100-meter dash at 9.3 seconds and the 200-meter dash at 20.0 seconds—both world records in the 1950s. He held nine world records at one point. Following his success in baseball and track, the Duke football coach asked permission for Sime to play for him. On the first play of his first football game, Sime caught a pass for a touchdown. On his next play, he caught another pass for a touchdown. For the rest of the game, Notre Dame had three defenders covering him, but Duke still won. He graduated from Duke in 1958 and was voted the best athlete in Duke history. He was drafted by the Detroit Lions. He returned to Duke to attend Medical School where he got a degree in ophthalmology. He opened his own practice in Coral Gables, Florida, and became the eye doctor for the Miami Dolphins. (Courtesy of Dr. Dave Sime.)

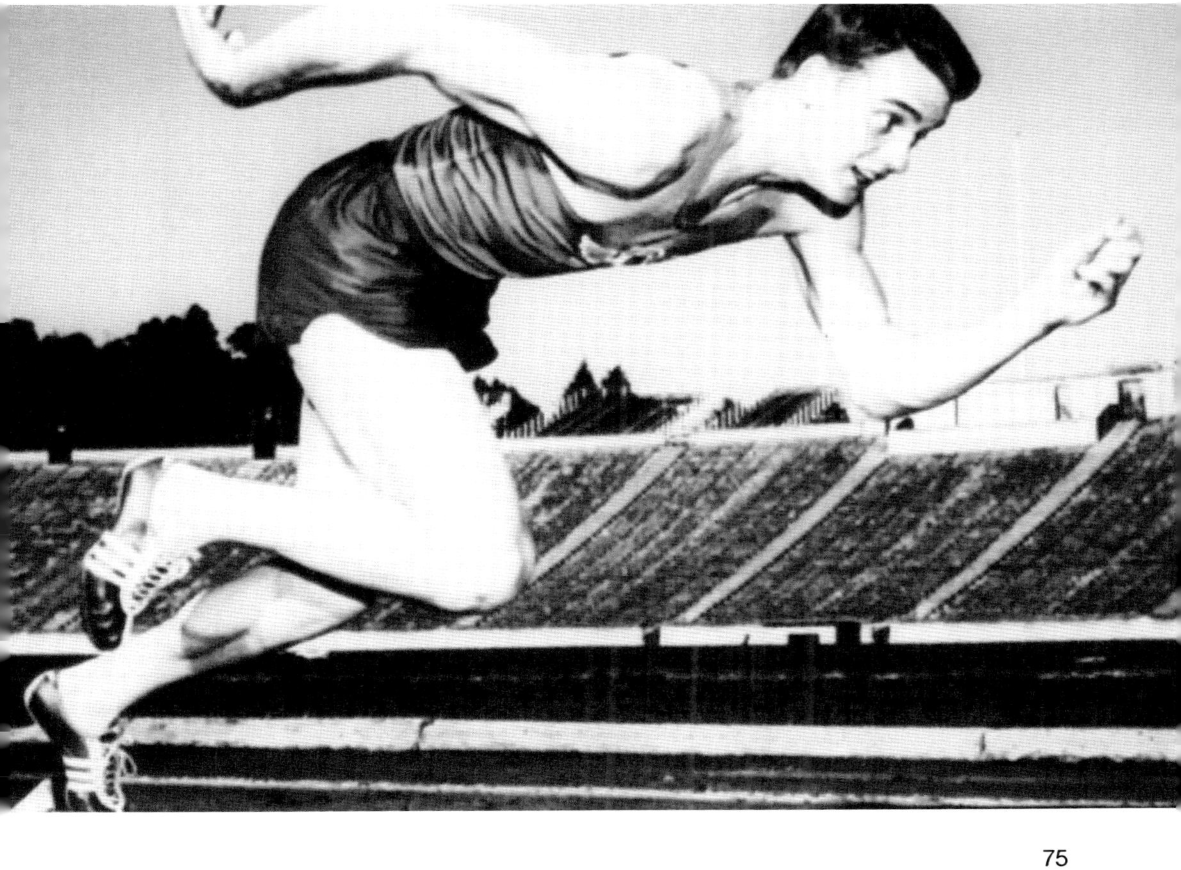

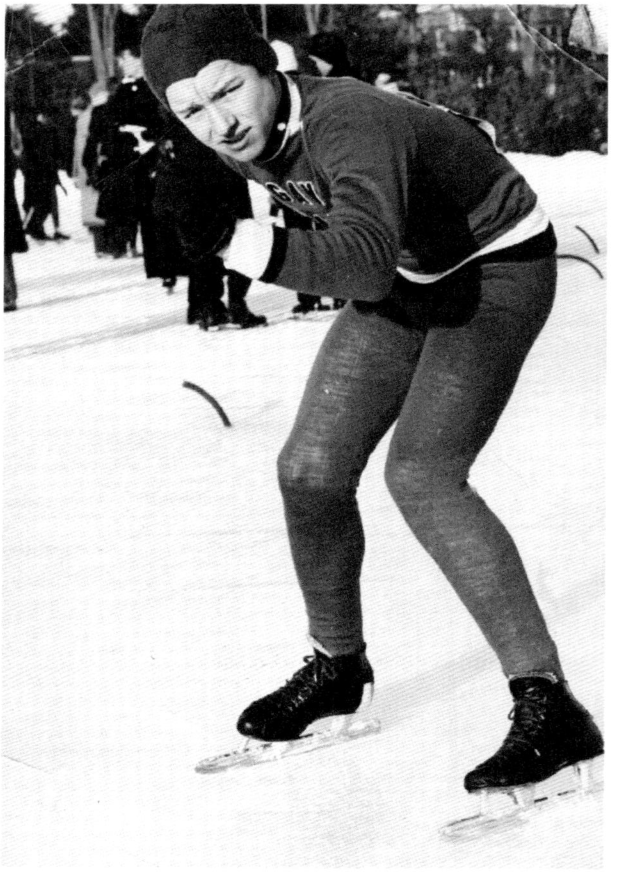

Silver Skates Winner
Jack Van Olden won the Madison Square Garden Silver Skates event and took third at the Boston Garden Silver Skates. In 1943, he was the captain of the first Fair Lawn High School football team and was an original "Cutter"—one of the players who cut class to go to the movies and was benched from a game, resulting in the nickname for the team. (Courtesy of Wayne Van Olden.)

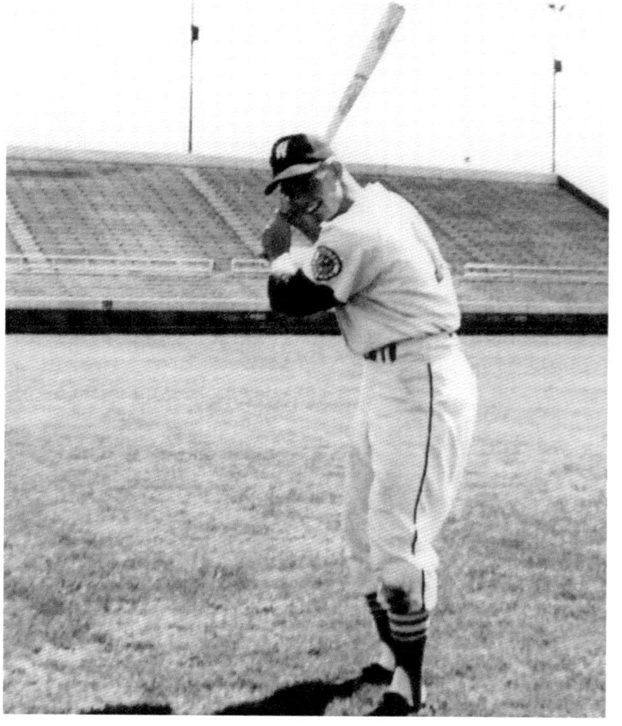

Player for Three National League Teams
Jon "Hank" Goin played for the St. Louis Cardinals, the Philadelphia Phillies, and the Washington Senators from 1959 to 1963. As captain of the Rutgers baseball team in 1959, he was chosen All Big East and led the nation in stolen bases. At Fair Lawn High School, he played on the two-time state champion team, which was coached by Virgil Sasso. (Courtesy of Jon Goin.)

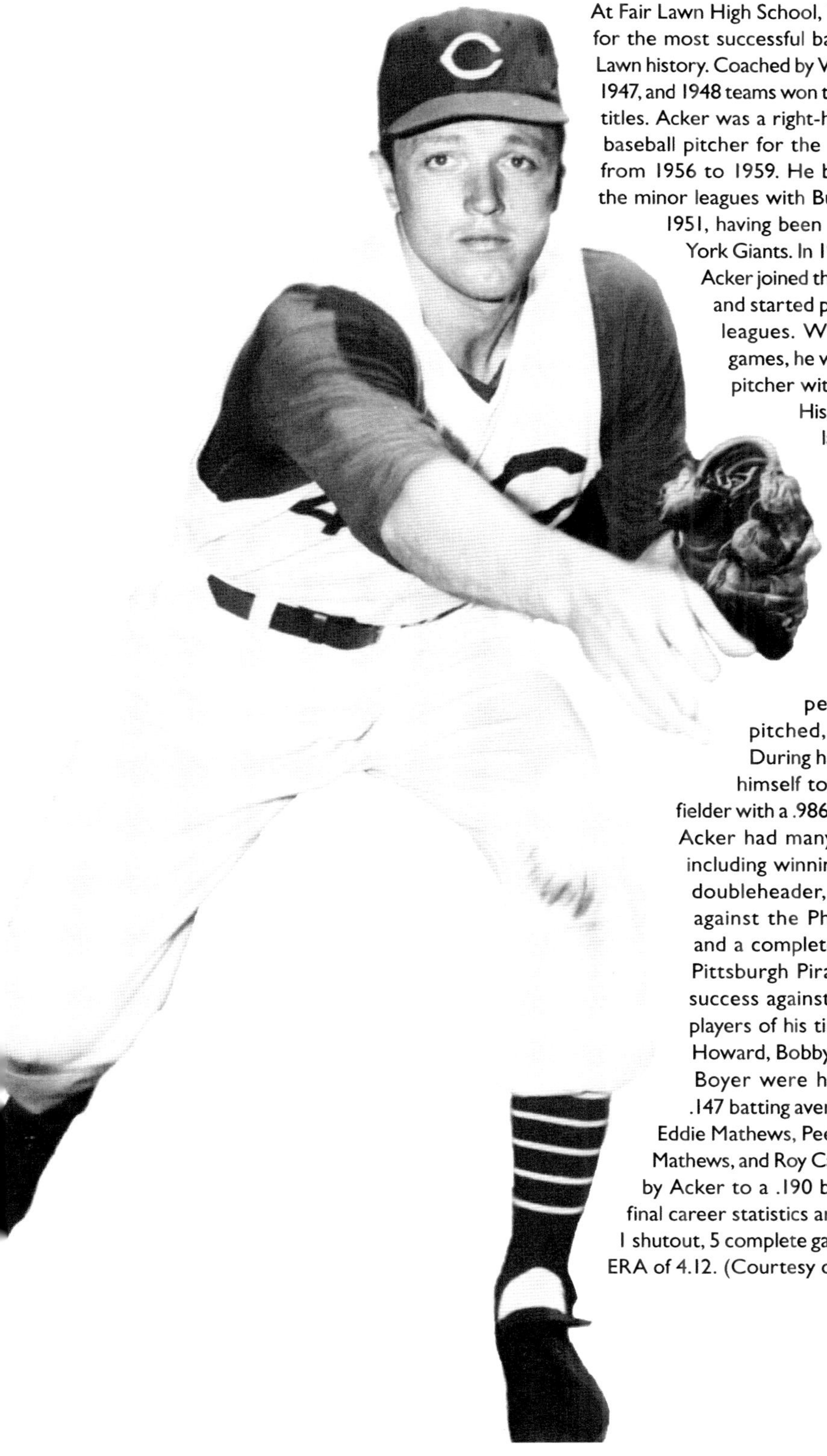

Cincinnati Redlegs' Starting Pitcher
At Fair Lawn High School, Tom Acker pitched for the most successful baseball team in Fair Lawn history. Coached by Virgil Sasso, the 1946, 1947, and 1948 teams won their league and state titles. Acker was a right-handed professional baseball pitcher for the Cincinnati Redlegs from 1956 to 1959. He began his career in the minor leagues with Buffalo from 1949 to 1951, having been signed by the New York Giants. In 1956, at the age of 26, Acker joined the Cincinnati Redlegs and started pitching in the major leagues. While he started 23 games, he was primarily a relief pitcher with 153 appearances. His major-league career lasted four seasons, during which in just 380.3 innings, he totaled 256 strikeouts. His best year was 1957 when he was in the top 10 for the National League in winning percentage, games pitched, and hit batsman. During his career, he proved himself to be an outstanding fielder with a .986 fielding percentage. Acker had many career highlights including winning both games of a doubleheader, a complete game against the Philadelphia Phillies, and a complete game against the Pittsburgh Pirates. He had great success against some of the best players of his time. All-Stars Frank Howard, Bobby Thomson and Ken Boyer were held by Acker to a .147 batting average. Hall-of-famers Eddie Mathews, Pee Wee Reese, Eddie Mathews, and Roy Campanella were held by Acker to a .190 batting average. His final career statistics are 19 wins, 13 loses, 1 shutout, 5 complete games, 8 saves, and an ERA of 4.12. (Courtesy of Tom Acker.)

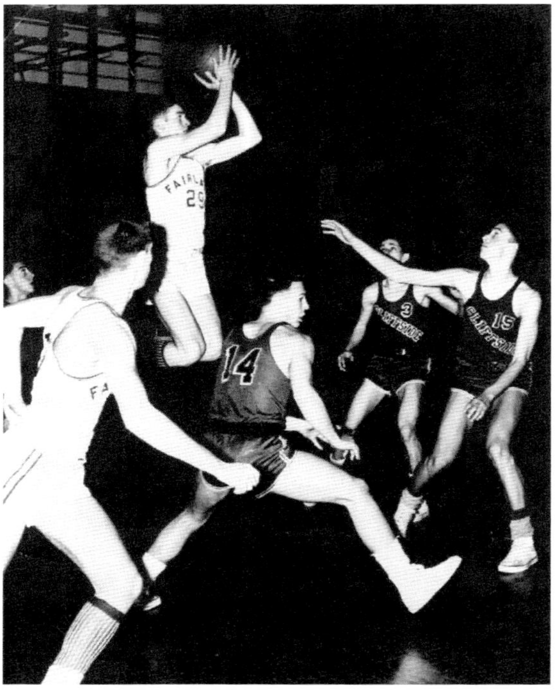

The Town's Greatest Basketball Player

Considered the best basketball player in Fair Lawn High School history, Bill Lundberg was All-League and All-County and led the team to the league championship during a year in which he scored 607 points. He went on to star for Southern Mississippi's basketball team, where he was named Player of the Year in Mississippi. (Courtesy of Bill Lundberg.)

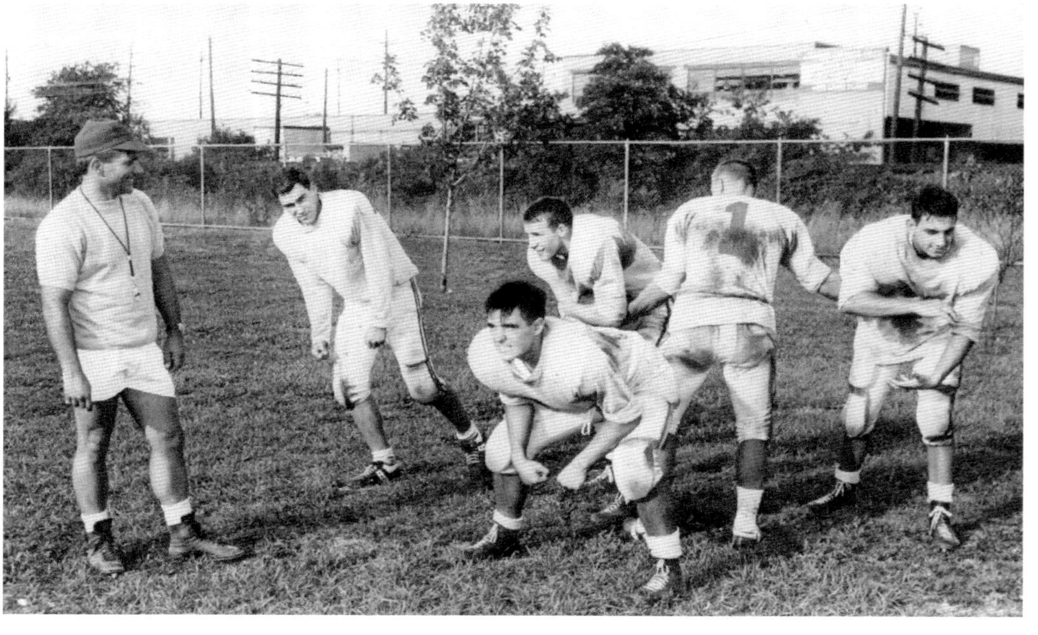

Coached a 24-Game Winning Streak

Frank Devens (at left) was the Fair Lawn High School football coach from 1965 to 1971, during which the team had a 24-game winning streak and two league titles. He was chosen *Daily News* Coach of the Year in 1965 and 1966 for teams led by Bruce Jankowski (center, holding the ball) that had a combined record of 16-1-1. (Courtesy of Bruce Jankowski.)

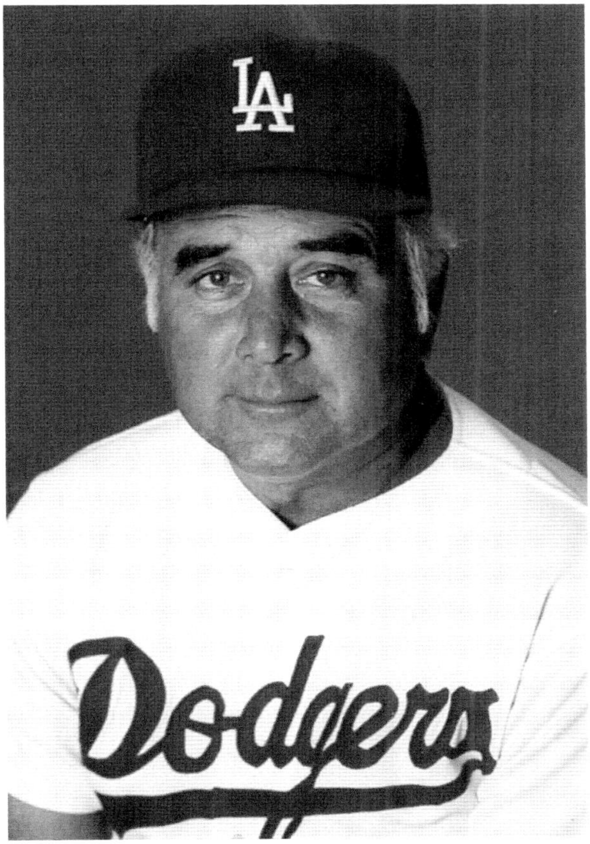

Los Angeles Dodgers' Relief Pitcher

Ron Perranoski was one of professional baseball's best relief pitchers when he played for the Los Angeles Dodgers from 1962 to 1967 and then for the Minnesota Twins from 1968 to 1970. In 1963, Perranoski won 16 of 19 relief decisions for the Dodgers, a team that won the 1963 World Series in four consecutive games over the New York Yankees. He appeared in one World Series game that season and earned a save. He had an earned run average of 1.67 and led the National League in win-loss percentage (.842) and games pitched (69). Perranoski used fastballs, curves, and sinkers to get the hitters out. In 1964, he led the National League in games finished (52).

In 1965, he again helped the Dodgers win the World Series. In 1967, he led the National League in games pitched (70) and was then traded to the Minnesota Twins. He continued to be a dominant relief pitcher in the American League until retiring in 1973. He led the American League in 1969 in games pitched (52) and saves (31) and again in 1970 in saves (34). He was chosen the *Sporting News* Relief Pitcher of the Year in both 1969 and 1970. He retired having saved 179 games.

Perranoski then turned to coaching and was the Dodgers' minor-league pitching coordinator (1973–1980) and then their major-league pitching coach for 14 seasons (1981–1994), during which they won the World Series twice. He joined the San Francisco Giants as minor-league pitching coordinator in 1995, was Giants' general manager Brian Sabean since 2000.

Perranoski was a starting pitcher for Michigan State University with teammate and friend Dick Radatz, who would also become a top relief pitcher in the 1960s. Perranoski was signed by the Chicago Cubs in 1958 and then traded to the Dodgers who switched him from a starting pitcher to a relief pitcher. At Fair Lawn High School, he was a starting pitcher for Coach Virgil Sasso in 1953 and 1954. Perranoski pitched 57 scoreless innings and 10 shutouts in 1954 when Fair Lawn won league and state titles. (Courtesy of Ron Perranoski.)

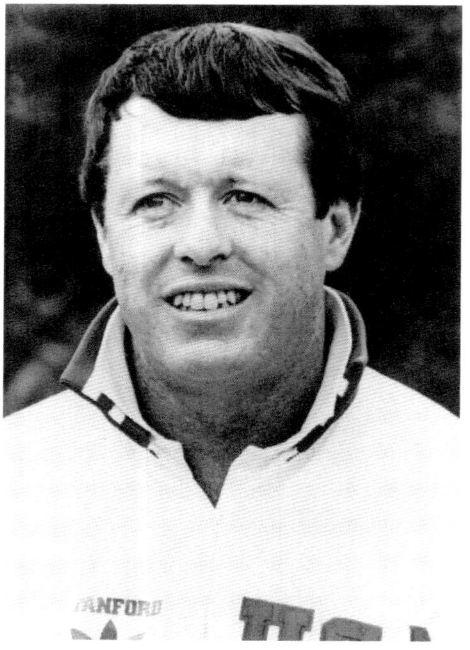

Record-Setting Tennis Coach

Frank Brennan was coach of the Stanford Women's Tennis Team which had an astounding 21-year record of 510-50. His teams won 10 National Collegiate Athletic Association (NCAA) titles, beginning in 1982 and including a record six in a row. He was twice named the NCAA Tennis Coach of the Decade and is a member of the US Tennis Association International Hall of Fame as well as the Stanford University Athletic Hall of Fame. He is a graduate of Fair Lawn High School. (Courtesy of Frank Brennan.)

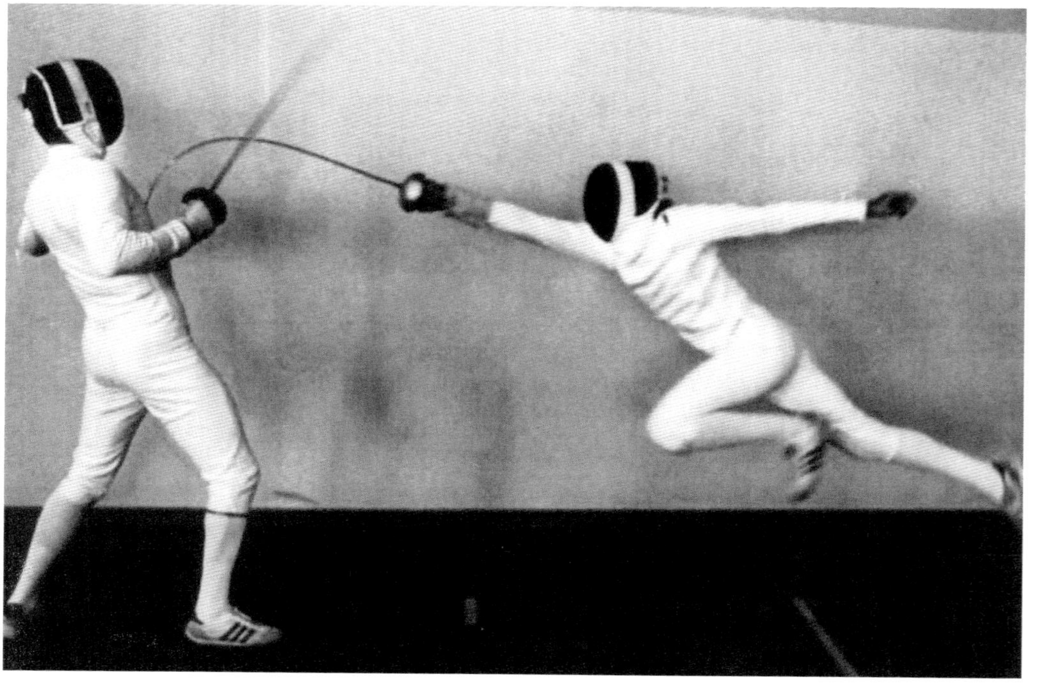

Olympic Alternate Fencer

A nationally ranked fencer, Steven Griffiths (right) made the US Olympic team as an alternate in 1984. A star fencer at Fair Lawn High, he is considered the greatest fencer to come out of any school in Bergen County. He was named to the 1980s All-Decade Team and All-State Teams in 1983 and 1984. This épée fencer is a two-time winner of the New Jersey state championships. (Courtesy of Steven Griffiths.)

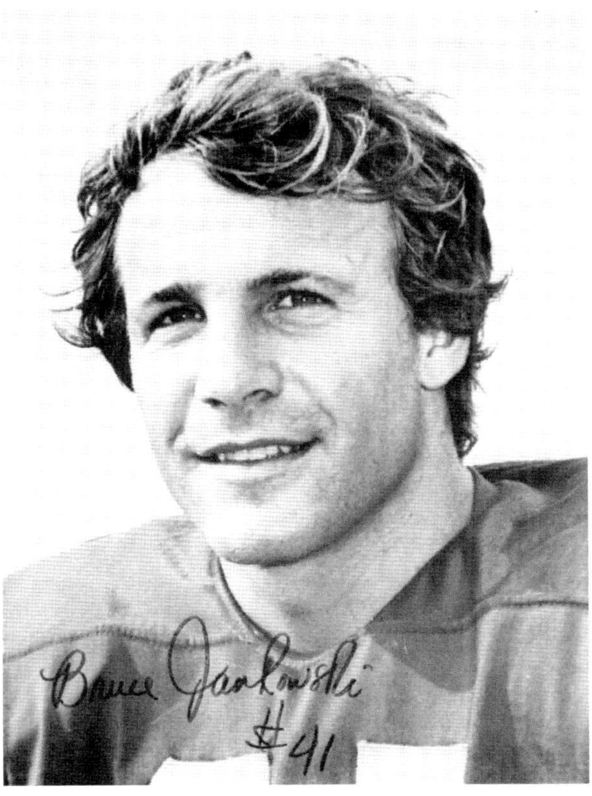

Kansas City Chiefs' Wide Receiver

Bruce Jankowski is considered to be the greatest football player to ever play for Fair Lawn High School. The 1965 and 1966 seasons were two football years that have never been reproduced by any Fair Lawn football team. Jankowski led the team on a 24-game winning streak, and the crowds at Sasso Field reached levels of 8,000 to 10,000. On Thanksgiving Day 1967, the crowd was estimated to be between 15,000 and 17,000. Jankowski scored in every game those two seasons, scoring three times in 30 seconds against Bergenfield and six touchdowns in one game.

He made the *New York Daily News* All-Star football team and also Player of the Year. He was First Team All-State as a backfielder. Jankowski was one of two high school All-Americans that Fair Lawn has produced (the other being John Schmunk in lacrosse). Jankowski also played basketball and baseball. He pitched a no-hitter in 1967, leading his team to the league title. NBA coach and ABC broadcaster Hubie Brown, as basketball and baseball coach and football assistant, coached him at Fair Lawn High School in three sports. In junior high school, he was known for doing three or more workouts a day and running with weighted vests.

Jankowski won a scholarship to Ohio State University and played for legendary coach Woody Hayes. He made the cover of *Sports Illustrated* in November 1968 for his over-the-shoulder catch against rival Michigan State. He became a professional football player as a wide receiver for the Kansas City Chiefs from 1971 to 1973. Torn ankle ligaments ultimately ended his football career, which had also included a season with Shreveport of the World Football League. Three hall-of-fame coaches—Hubie Brown in high school, Woody Hayes in college, and the Chiefs' Hank Stram in the pros—coached him.

Bruce and Sharon, his wife of 39 years, make their home in Leawood, Kansas. After football, his career has been in technology sales and management for companies such as IBM and Cisco Systems. The Jankowskis enjoy traveling, playing golf, and spending time with their granddaughter. (Courtesy of Bruce Jankowski.)

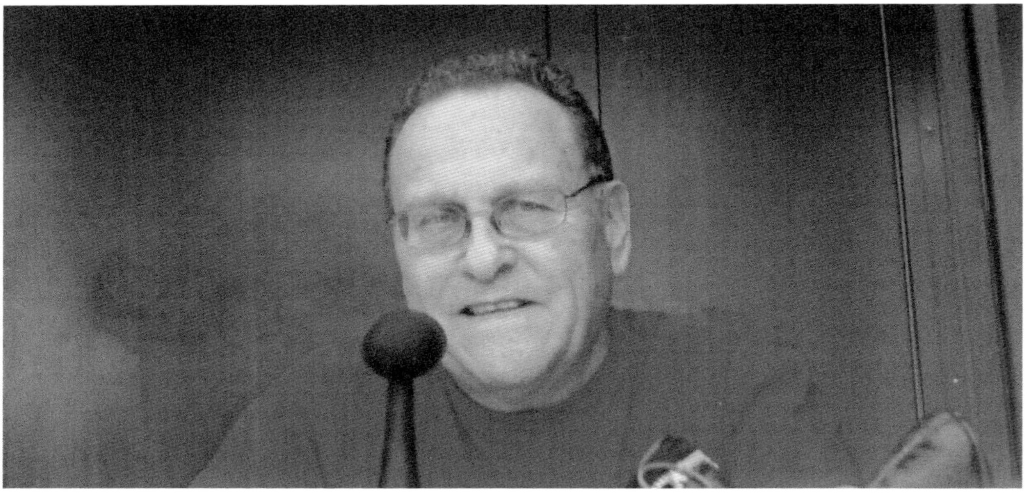

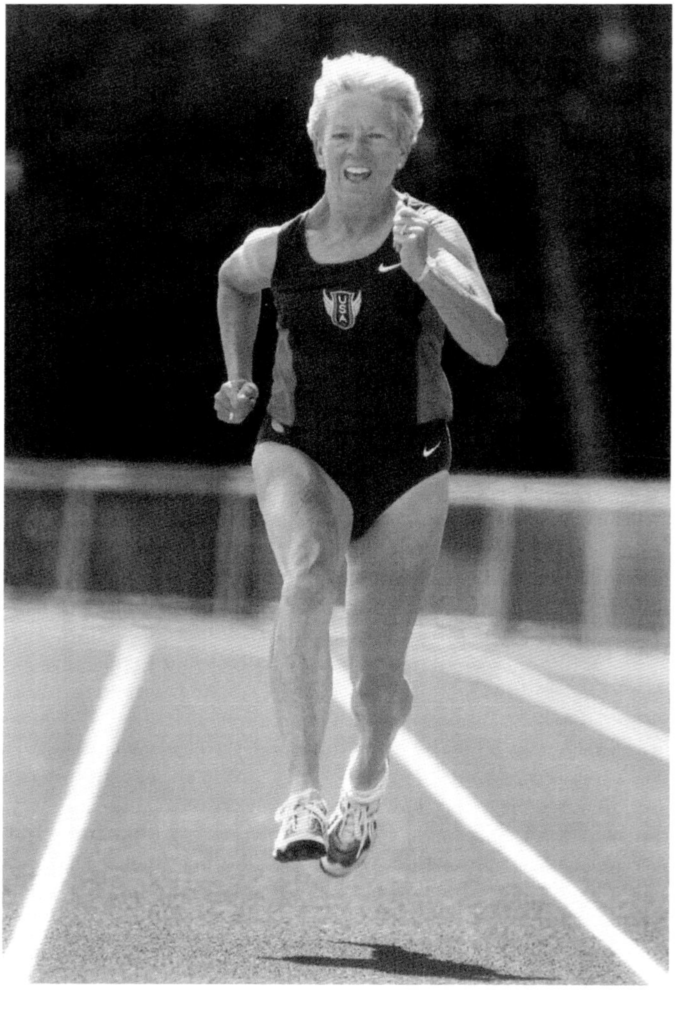

Voice of the High School Football Cutters
Dick Engelhardt has compiled a complete history of every football game Fair Lawn High School has ever played. For 30 years, he and his brother were "spotters" for Fair Lawn's football announcer. In 1997, Engelhardt became the football game announcer, a job that he continues to this day. He writes the "Gridiron" column of school football news for the local newspaper. (Courtesy of Dick Engelhardt.)

National Champion Hurdler
Barbara Jacobs Jordan is a Senior Olympic medalist who began her track career at age 50 and won National Championships in Masters track and field. She held world records in the short and long hurdles and many other events and was inducted into five halls of fame. At Fair Lawn High in the 1950s, Jordan was a majorette with the marching band. (Courtesy of Barbara Jacobs Jordan.)

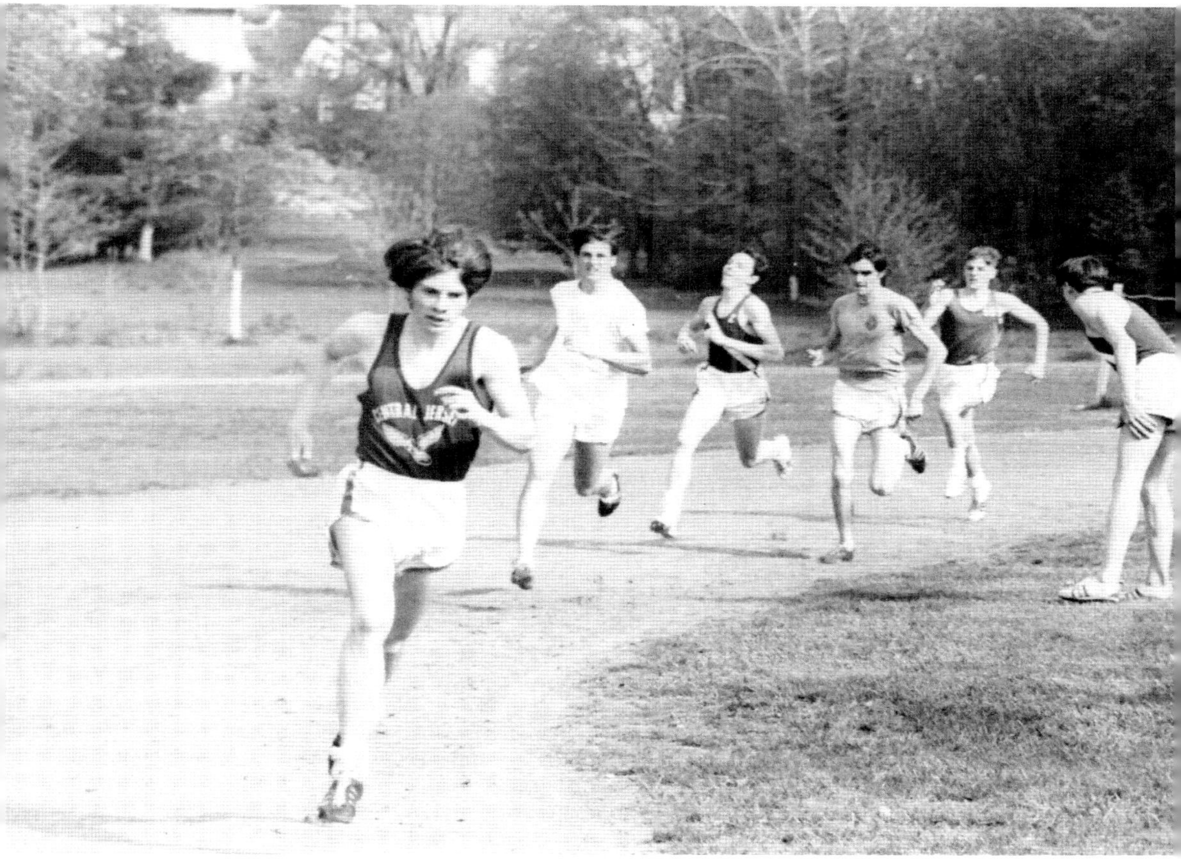

Greatest Cross-Country Team
Fair Lawn High's 1971 cross-country team is the greatest in school history, the only team to win league and state sectional titles. The team won the Northern New Jersey Interscholastic League (NNJIL) Championship meet to win the league title and the Group IV State Sectional Championship to finish ninth in the state finals. The team was ranked second in Bergen County and finished second in the Waldwick Invitational. Coached by Joe Hausmann and captained by Cuyler Christianson, pictured in the lead, the team finished in 1971 with a 12-1 record. Christianson was named First Team All-League and All-County. Other stars of the team were Tom Driscoll, Mike Belby, Craig Rubin, and Danny DeNicola. (Courtesy of Cuyler Christianson.)

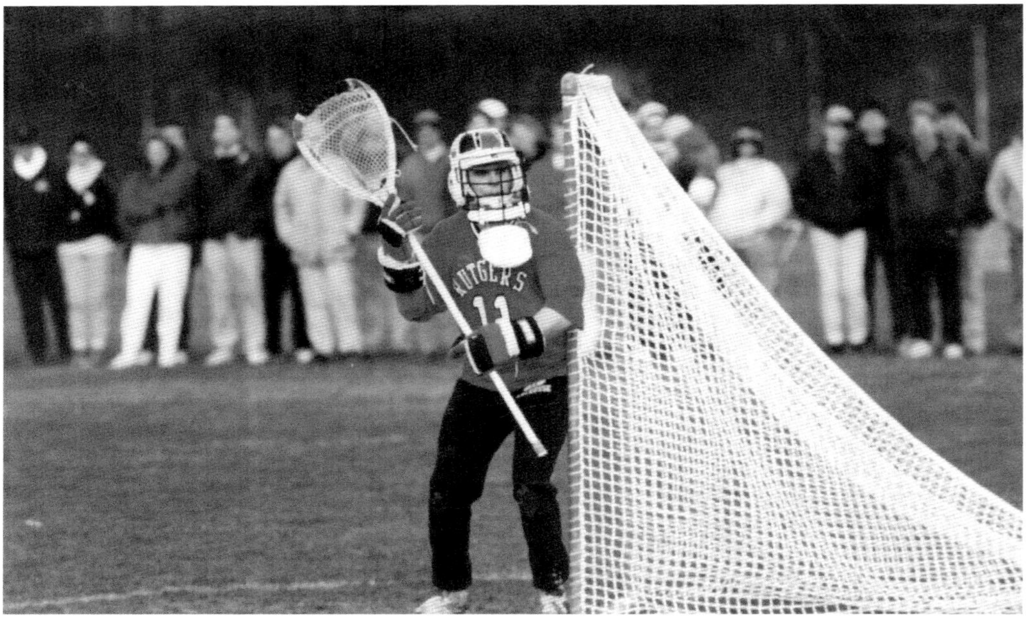

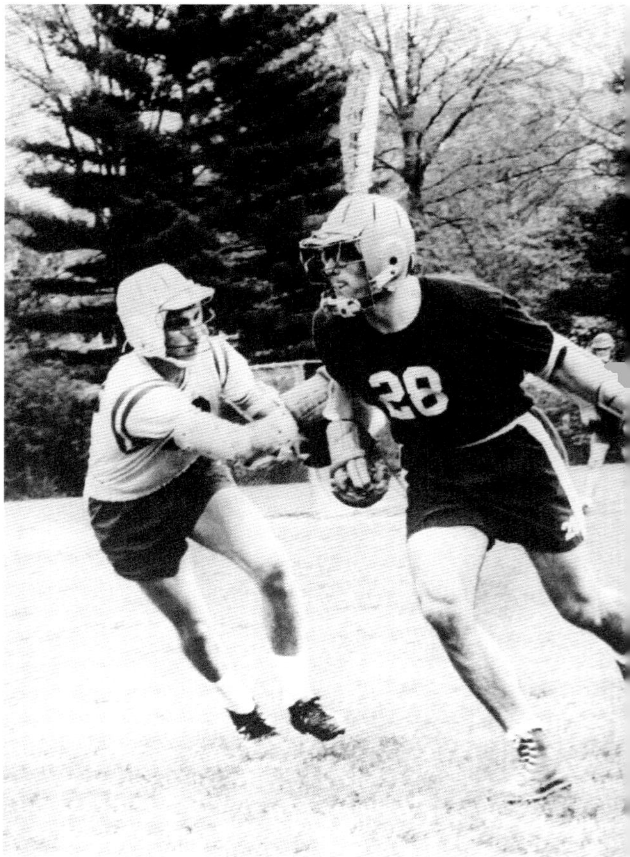

Professional Lacrosse Goalie
John Schmunk played professional lacrosse in the North American Lacrosse League, playing goalie. He is considered the greatest lacrosse goalie in Rutgers history, as well as in Fair Lawn High history. He was an All-American at Rutgers. He and Bruce Jankowski are the only Fair Lawn athletes to be named All-American in any sport. He was All-League, All-County, and All-State. (Courtesy of John Schmunk.)

World Champion Lacrosse Coach
Steve Jacobson was assistant lacrosse coach when the USA team won the World Lacrosse Championship in 1996. He was head coach for the USA team in the 2006 World Lacrosse Games. He is the founder of the New Jersey Lacrosse Coaches Association. At Swarthmore College, Jacobson was a two-time All-American in lacrosse. At Fair Lawn High School, he coached the lacrosse team to state championships in 1968 and 1970. (Courtesy of Steve Jacobson.)

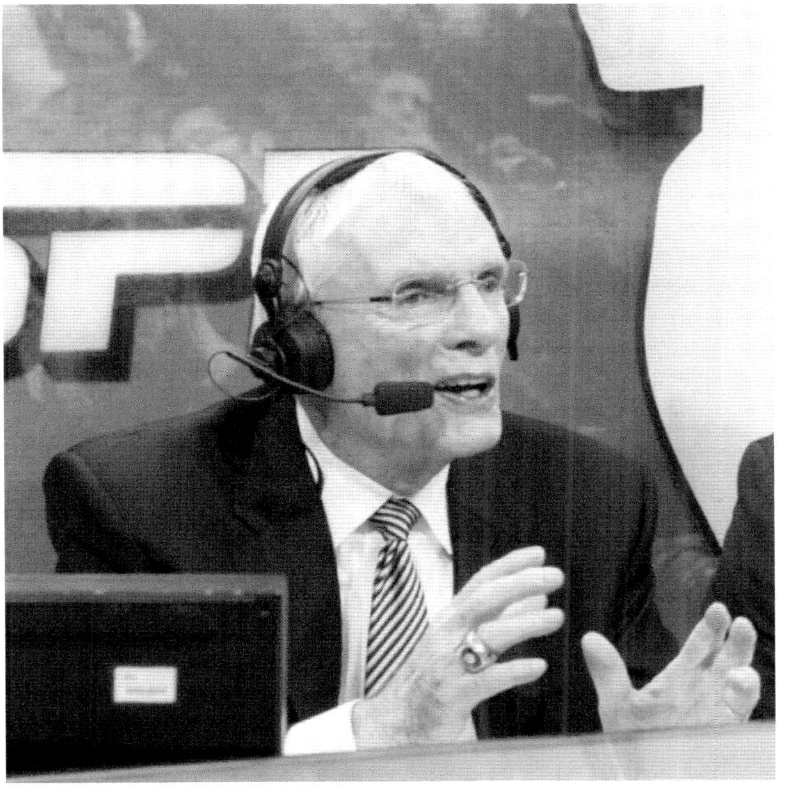

Fromer Coach to ABC Sports Broadcaster

Hubie Brown was a professional basketball coach and is a two-time NBA Coach of the Year and member of the Naismith Memorial Basketball Hall of Fame. He began his professional career as an assistant coach with the Milwaukee Bucks, which had two players who would be in the hall of fame: Oscar Robertson and Kareem Abdul-Jabbar. In 1974, the team reached the NBA finals but lost in seven games to the Boston Celtics. He got his first head-coaching job with the Kentucky Colonels in the American Basketball Association (ABA) and won the championship in 1975. Brown continued as the Colonels' coach until the ABA-NBA merger in 1976 when the Colonels franchise folded. He returned to the NBA coaching the Atlanta Hawks, turning a losing team into the Central Division champions and winning his first Coach of the Year award. He coached the New York Knicks into the playoffs in both 1982–1983 and 1983–1984. Then two losing seasons followed due to injuries to Patrick Ewing and Bernard King, the team stars. In 1986, when the team began the season with a dismal 4-12 record, the Knicks fired him. In 2002–2003, the Memphis Grizzlies made the controversial decision to hire Brown as the NBA's oldest coach at age 69. Brown coached the team to their most wins of all time. The following year, 2003–2004, he coached Memphis to its first playoff appearance, earning Brown his second NBA Coach of the Year. During the 2004–2005 season, Brown had health issues that were later cleared up, but he decided it was time to retire from basketball coaching. He turned to a new career as a broadcaster and became the lead commentator for the NBA on ESPN and ABC Sports. At Fair Lawn High School, he coached Bruce Jankowski in three sports: basketball, baseball, and football. Then, Brown coached basketball at the College of William & Mary and Duke. He played basketball in college at Niagara and for the Army's team, and briefly, he played professional basketball for the Rochester Colonels. (Courtesy of ESPN.)

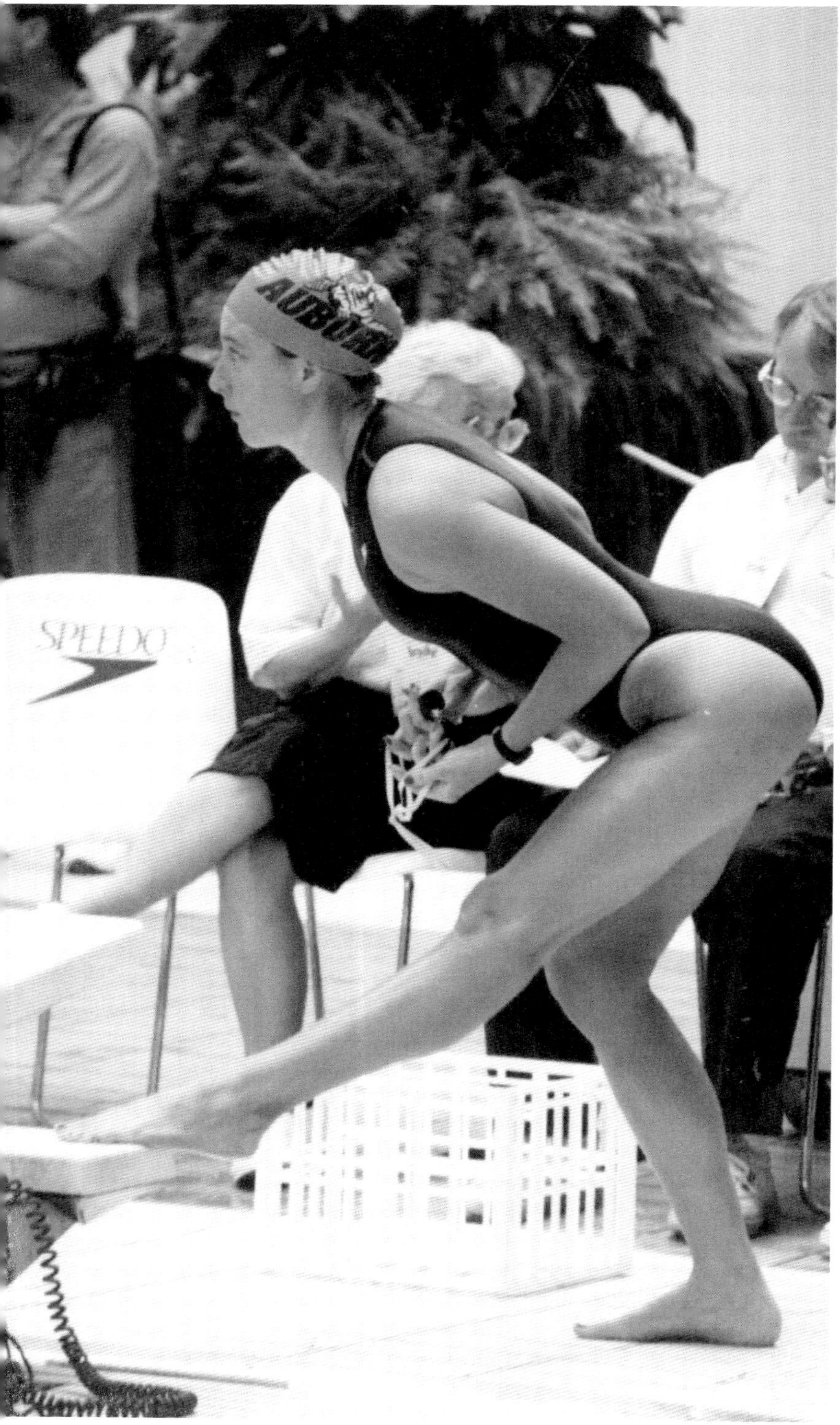

Best Swimmer
Rachel Pchola Schirmer is considered Fair Lawn's greatest female swimmer. She was a US Olympic trials finalist in the 100-meter and 200-meter backstroke races for the 1988, 1992, and 1996 games. She beat Olympic gold medalist Janet Evans in the 200-meter backstroke. At Auburn University, she was SEC Champion in 100-meter and 200-meter backstroke and was All-American all four years. In 1991, she was the US Open Champion in the 200-meter backstroke. At Fair Lawn High, Rachel was state champion all four years in backstroke and butterfly events and All-American all four years, setting the New Jersey state record in the 100-meter and 200-meter backstroke. She made the *Star Ledger*'s Top 10 Swimmers of the Decade list for 1990 through 1999. (Courtesy of Rachel Pchola Schimer.)

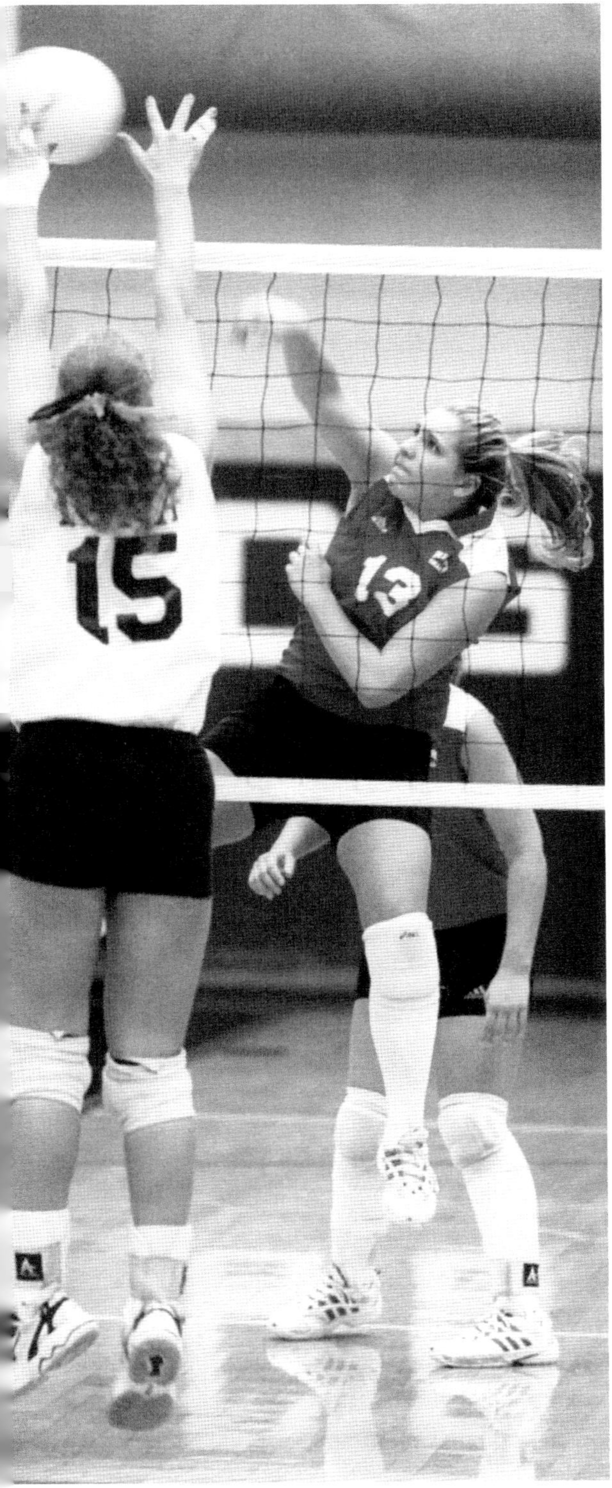

Volleyball player
Evette Hoeffner Picinic
She was only five feet, six inches, but Evette Hoeffner Picinic was one of Fair Lawn High School's best-ever volleyball players. In 1997, as captain, she led her team to a 27-1 record—the top ranking in New Jersey—and the state title. At the state championship game, she had 31 digs, 15 service points, five aces, and 13 spikes for points. In her three years on the team, Fair Lawn won 70 games and lost 10. Picinic was All-League for three years, All-County for three years, and All-State in her senior year. As an NCAA Division I volleyball player at Rider College, she led the nation in digs in 2000 and 2001. (Courtesy of Rider College.)

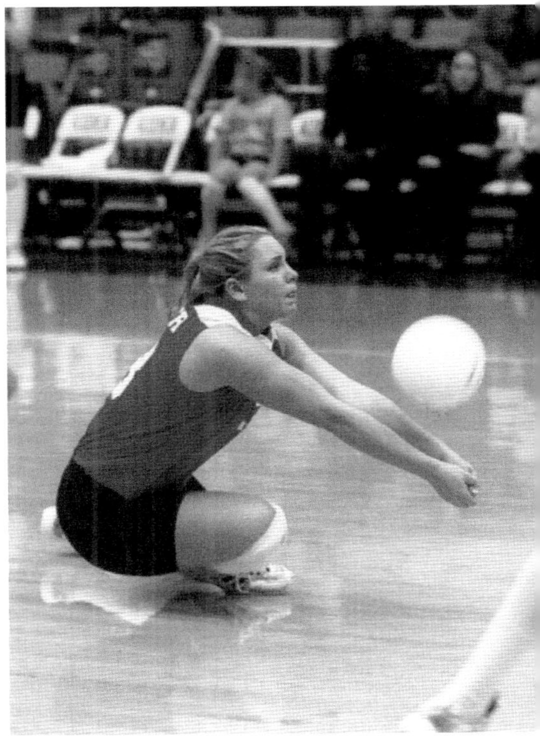

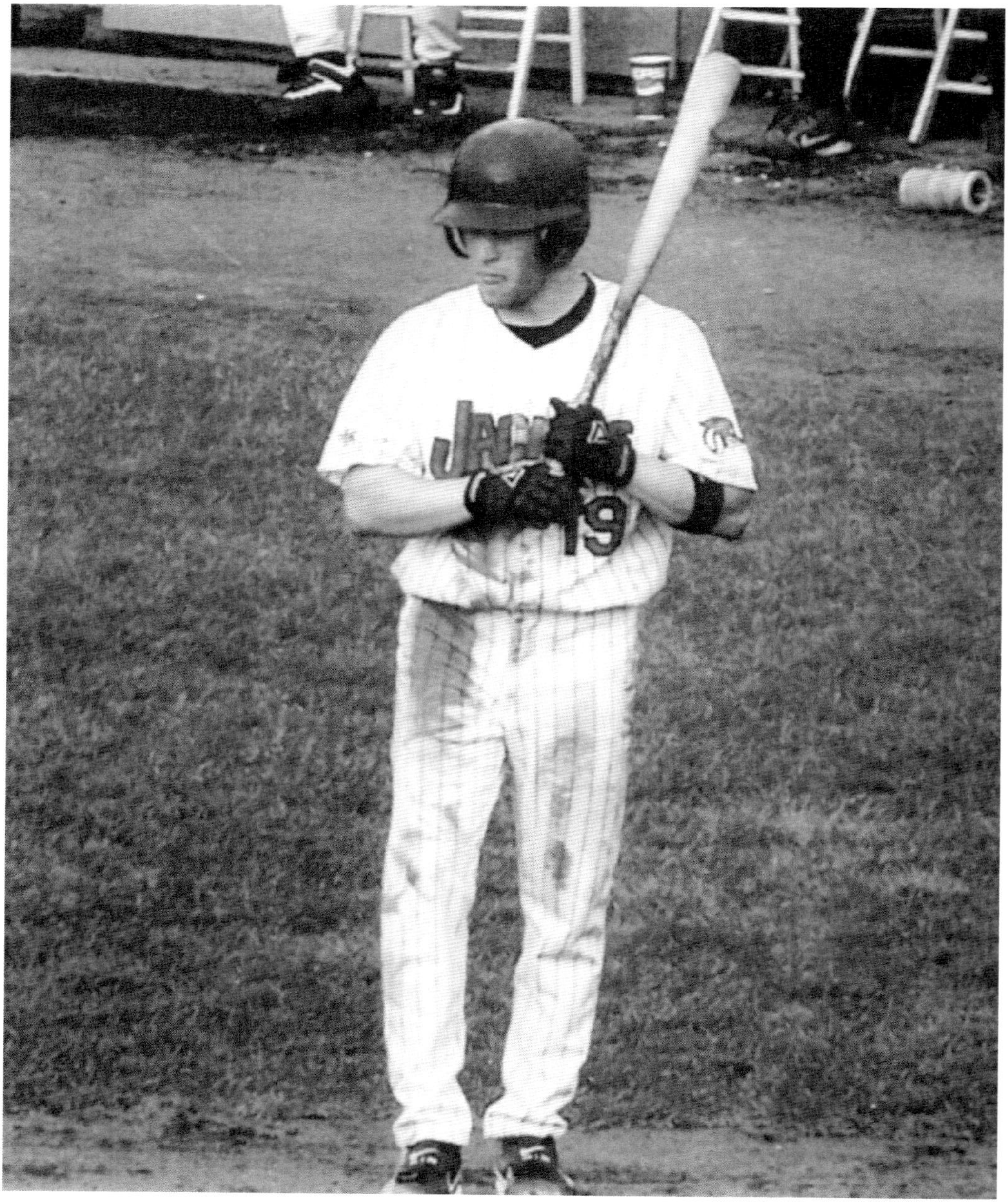

Professional Baseball Player Zack Smithlin

At Fair Lawn High School, Zack Smithlin was chosen All-League, All-County, and All-State in baseball, was an All-State sprinter, and was an All-League wide receiver on the football team. At Penn State, he ranked in the top 10 all-time in hits, runs, and RBIs and still has the career record stolen bases. Smithlin went on to play professional baseball with the New Jersey Jackals from 2004 to 2011, setting franchise records in hits, runs, and stolen bases. In 2011, the Jackals honored him by retiring his No. 4 jersey, only the third jersey retired in the organization's 14-year history. (Courtesy of Zack Smithlin.)

CHAPTER SIX

The Business People and Professionals

Fair Lawn has always thrived in commerce, and this chapter presents a representative sampling of its businesses and professionals. The oldest business is the Fair Lawn Cemetery, dating back to 1894. In 1911, Richard and Henry Kuiken established a wood-working shop, followed by a lumberyard and paint store that became Kuiken Brothers. Another early enterprise was a painting business started by Henry Landzettel, which became Lazon Paint. In 1927, the Fair Lawn Building and Loan Association began as the first banking operation in town. Today, it is a regional institution, the Columbia Bank, with headquarters in Fair Lawn and assets over $4 billion.

In 1929, the Radburn Plaza Building opened with many neighborhood stores. Across the street, George Sporn's Esso Station began selling gasoline; today, it is an Exxon. In 1954, the McBride family's industrial park opened on Route 208, and some of the original companies are still there today such as Nabisco, Sandvik, Inc., and Lea & Perrins. Nabisco currently bakes Oreos and Ritz Crackers at its factory. Sandvik, Inc., founded in Sweden in 1862, has its US headquarters in Fair Lawn. Lea & Perrins's famous Worcestershire sauce is served in most restaurants across the country. In fact, when Fair Lawn residents travel and mention the town they are from, the response is usually "Lea & Perrins."

Professionals from Fair Lawn include Dr. Albert Rosen, ESPN cofounder Steve Bornstein, and Stuart Brotman, who has been an advisor to four presidential administrations. Fair Lawn has one of the first McDonald's and first International House of Pancakes. With Fair Lawn's big population of Russians, several businesses have opened to cater to that market, led by B & B International Food and Fair Lawn Pharmacy. The Fair Lawn Chamber of Commerce is very active in town affairs, including the sponsorship of two annual street fairs. The Hunter Group is the leading accounting firm in the area. Many consider Ness Pizza to have the best pizza, Empress Diner to have the best dinner specials, and Benny's Luncheonette to serve the best breakfasts.

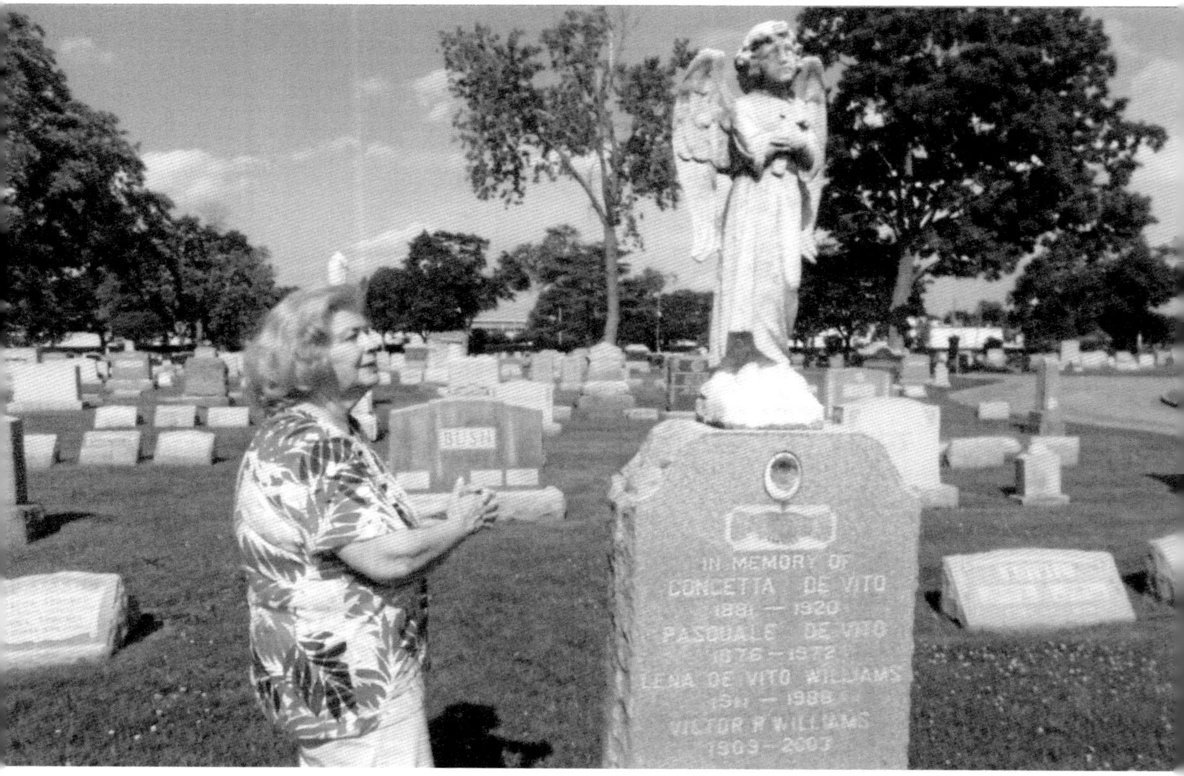

Fair Lawn's Oldest Business

The Fair Lawn Memorial Cemetery and Mausoleum on Maple Avenue was founded in 1894 and is the borough's oldest continuing business. Pictured on the right is Charles Schofield; he has been an employee for 36 years and has been the superintendent for 15 years. The cemetery has more than 50,000 people of all faiths interred there, including 1,000 veterans. Each year, Schofield works with local Boy Scout troops to decorate the veterans' graves with American flags on the Saturday before Memorial Day. Schofield holds photographs of founder Abraham Vermeulen and his son John (with mustache). The elder Vermeulen was a funeral director in Paterson who bought a cornfield in Fair Lawn and developed the cemetery, which is still run by family members today. Irene Slawenski, pictured above, lives adjacent to the cemetery and can be often seen praying there by her favorite angel tombstone.

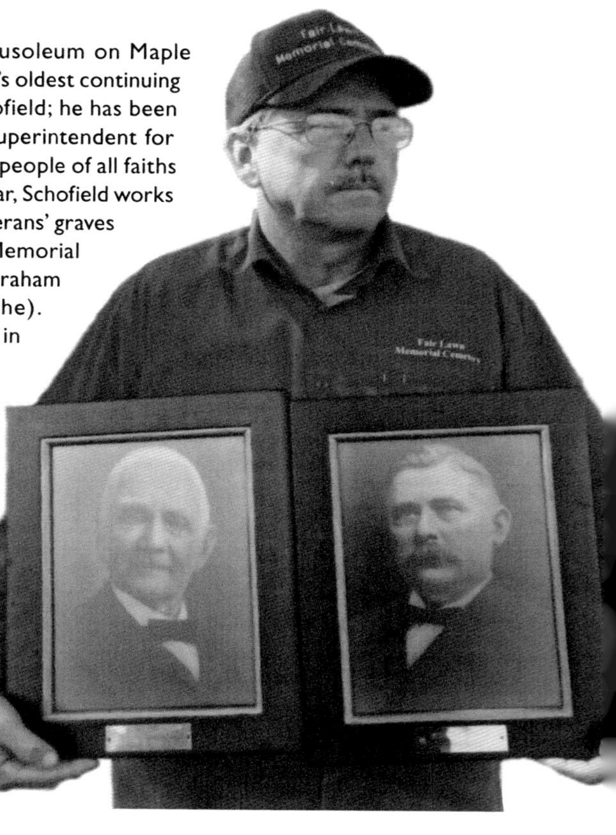

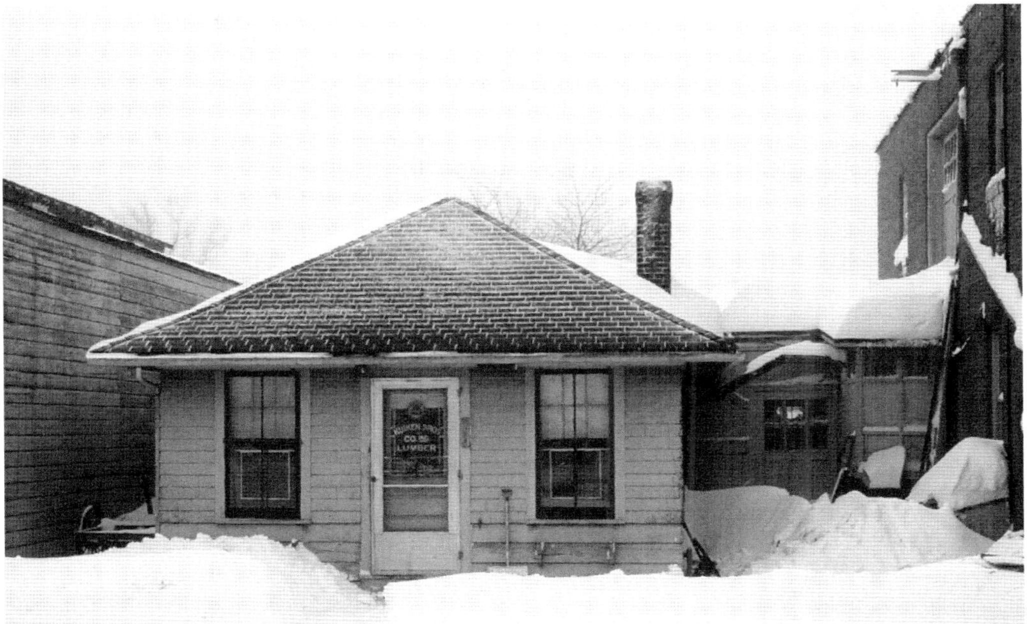

Oldest Local Company

The Kuiken Brothers Company is the oldest local company started by Fair Lawn residents and still owned by the family. In 1912, two Kuiken brothers Henry and Nicholas and their cousin Richard founded Kuiken Brothers and started building houses on George and Edward Streets and on the streets west of River Road. The windows were made in their mill workshop on Sixth Street. Brother Dirk joined the firm a few years afterward. A lumberyard and a paint store were added later. When the Depression brought building to a halt, the Kuikens added a hardware business. Today, the company is run by the third and fourth generations of the family and has expanded to eight other locations in New Jersey and New York. Third-generation Doug Kuiken is pictured below, right. (Above, courtesy of Doug Kuiken.)

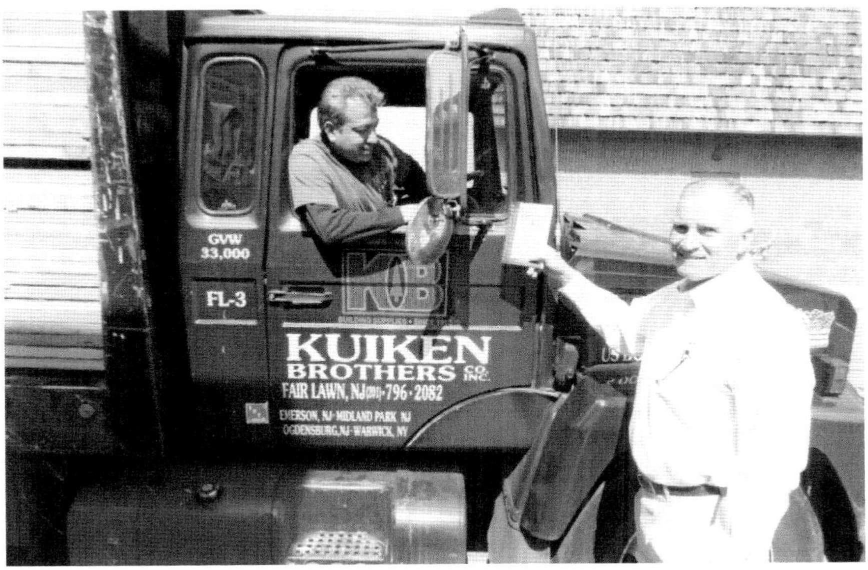

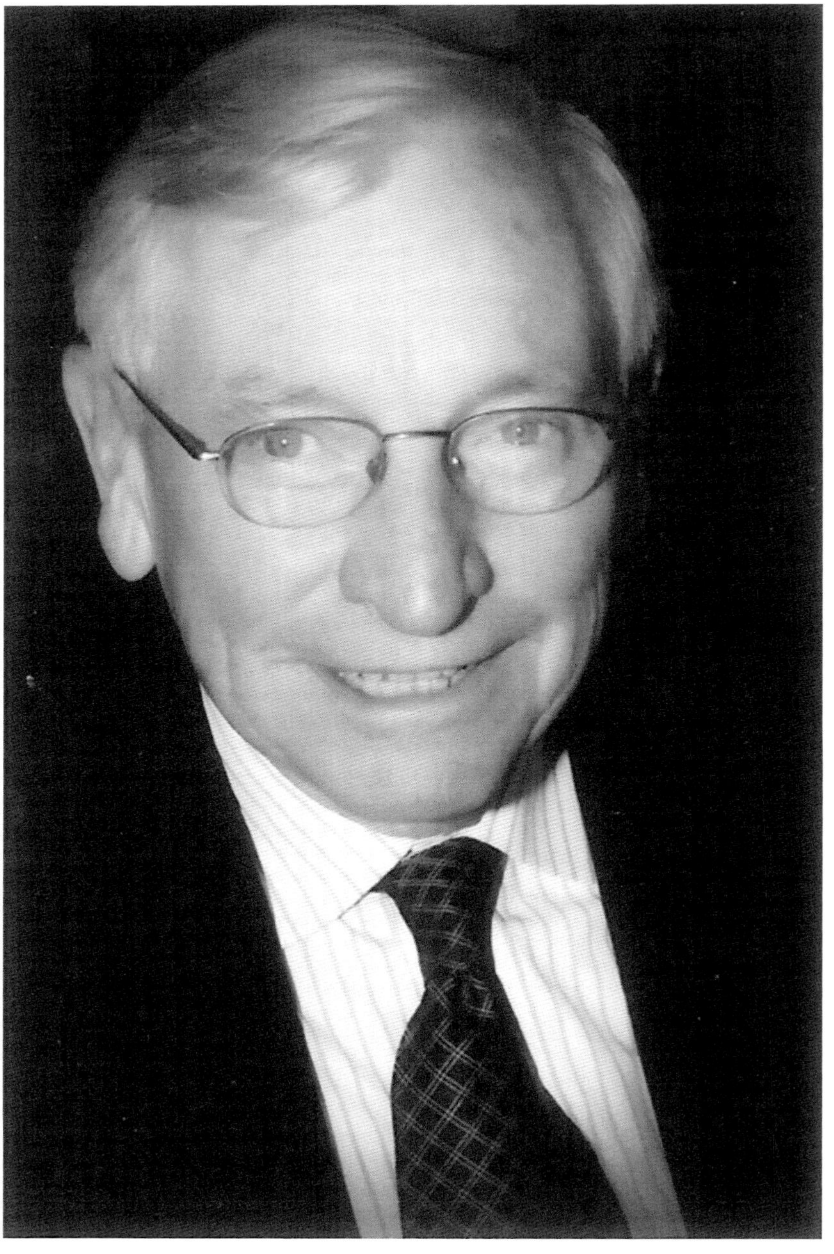

Business Booster

Robert Landzettel, known by all as Bob, has been active in Fair Lawn affairs for more than 50 years. He served on the zoning board and the borough council and, in 1973–1974, as mayor. He was active in the chamber of commerce and was one of the founders of the River Road Improvement Corporation. As its longtime president, he was instrumental in the revitalization of the River Road business district. Bob Landzettel is the third-generation president of his family business, Landzettel & Sons. In 2013, he was honored by the chamber of commerce as Person of the Year for his long public and community service. (Courtesy of Robert Landzettel.)

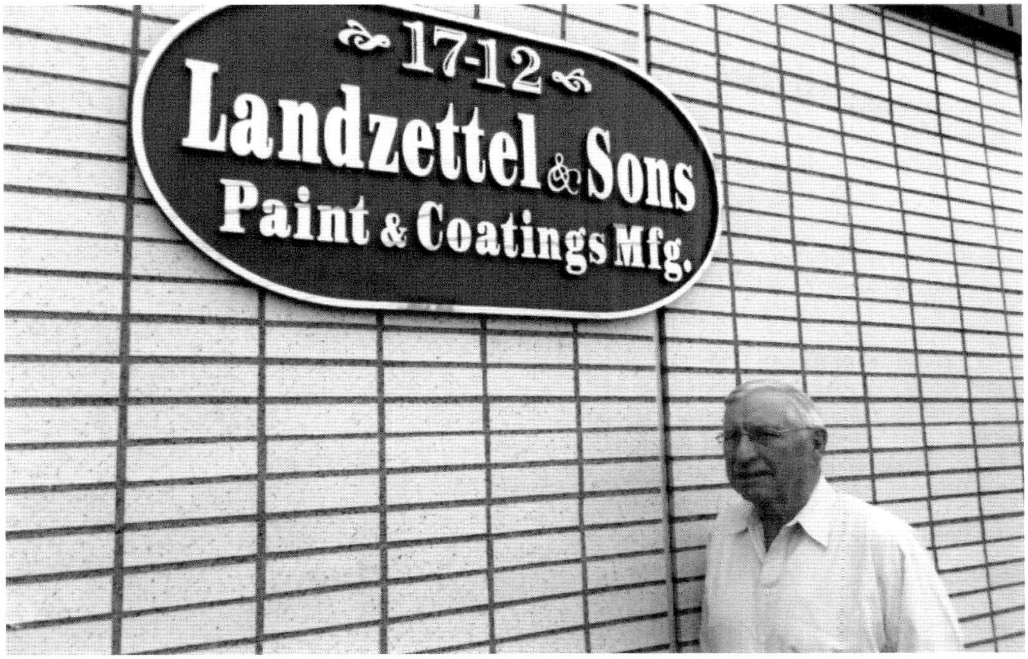

Making Paint for 80 Years

In 1932, Henry Landzettel and sons William and Walter founded Landzettel & Sons and started manufacturing and selling paint in their factory and store on Fourth Street. The business was called Lazon Paint. It expanded in the era of "do it yourself" and moved to a new retail store and plant on River Road in 1949. Pictured below are, from left to right, William Landzettel, Clarence VanHandel, and Walter Landzettel. In 1961, Robert "Bob" Landzettel (pictured above), William's son, became manager of the business with his uncle Walter continuing as manager of manufacturing. Bob's brother Don then joined the company as head of retail sales. Today, Walter Landzettel III is in charge of manufacturing the various paint products. In 2006, the retail stores were leased to Ricciardi Brothers. The manufacturing business continues and ships to customers throughout the country as well as to the Far East.

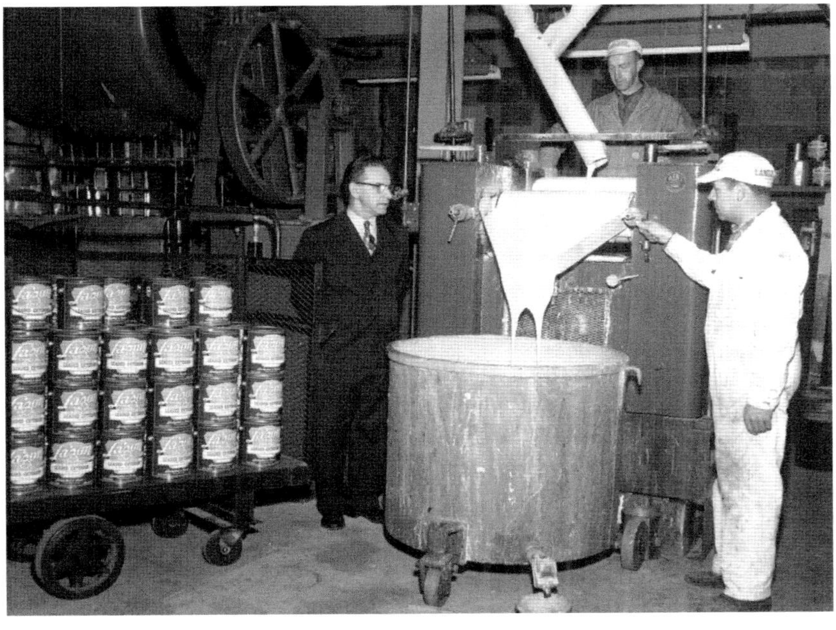

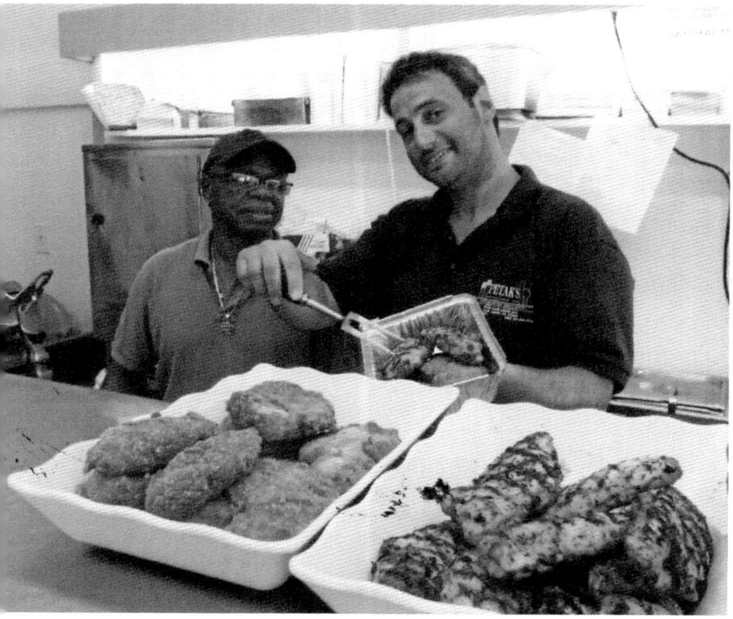

1928 Deli

Petak's Glatt Kosher Fine Foods owner Gary Rubin (right) is shown serving fried chicken. Each year, Rubin helps the Jewish Federation of Northern New Jersey to raise hundreds of thousands of dollars in its phone-a-thon, which supports organizations in need. The deli is run under the supervision of the Rabbinical Council of Bergen County. On any day of the week, Petak's serves kreplach, matzo balls, chopped liver, gefilte fish, kugels, and knishes. The deli also provides a variety of French, Italian, Oriental, Middle Eastern, and Latin American cuisines, all prepared with kosher integrity. Petak's attracts customers who come for its traditional kosher cuisine from all over Bergen and Passaic Counties.

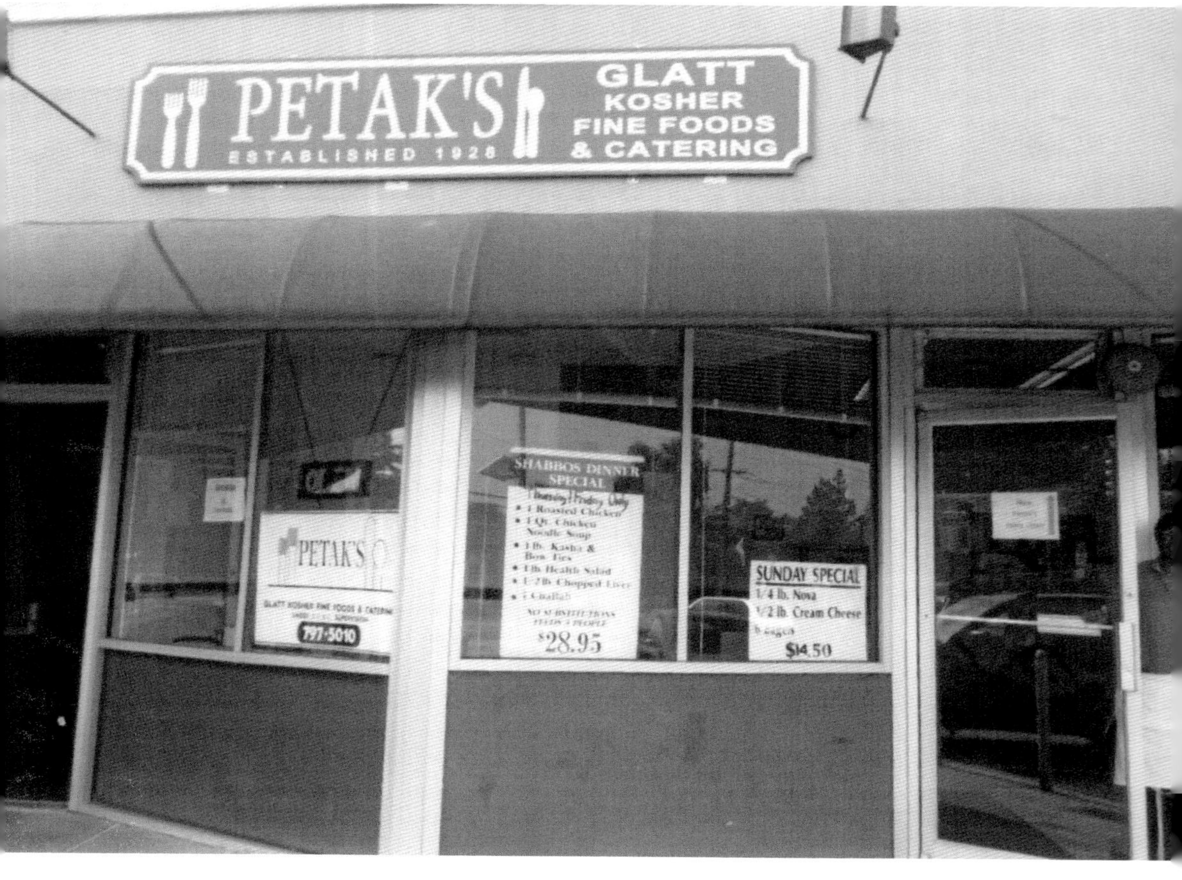

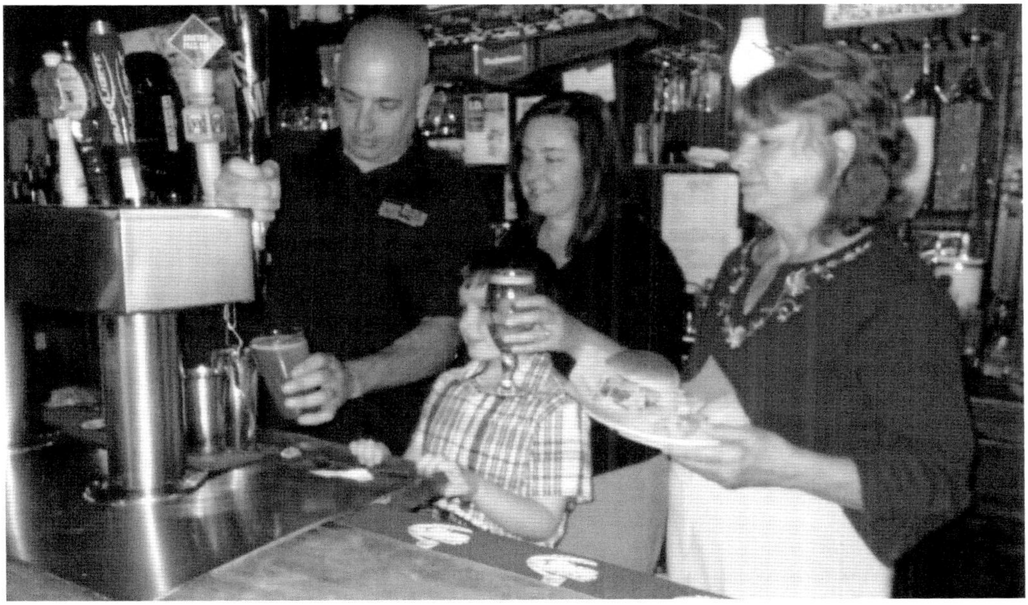

Dutch House Tavern

The historic Dutch House Tavern is owned and operated by Fair Lawn residents Frank David, Marlies, and Penny Drahouzal (pictured above from left to right). Customers tell Frank David that they consider the Dutch House a landmark, and "they tell me it's one of the few things that hasn't changed in Fair Lawn." A tavern since 1933, the business was acquired in 1961 by Frank J. Drahouzal and continues to be a popular pub and restaurant. Also pictured above is Frank David's son Sean, age eight, who likes to go fishing with his father in the Saddle River. The Dutch House has occupied its site since before the American Revolution.

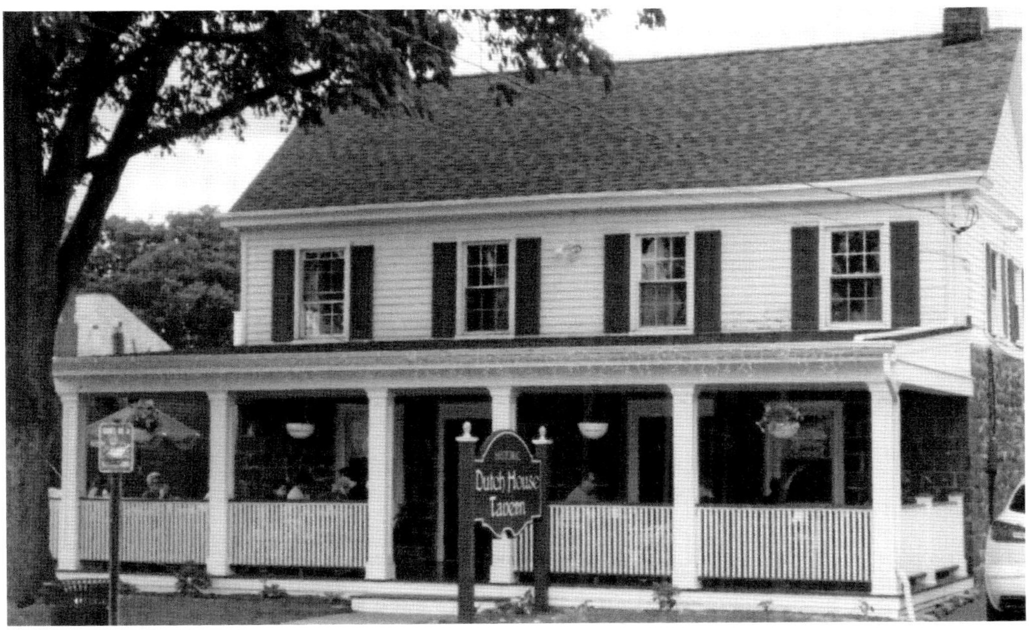

New Jersey's Largest Mutual Bank

For Columbia Bank's president and chief executive officer Thomas Kemly, it is important to be a community leader, a problem solver, have keen strategic sense, and be great with numbers. Headquartered in Fair Lawn, Columbia Bank is America's fourth-largest mutual financial institution with an asset base of approximately $4.3 billion and 44 full-service offices throughout New Jersey including 19 branches in Bergen and Passaic Counties. It began in Fair Lawn in 1927 as the Fair Lawn Building and Loan Association, formed by Mayor Robert A. Smith and 12 prominent local citizens. In 1941, the name was changed to the First Savings and Loan Association of Fair Lawn, and a new bank building was opened on the corner of River Road and Fair Lawn Avenue. (Courtesy of Columbia Bank.)

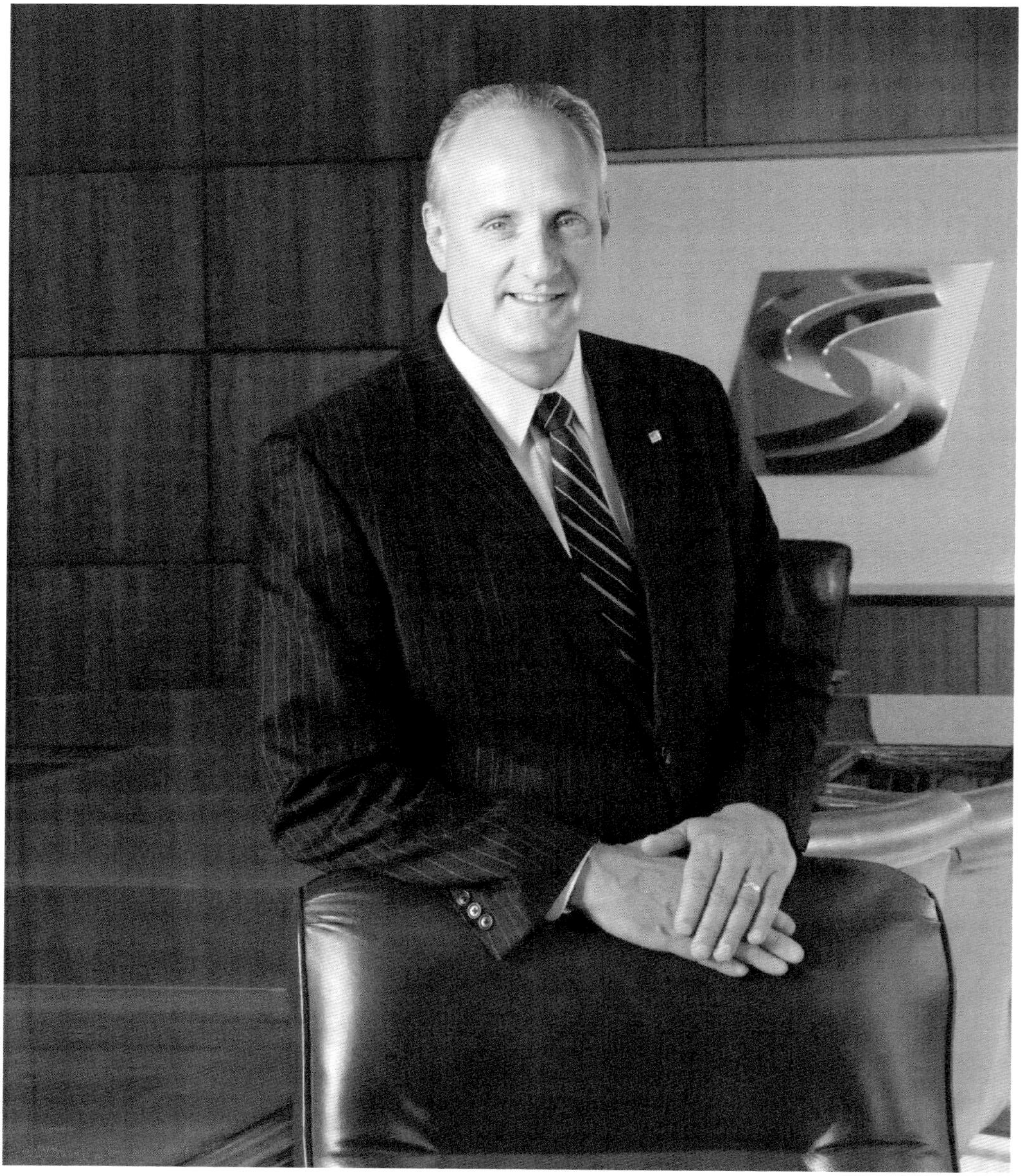

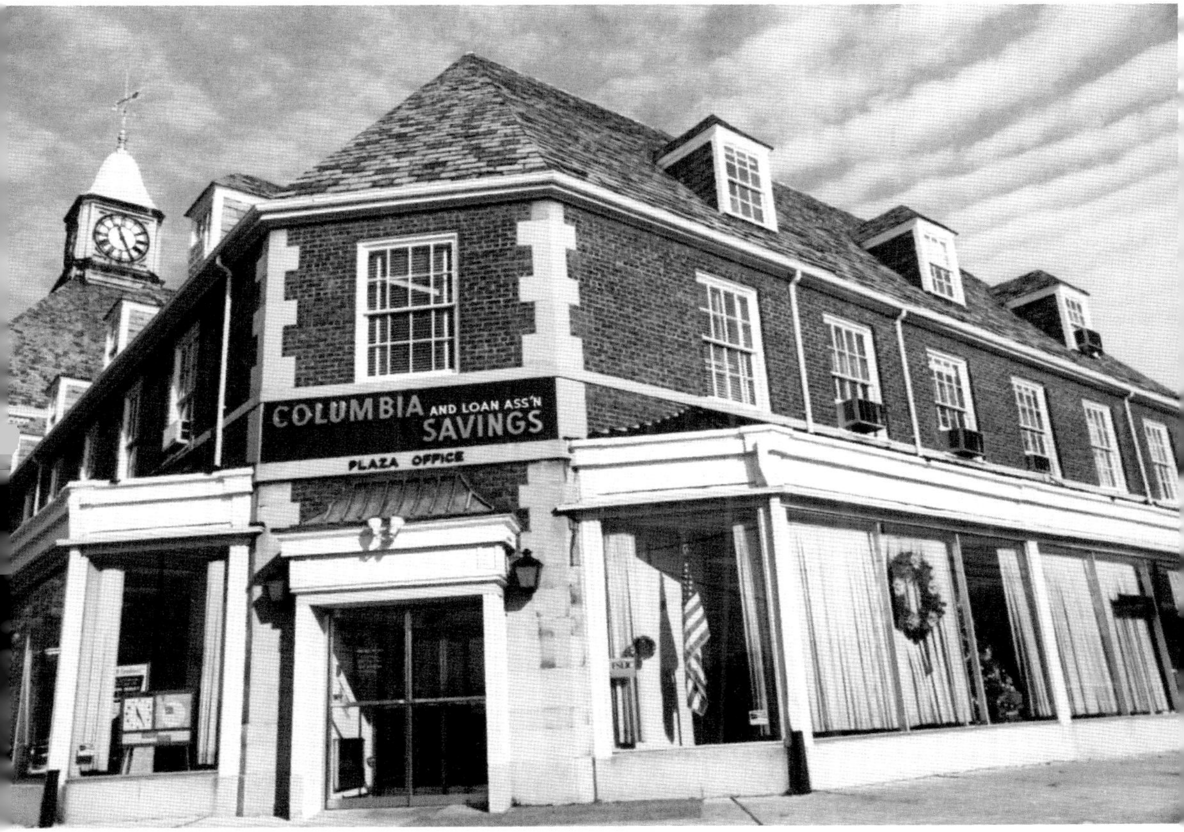

Best Bank in Town

The Columbia Bank's Radburn branch in the Plaza Building was completely destroyed by a spectacular fire in 2002. At the time, it was called Columbia Savings and Loan Association. It has since been rebuilt and is one of six branches in Fair Lawn. By 1985, Columbia's assets surpassed the $1 billion mark. The bank began offering commercial loans in 1993 and small business administration loans in 1994. Today, with assets over $4.3 billion, Columbia Bank remains New Jersey's largest mutual bank. Columbia's uniqueness lies in the fact it is both a full service "community" bank for individuals and families and a commercial bank for businesses. Columbia was named Best Bank in Fair Lawn by a poll of *Patch* readers. (Courtesy of Columbia Bank.)

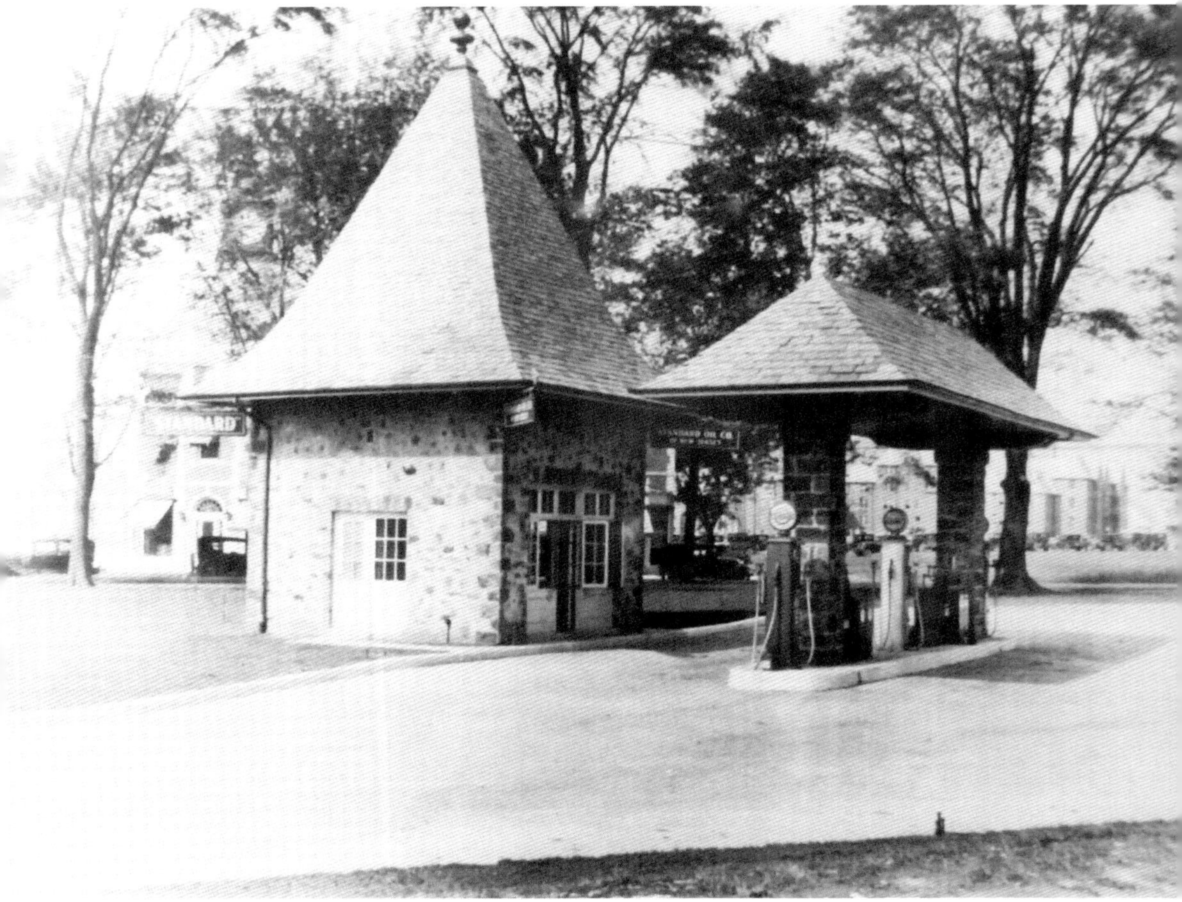

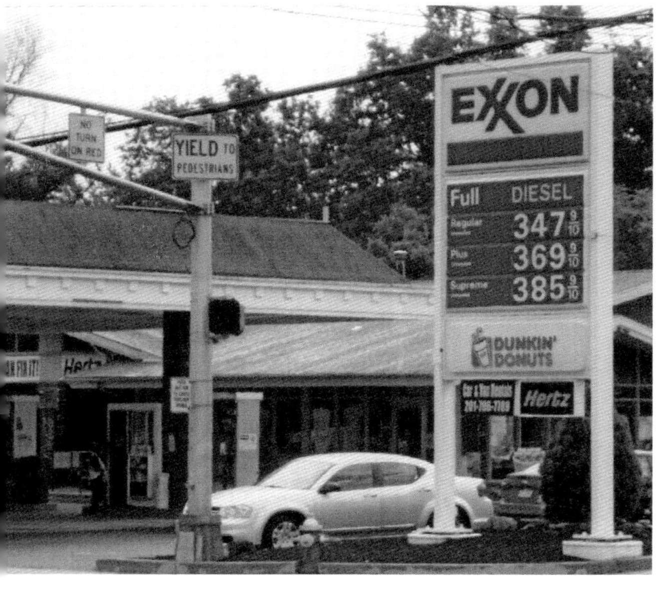

Radburn Exxon Station

George Sporn was the proprietor of the Radburn gasoline station when it opened in the new town around 1929 as a Standard Oil station on the southeast corner of Fair Lawn Avenue-Plaza Road. The business outgrew the location in its quaint stone building, and Mr. Sporn located across the road to the present site. By then, the business was known as Radburn Esso. George Sporn was active in local affairs, a member of the Radburn fire department, and an early member of the chamber of commerce. When he joined the service in World War II, his wife, Edna, ran the station. The name has now been changed to Radburn Exxon, and Karl and Dan Sewall own the establishment. Karl is a longtime resident and grew up in Fair Lawn. They both like to go deep-sea fishing on weekends. (Above, courtesy of Karl and Dan Sewall.)

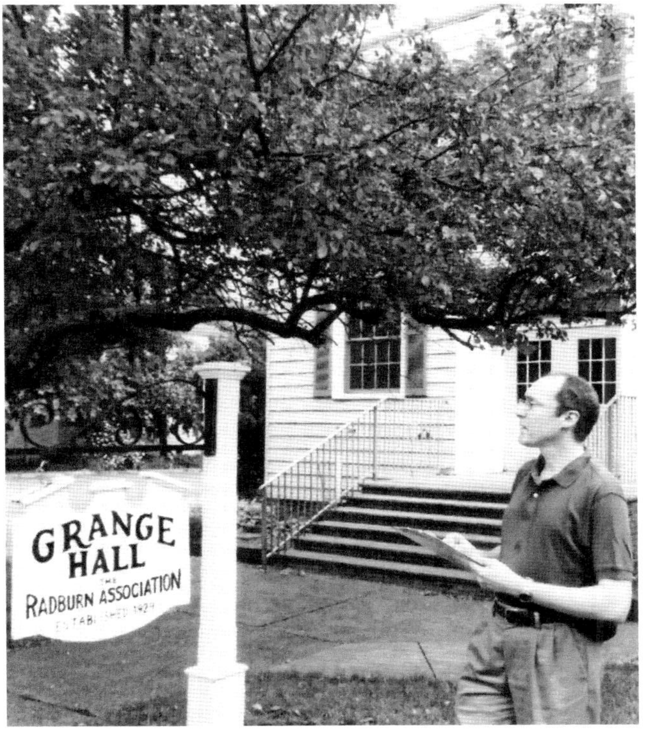

Radburn's Grange Hall and Tunnel

Eric Schutz, pictured at left, is president of the Radburn Citizens Association, which serves as a voice for residents in Radburn decisions and sponsors annually a family day, a Halloween party, and the yard sale treasure hunt. Schutz is a computer programmer who likes to work in his garden and take hikes with his kids in national parks. Founded in 1929, Radburn was one of America's first modern planned communities, a "Town for the Motor Age." Designed by town-planning pioneers Clarence Stein and Henry Wright, it was based on a design of cul-de-sacs connected to parks and a tunnel that allowed children to walk to school without having to cross a street. In 1975, Radburn was listed in the National Register of Historic Places and achieved National Landmark status in 2005.

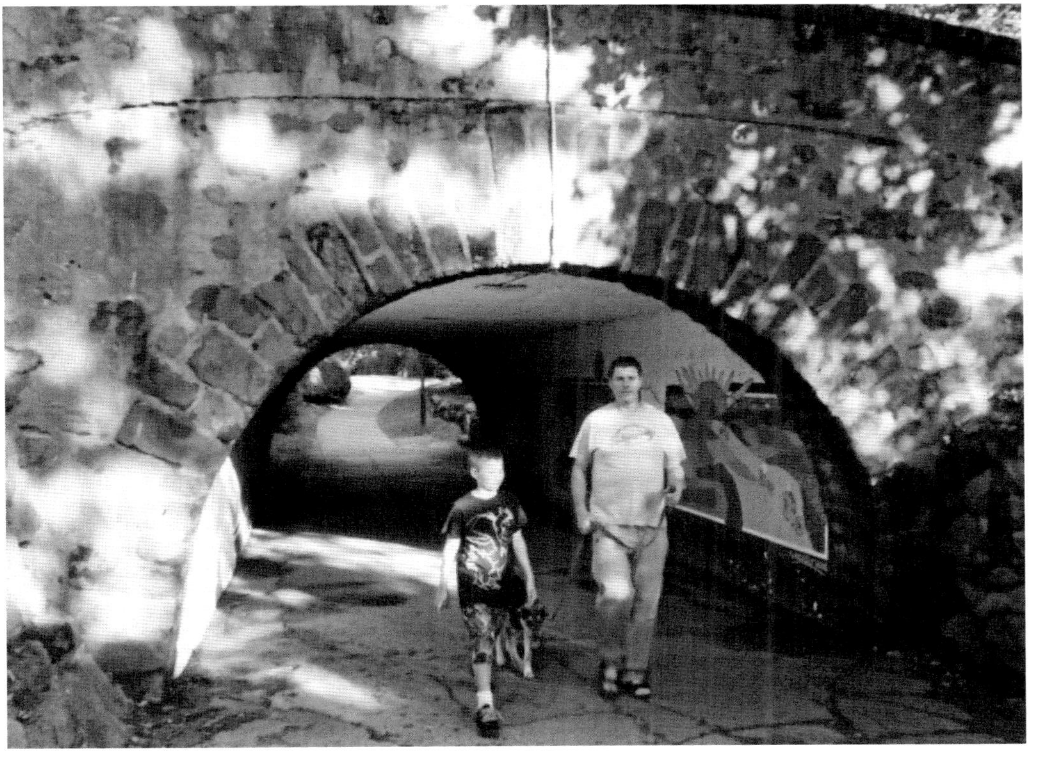

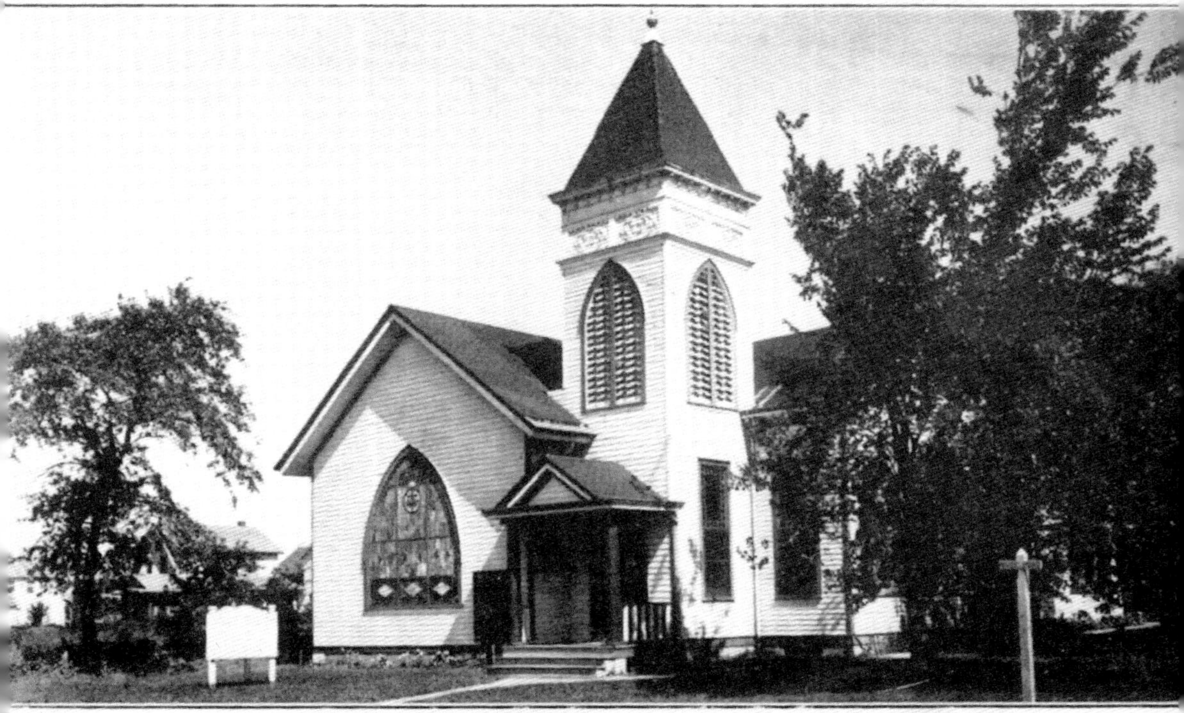

7-160 The Van Riper Ellis Memorial Church, Fair Lawn, N. J.

Created Foundation for Van Riper-Ellis Church

Eleanor Van Riper saw the need for a Sunday school in her neighborhood of Saddle River Township, so she organized a class in 1870 and held it in her home on Sloterdam Road (now River Road). Soon, the school needed a building, and she persuaded her husband, Henry, to donate land and her neighbors to contribute to the building of a chapel. Eleanor Van Riper served as superintendent of the Sunday school until her death in 1919 and was succeeded by her daughter Ida (née Van Riper) Ellis. Sunday afternoon services were conducted in the building by ministers of various Paterson churches until the Van Riper-Ellis Church was organized in 1929.

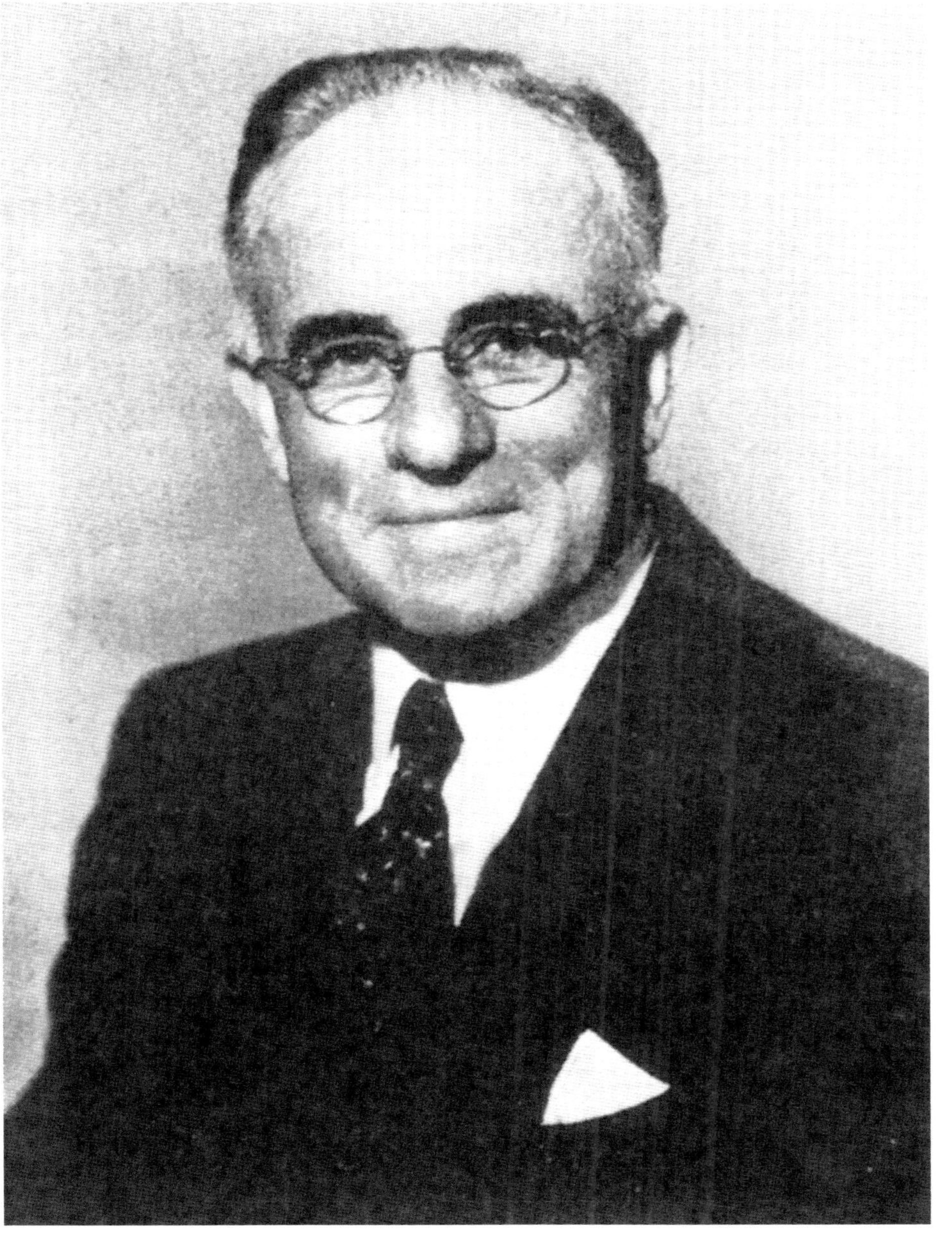

Rev. Peter Apelian

The Rev. Peter Apelian came to Fair Lawn in 1936 to be the second minister of the nondenominational Church in Radburn. Born in Turkey, Dr. Apelian, an Armenian, escaped to America as a young man after the persecution of his family. He had come home to find a trail of Bible pages; at the end, he found his mother dying. In America, he became a citizen and studied for the ministry. After World War I, he was secretary of the Near East Relief organization, heading the committee for Armenian and Syrian relief. Dr. Apelian joined the Rotary club and took an interest in Fair Lawn and national issues. He was a founder of The Forum, which featured speakers on public affairs on Sunday evenings.

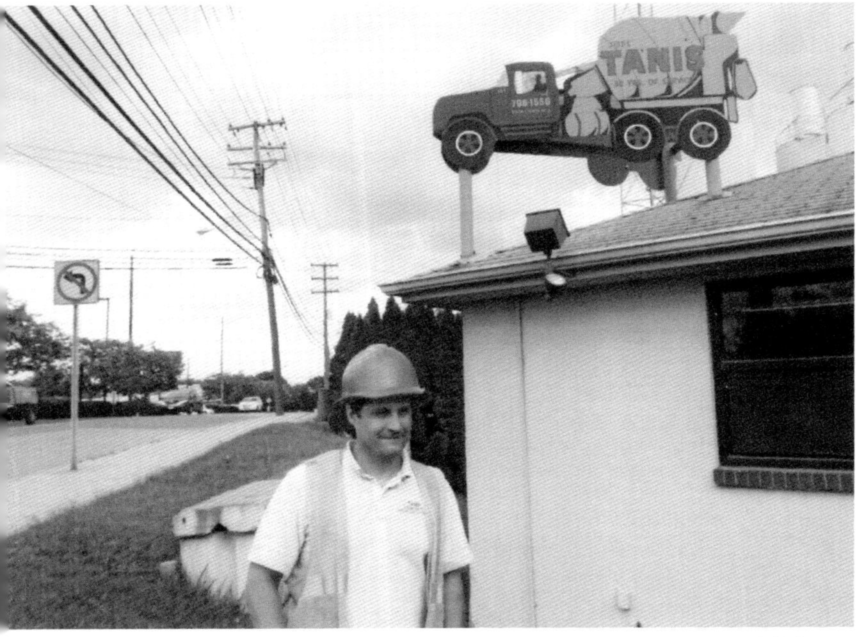

Seventy-five-year-old Concrete Business
The Tanis family no longer owns Joel Tanis & Sons Ready Mixed Concrete, but Todd Dages, grandson of the founder, works there in quality control. On weekends, Todd (pictured) likes to go hiking with his kids at the Delaware Water Gap. The company began in 1939 at the family home in Fair Lawn but soon moved to its present location on River Road.

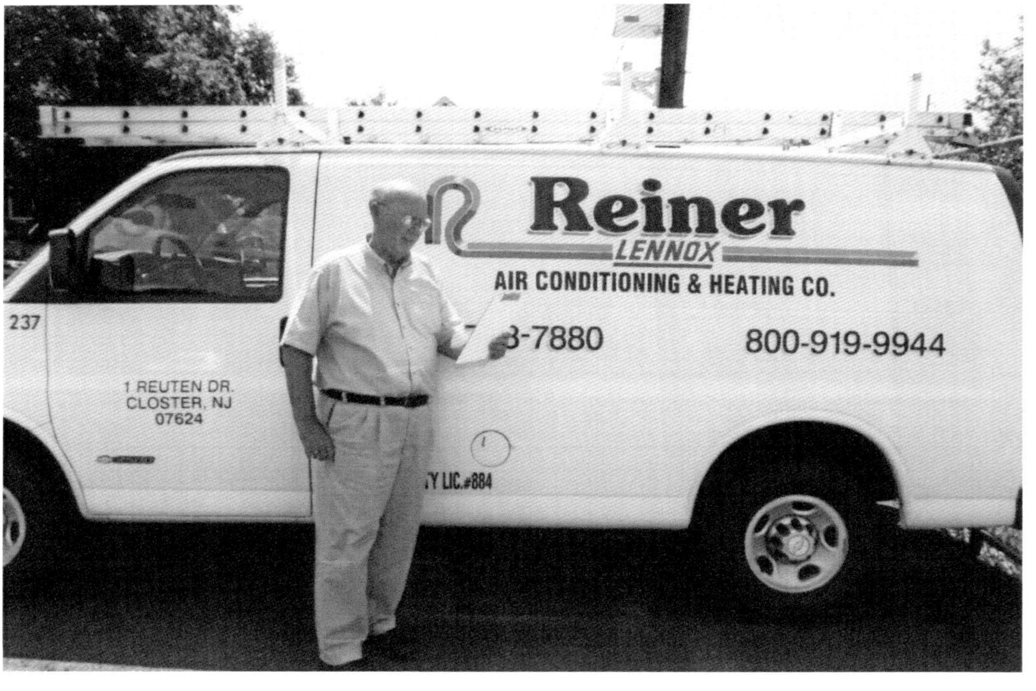

Heating and Cooling for 80 Years
In 1934, William Reiner established Reiner & Company in Fair Lawn for the installation and maintenance of all types of residential and commercial heating and cooling systems. Known as Reiner Group, Inc., today and still headquartered in Fair Lawn, Reiner currently employs more than 150 people in Fair Lawn and other locations. Vice Pres. Nick Kuiken, pictured, is the son of one of the founders of Kuiken Brothers.

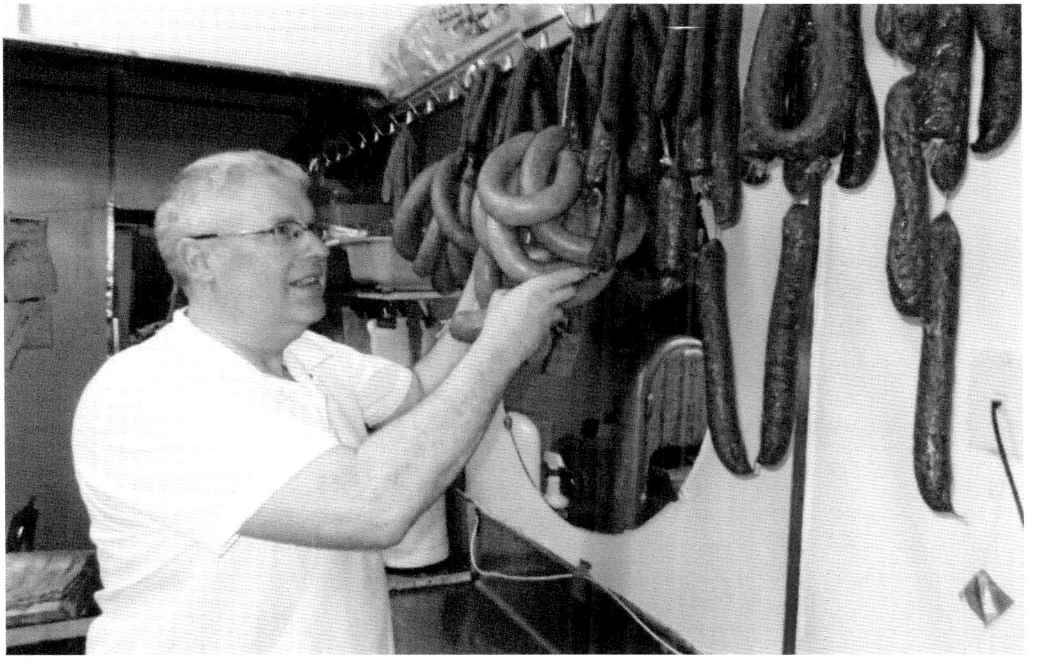

Best Butcher Shop in Town

Traditional butcher shops are becoming more and more scarce, but the Swiss Pork Store is thriving due to its age-old recipes and time-tested quality. Steve Struble has owned and operated the deli since 1997 and is shown with his handmade sausages. Struble likes to play tennis on weekends, usually in Radburn where he lives. A Swiss and a German opened the store in 1950, and being concerned about anti-German sentiment after World War II, they named the shop the Swiss Pork Store. Customer favorites include smoked meats, bratwurst, knockwurst, sausages, and steaks. Some customers claim the store has the best hot dogs and hamburger meat in town. The store was named Best Butcher Shop and Best Specialty Food Store by a poll of *Patch* readers.

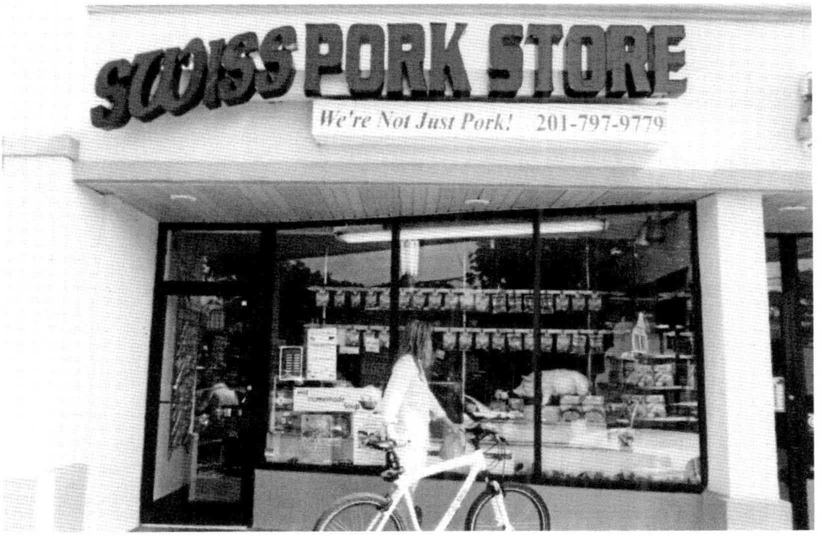

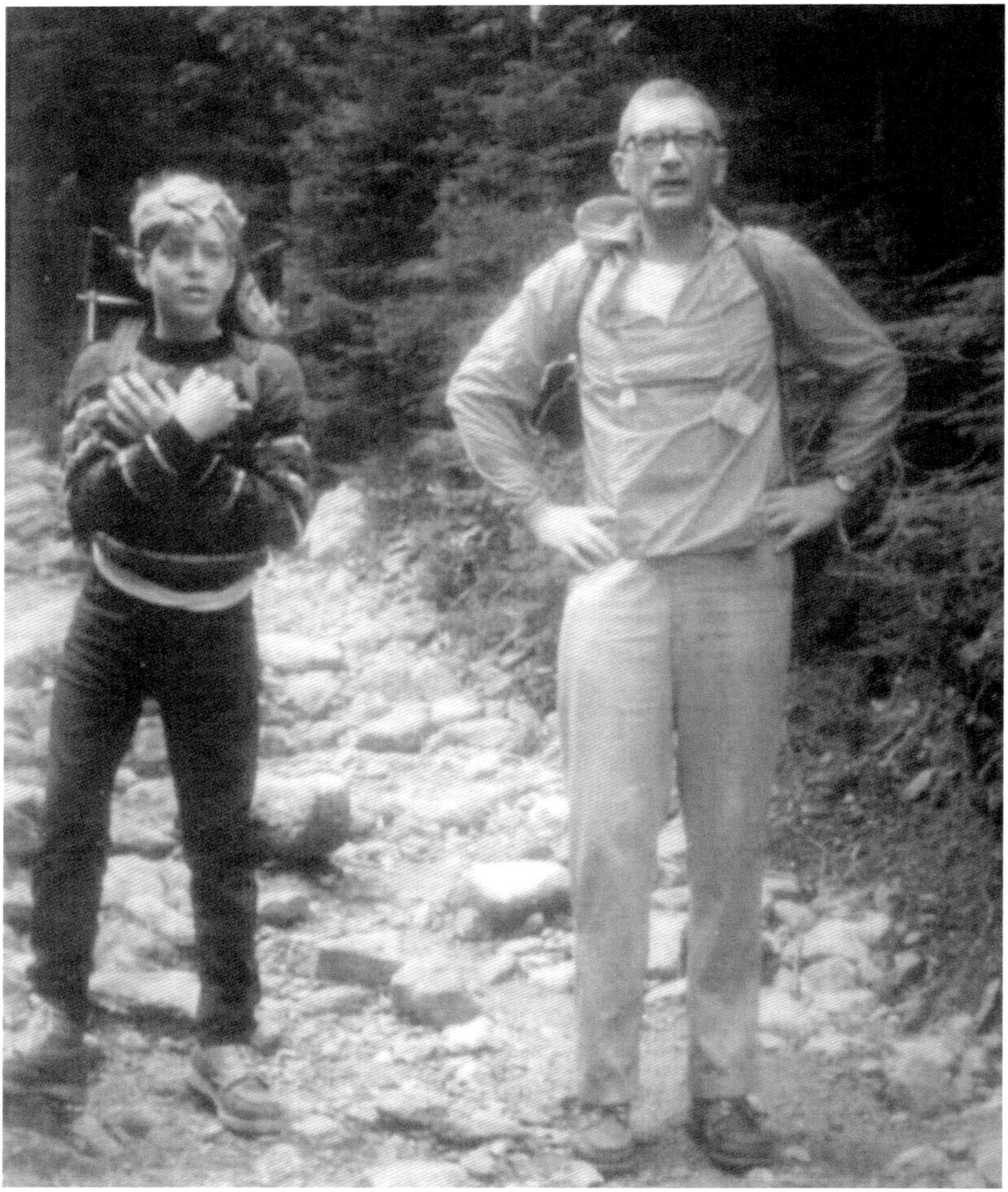

Much-loved Pediatrician

Dr. Albert Rosen was a much-loved pediatrician who remembered his former patients when they brought their children to him. He was a founding member of the medical staff of Valley Hospital and was the first recipient of its Distinguished Physician Service Award. Dr. Rosen was an enthusiastic mountain climber, climbing on every continent. An avid hiker, he promoted its health benefits through his community school course on hiking. He published a book, *Health Hints for Hikers*, which was sold in local sports stores as well as bookstores. The doctor also loved gardening and had a small farm, which included bees and farm animals, behind his Fair Lawn Avenue home and office. Dr. Rosen is pictured hiking with his son Jonathan. (Courtesy of Jonathan Rosen.)

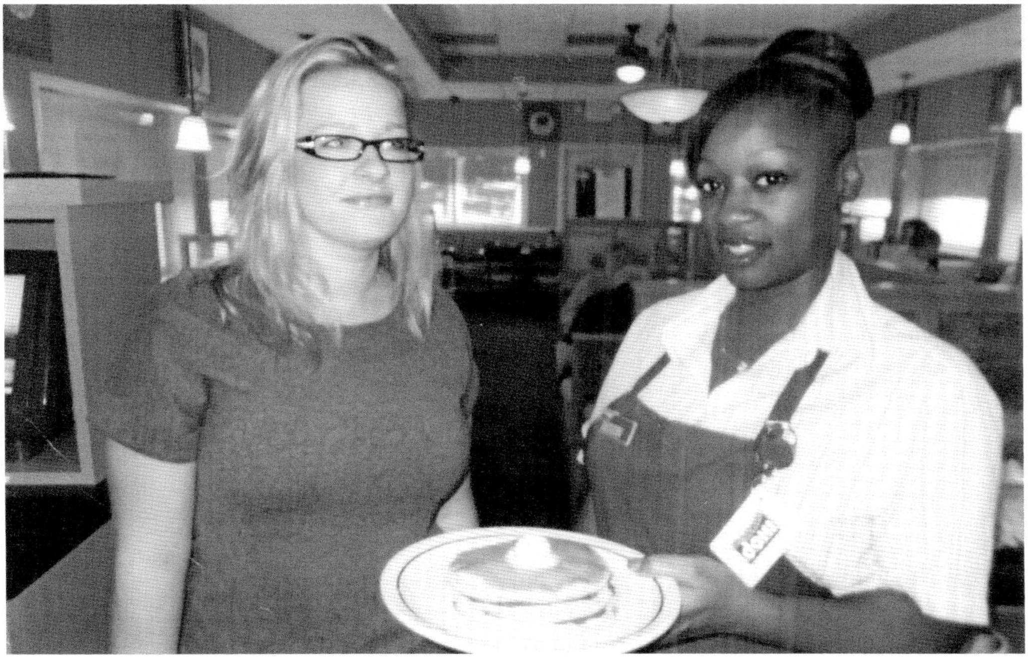

Early International House of Pancakes

Jennifer Alaimo (left) has been the IHOP franchise owner for eight years, taking over from her father, John Alaimo, who started the restaurant in 1963. John was active in the Rotary Club and founded the Fair Lawn Chamber of Commerce in 1954, serving as its first president. Now called just IHOP, this famous pancake house chain has more than 1,500 restaurants across America. Known for its breakfast foods, such as pancakes, French toast, and omelets, it also offers a menu of lunch and dinner items. Also shown in the photograph is longtime waitress Latrice Sanders, who has worked at IHOP for 12 years.

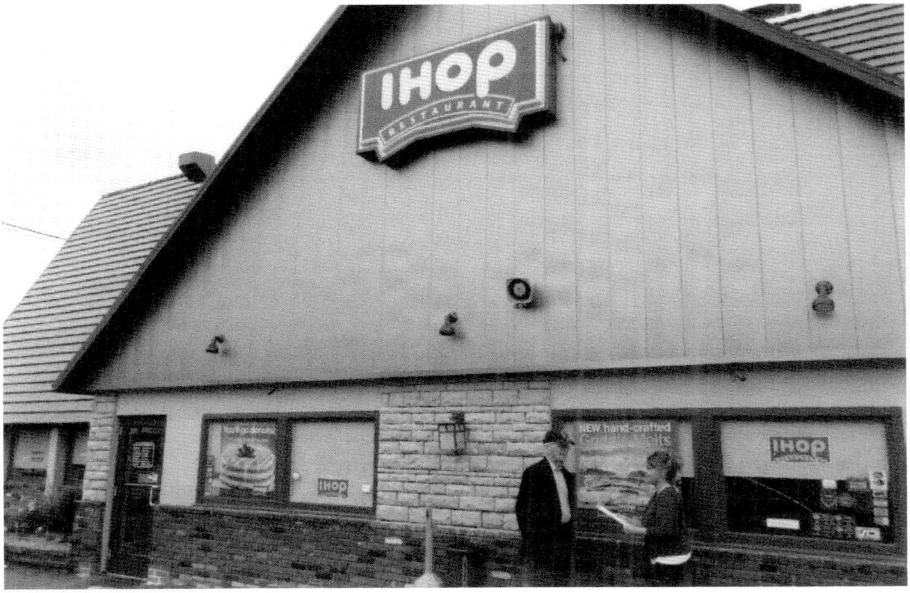

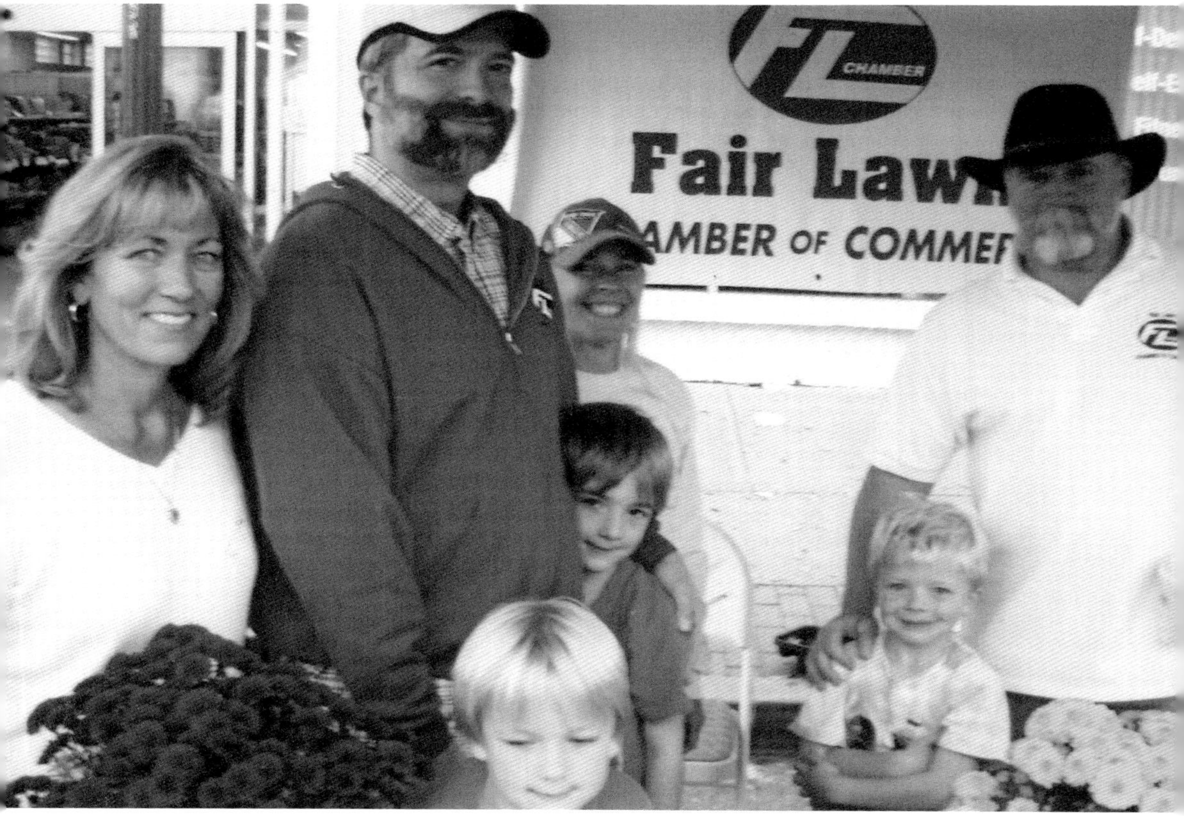

Spring and Fall Street Fairs

The Fair Lawn Chamber of Commerce sponsors two street fairs each year, one in the Radburn Shopping Center in the spring and one on River Road in the fall. "The street fairs bring together families who get to enjoy a casual day of shopping, rides, great food, and live entertainment," said current chamber president Mitch Palin, owner of Minuteman Press. He goes on to say, "Our members have an opportunity to participate by having a table to display their products and services directly to our community for a relaxing and fun time." Members of the board of directors, shown in the booth at the street fair, are, from left to right, past president Mary Marrara, past president Tod Christianson and family, and current vice president Jack Donohue.

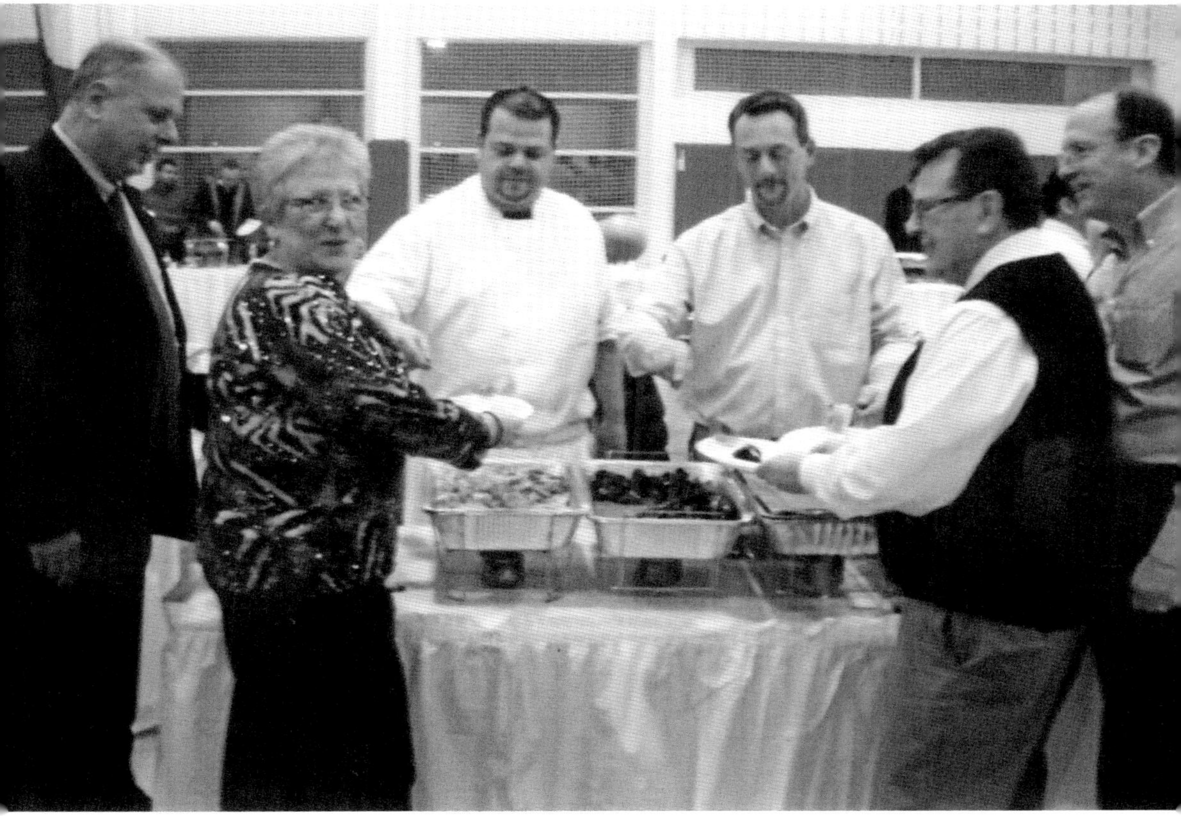

Taste of Our Town

The Fair Lawn Chamber of Commerce's newest event is its annual Taste of Our Town, during which hundreds of people pay $20 to sample specialties from 20 local eateries that donate their fine food in order to help families in the community. Pictured from left to right are the following chamber board members: administration vice president Rick Kellerman, programming vice president Annette Wanamaker, executive director Hank Pawski, and finance vice president Stu Herrmann. They are being served award-winning chicken by Rob DeLaurentis, owner of Sage Restaurant, at Taste of Our Town. The net proceeds from the event benefit the borough's food pantry. Funded by private donations, Fair Lawn's pantry assists families on a regular basis by providing food and grocery store gift cards.

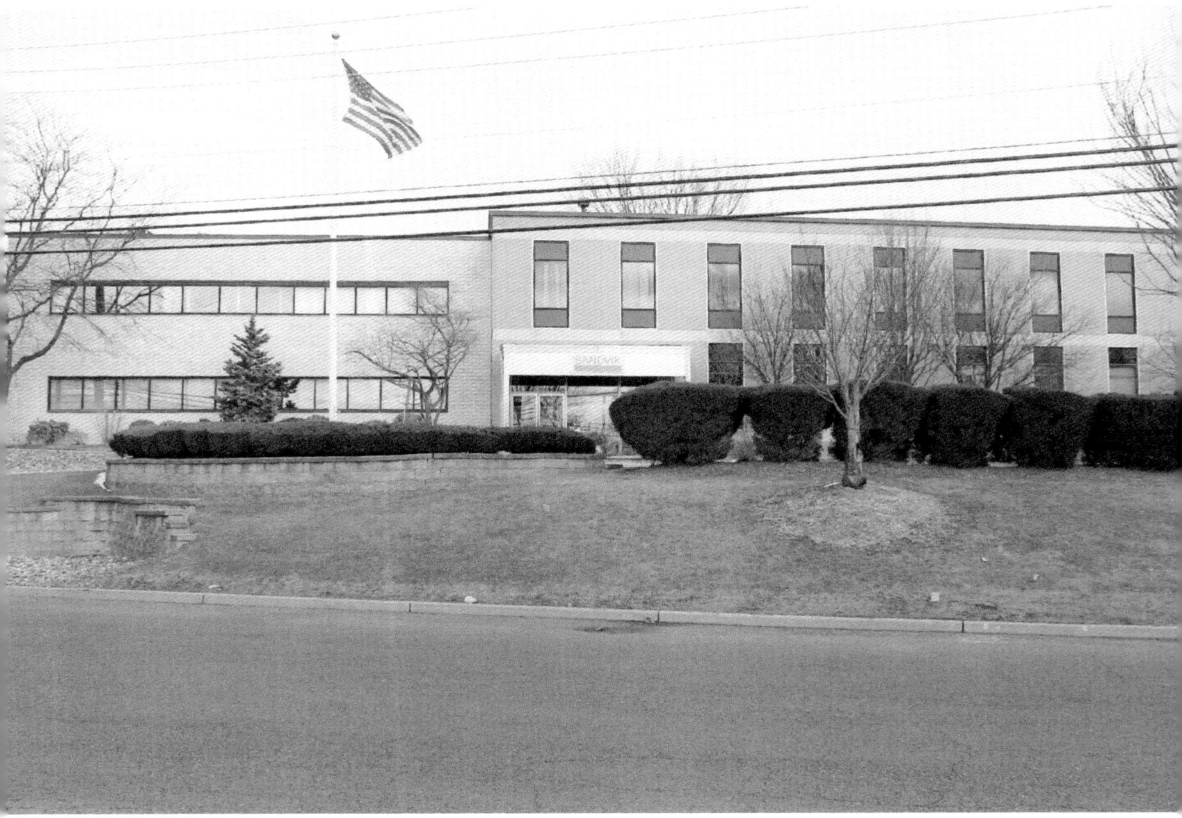

Swedish Company Donates to Community

In 1955, Sandvik, Inc., opened a steel products factory in Fair Lawn's new industrial park. The company has actively contributed money to the Fair Lawn Rescue Squad; the Fair Lawn Volunteer Ambulance Corps; the chamber of commerce for the "Commerce Flag Program," which honors all veterans who served the United States; and Relay for Life, which raises money for the American Cancer Society. Today, Sandvik no longer manufactures in Fair Lawn, but the office still serves as the US headquarters for its many product lines. Sandvik was founded in Sweden in 1862 where it built the world's first steel mill. (Courtesy of Sandvik, Inc.)

Fair Lawn's Leading Accounting Firm

Hunter Group CPA, LLC, was founded in 1956 by Robert D. Hunter and has grown to 47 employees with eight partners (directors). While Hunter passed away in 2004, his leadership, dynamic business skills, and personality are still a benchmark for the personal service offered by the firm.

Hunter is proud to provide audit, tax, and accounting services to several of Fair Lawn's prominent nonprofit organizations at a discounted rate. The firm is a leading supporter of the Fair Lawn Chamber of Commerce.

Shown in the photograph are the Hunter partners, from left to right, (first row) Frank Pawlowski, Leonard Manis, Elliott Koplitz, Kevin Hansen, Thomas Cairoli, and Andrew Trivento; (second row) Tod Christianson and Maria Plucinsky.

"We have clients throughout northeastern New Jersey," Pawlowski said. "We specialize in family-owned businesses in a wide range of industries."

"Our clients rely on us as trusted advisors," said Manis. "We consult on business succession, estate and business planning, company valuations as well as litigation support." The firm has considerable expertise in benefit plan and pension plan auditing.

Hansen oversees Hunter Financial Resources, which he says, "is our recruiting firm that helps companies find temporary or permanent employees." Plucinsky said, "Hunter Financial Services is our financial planning arm, which helps our clients reach their personal financial goals."

Christianson, who has lived in Fair Lawn his whole life, heads up the 401k department, of which he says, "Hunter has significant expertise in 401k investment and is looking to grow this area of our practice." Cairoli said, "Hunter Group is also an active member of CPAmerica, which is a national network of mid-sized accounting firms that share information and resources." (Courtesy of Hunter Group CPA, LLC.)

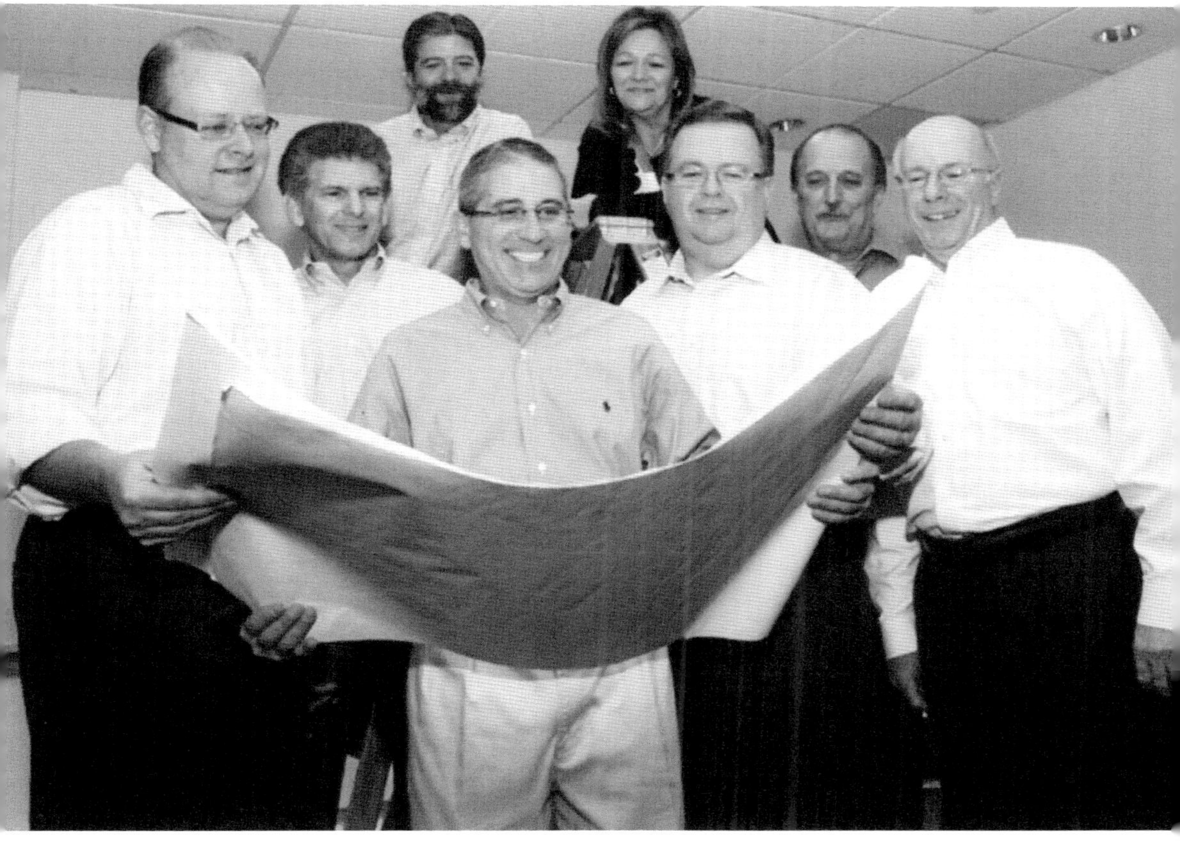

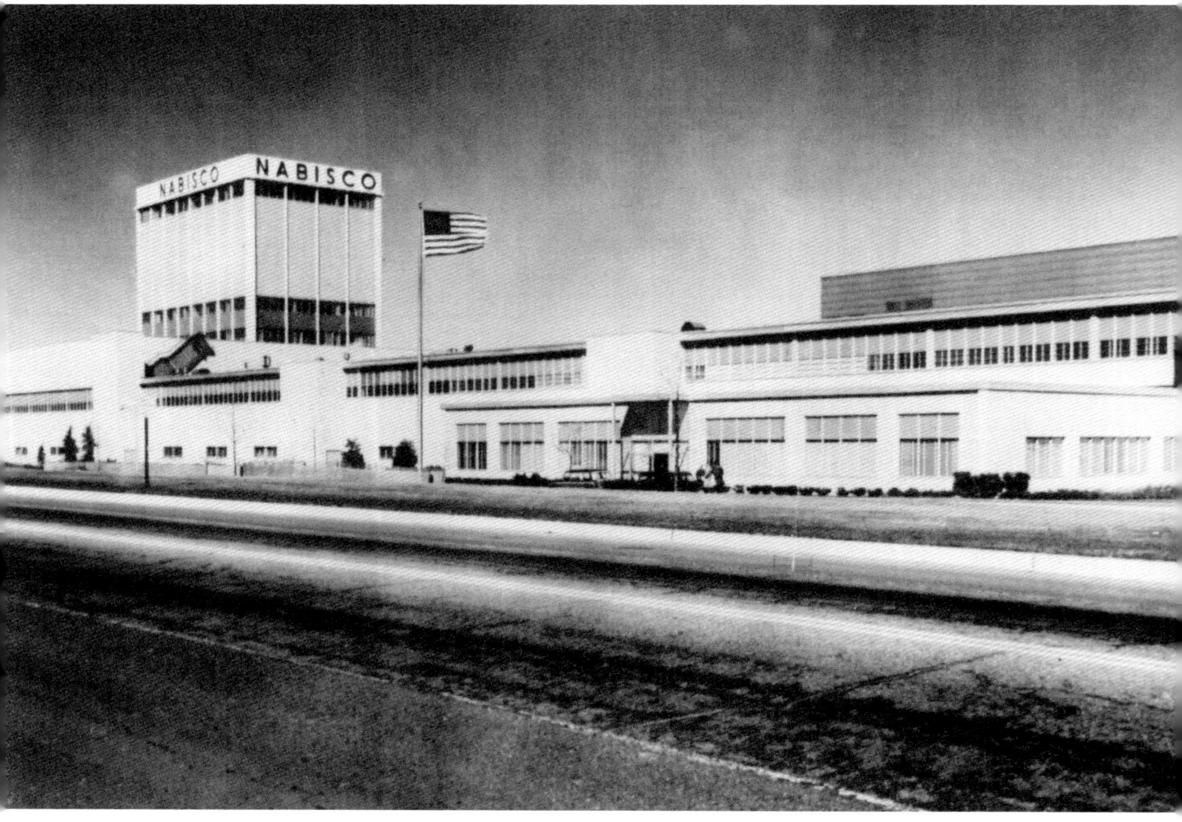

Nation's Biggest Producer of Oreos

Michael Wallace is the new plant manager for Nabisco Bakery. Fair Lawn residents claim that when the wind is blowing just right, they can smell the freshly baked cookies. The bakery is Fair Lawn's tallest building and most famous manufacturer, now owned by the American conglomerate Mondelez International, which purchased Kraft Foods. The factory was constructed in 1955 for $15 million with eight industrial ovens, a 160-foot tower for storage of raw materials, and a total floor area of 500,000 square feet. It was dedicated in 1958. Today, the factory has 550 employees and a research and development division. In addition to Oreos, the plant bakes Ritz Crackers, Premium Saltines, and Barnum Animal Crackers. At public meetings, Nabisco has said it has no plans to leave Fair Lawn since it has been very successful here. (Nabisco is a registered trademark of Mondelez International, Inc. Image and text is used with permission. Courtesy of Mondelez International, Inc.)

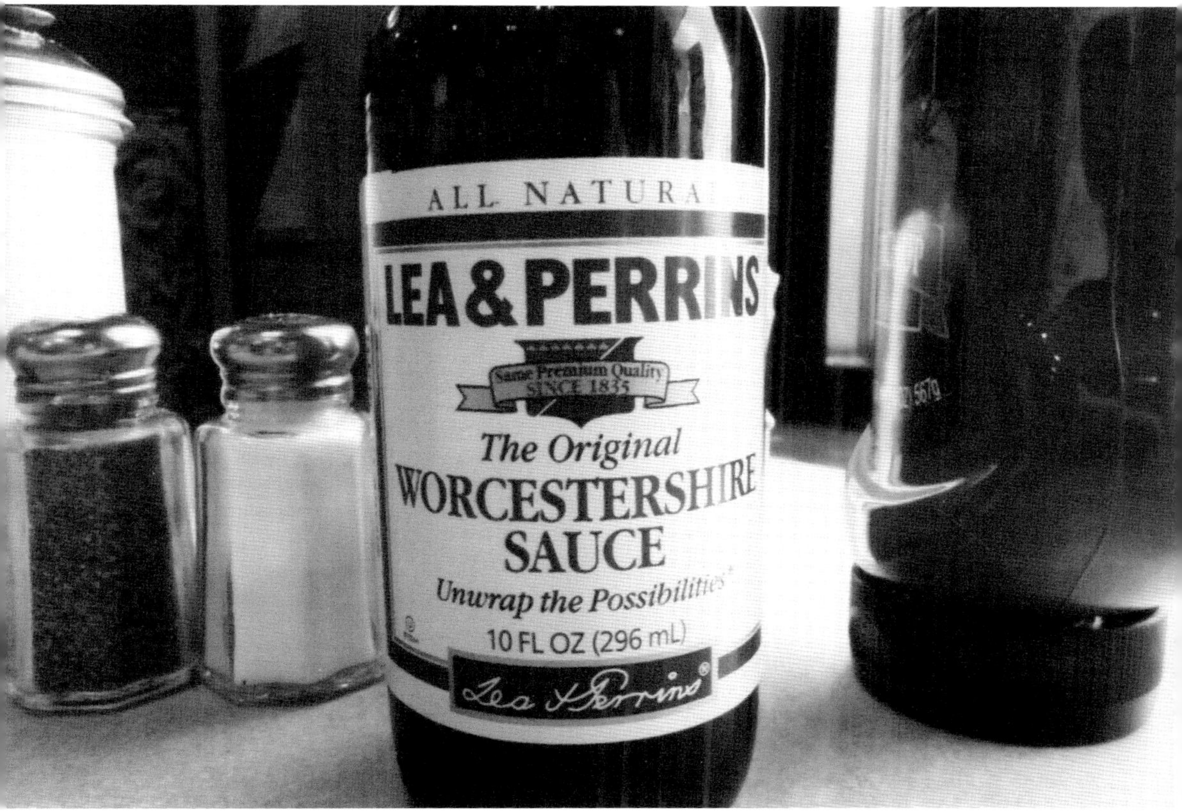

The No. 1 Steak Sauce in America
Lea & Perrins factory manager Kish Patel takes pride that, when Fair Lawn residents travel the country and tell people what city they are from, the response is often "Lea & Perrins Worcestershire Sauce." This famous steak sauce is found on most restaurant tables, with the distinct address of Fair Lawn, New Jersey. Patel is proud that Lea & Perrins supports the local food pantry with Heinz products and financial contributions. On page 27, Ike Herman of Lea & Perrins is presenting a grant to Carl Koenig for the Cadmus Museum. Lea & Perrins began in England in 1838. In 1957, it opened a factory in Fair Lawn's Industrial Park and sold the first commercially produced Worchester sauce in America. The ingredients include fish from Argentina, garlic from California, red onions from Washington, and anchovies from Italy.

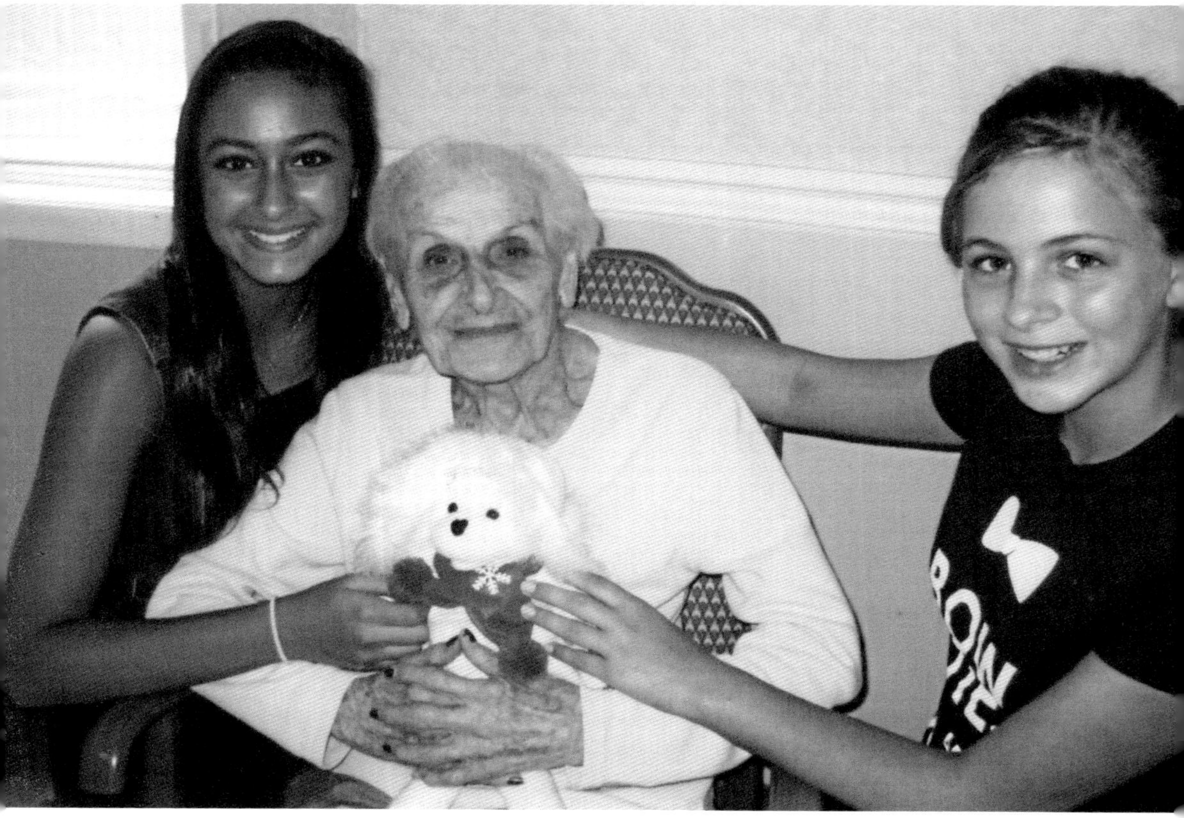

Stuffed Animals for the Elderly

Maple Glen Center resident Marie Kuklias (center) was filled with warmth and joy when given a stuffed animal that plays music. It was a gesture of love by two young teens who gave stuffed animals to all the elderly women after going door-to-door in Fair Lawn and getting donations from 50 people. Thirteen-year-old Thomas Jefferson Middle School eighth-grader Nicki Kissil (left) swims for the Radburn swim team, is a cheerleader, sings, and acts. Thirteen-year-old Fair Lawn High School ninth-grader Charlotte Glassett (right) plays clarinet, sings, and acts. Maple Glen Center is a Genesis HealthCare nursing home facility with 160 beds at the former location of the Fair Lawn Memorial Hospital, which was built in 1960.

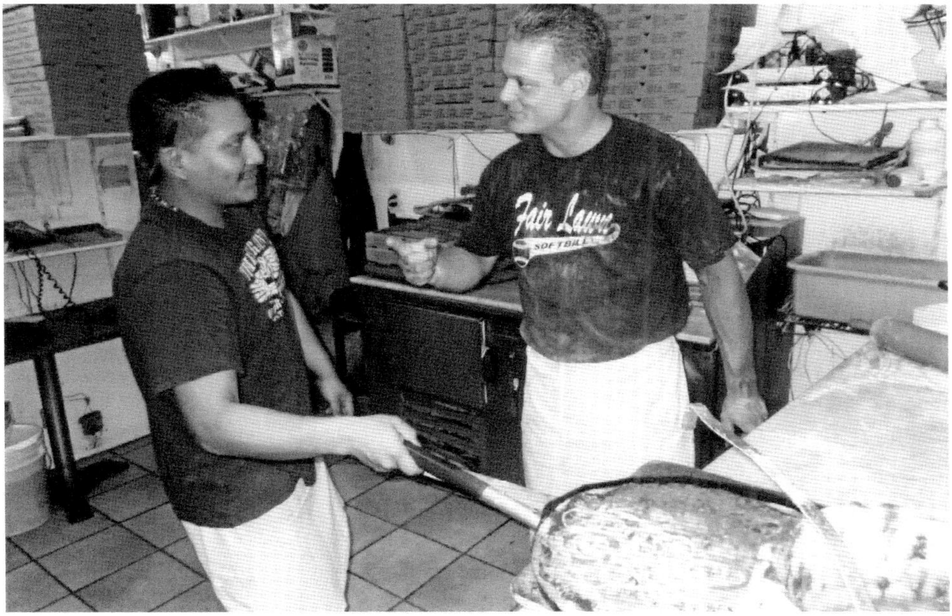

Fair Lawn's Best Pizza

The owner and operator of Ness Pizza House, Steve Jubelt (right), grew up just two blocks away from the store, frequenting it often. And now he has owned it for more than 15 years. In fact, he expanded it to include a full Italian menu. In addition to pizza—still the original special recipe—are appetizers, salads, and a large variety of heroes, wraps, dinners. and pastas. The penne vodka and Sicilian pies are very popular, as are shrimp parmigiana, grilled salmon, eggplant parmigiana, meatball heroes, and BLT classic wraps. Ness was named Best Pizza in Fair Lawn by a poll of *Patch* readers.

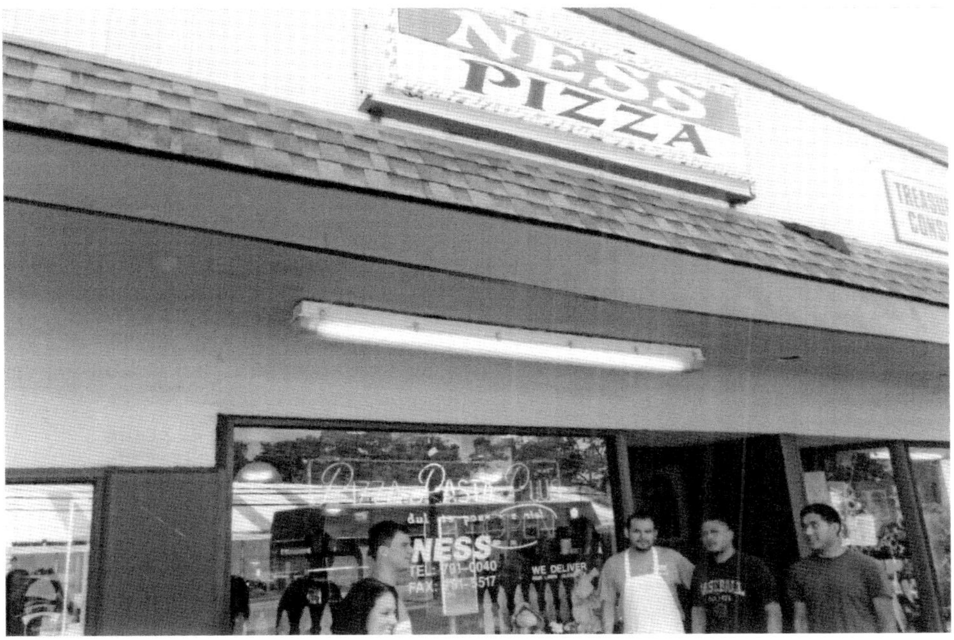

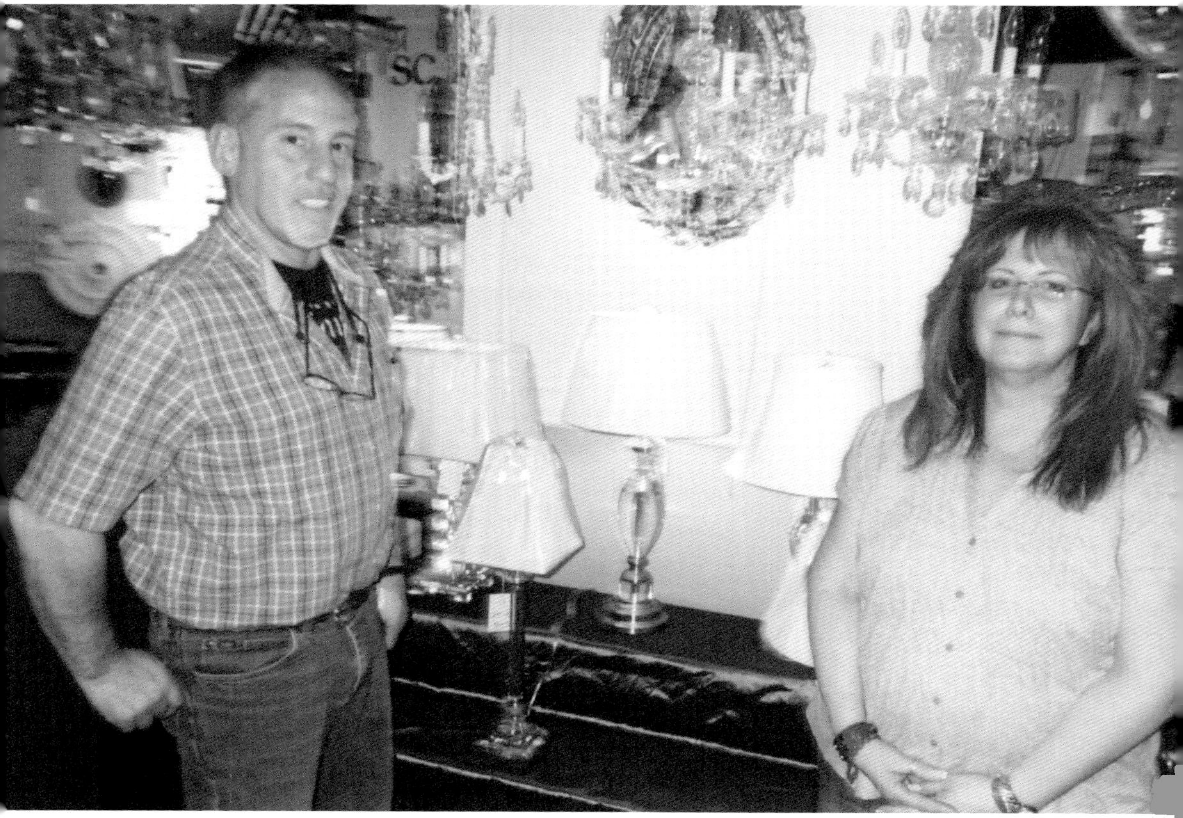

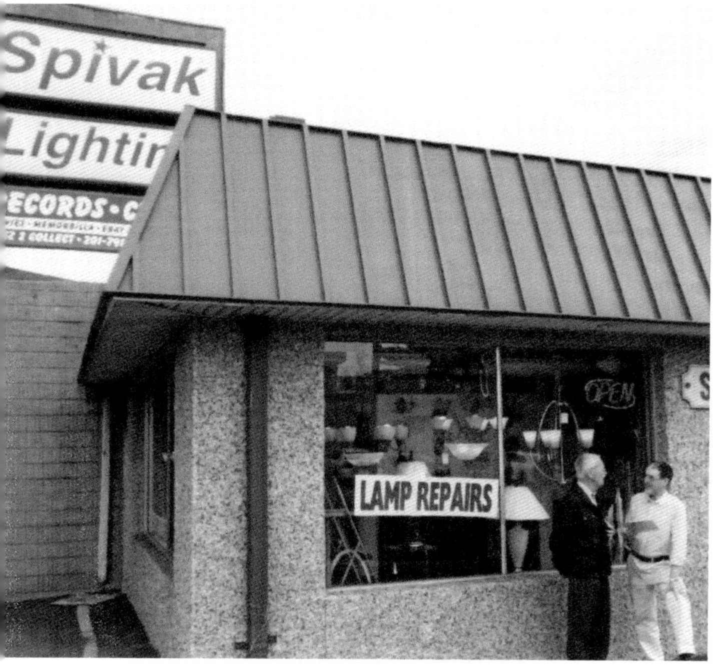

Lighting Consultant for 35 Years
Albert Spivak emigrated from Russia to the United States around 1900, and his trade evolved into an electrical supply business. In 1920, Albert and his brothers opened their first showroom, Spivak Electrical Supply, in Paterson. The business thrived on the postwar building boom, and in 1970, the showroom was relocated to Elmwood Park and rebranded as Spivak Lighting. Today, the showroom is located on Broadway in Fair Lawn. In 2002, Jay Koransky (left) became the sole owner and manager of the store and has been running it for the past 35 years. Koransky likes to build and restore vintage cars on his day off. Spivak offers all types of residential and commercial lighting from chandeliers to landscape lighting, as well as lamp repairs and lighting layouts for kitchens. Paula Radest is shown to the right.

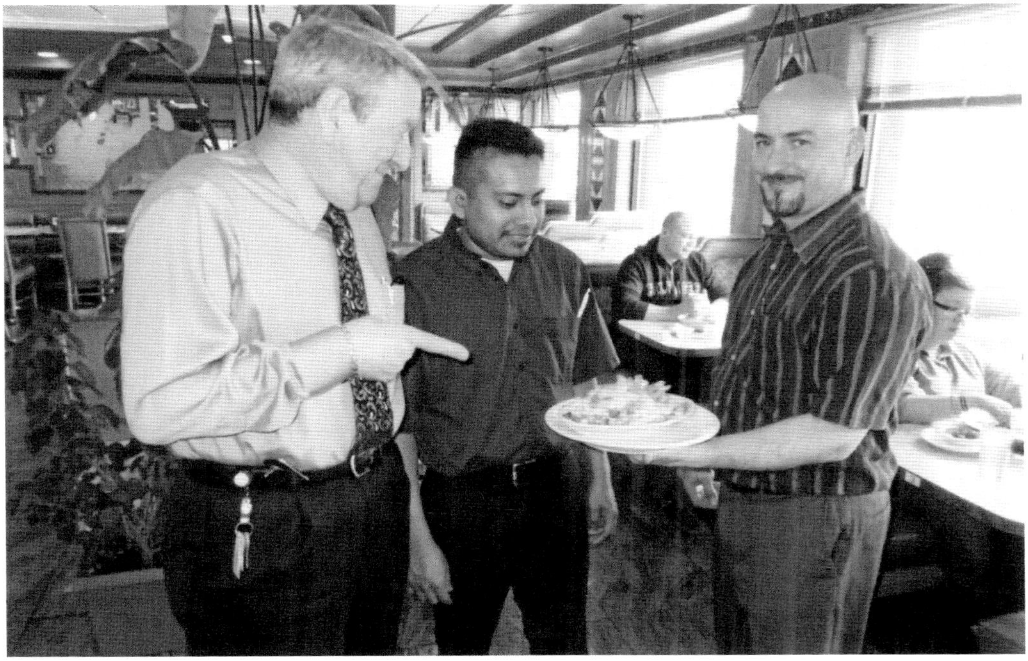

Best Dinner Specials in Town

The Empress Diner has been owned and operated since 1965 by Nick Melissas (left) and his son John Melissas (right). The two men like to go deep-sea fishing together off the Jersey shore. Longtime waiter Eddie Bravo (center) is shown admiring local favorite Jersey Disco Fries with gravy and cheese. The Empress Diner offers a huge menu for breakfast, lunch, and dinner, as well as a fully stocked bar. Breakfast is available all day and includes omelets, French toast, waffles, and pancakes. For lunch and dinner, specialty burgers, such as the Grecian and Cordon Bleu, are available. Also on the menu are "Mexican Delights," Philly steak sandwiches, and "triple-deckers." A local food critic determined the honor of Best Dinner Specials in Fair Lawn, and the Empress Diner won.

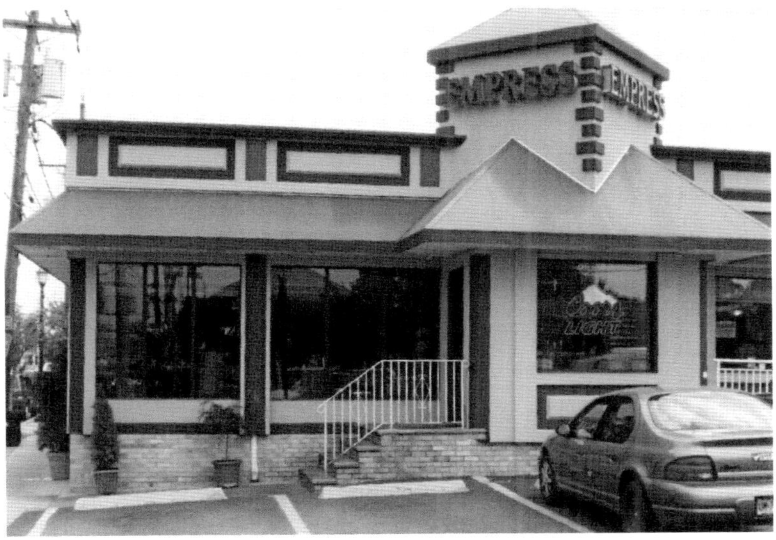

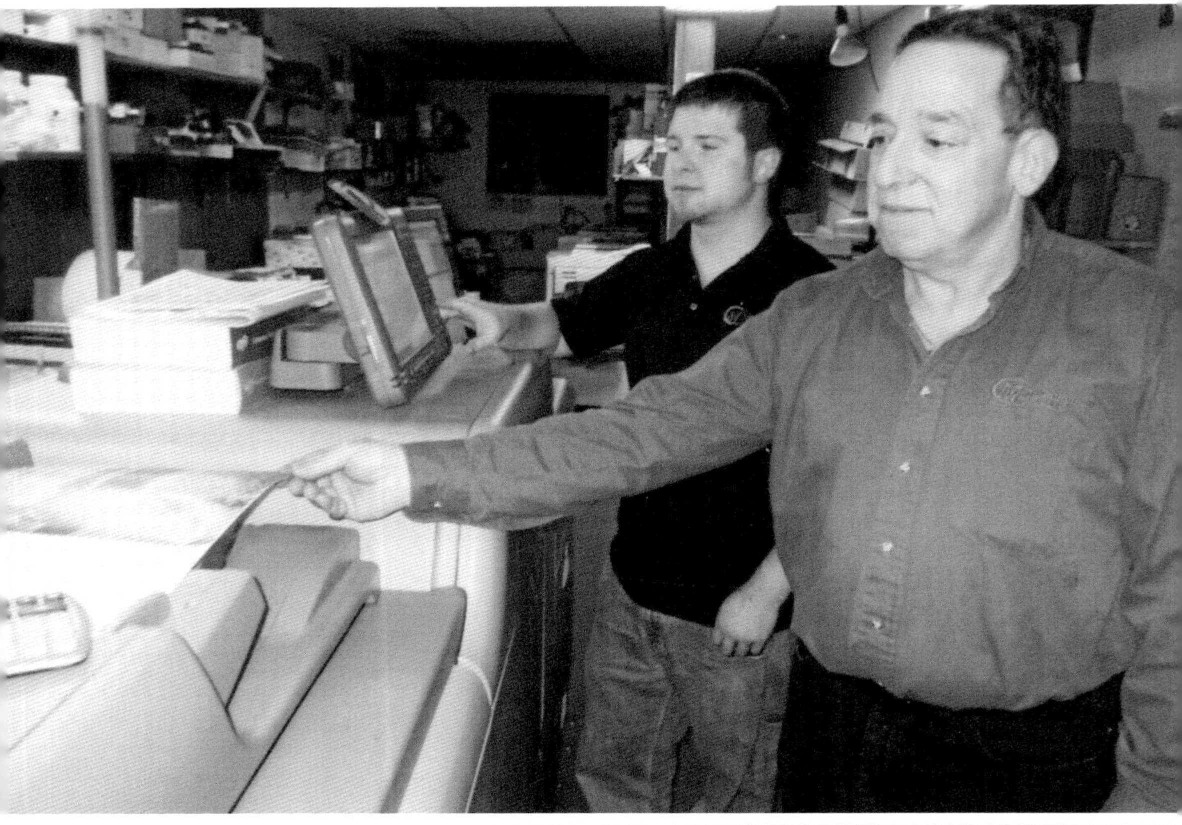

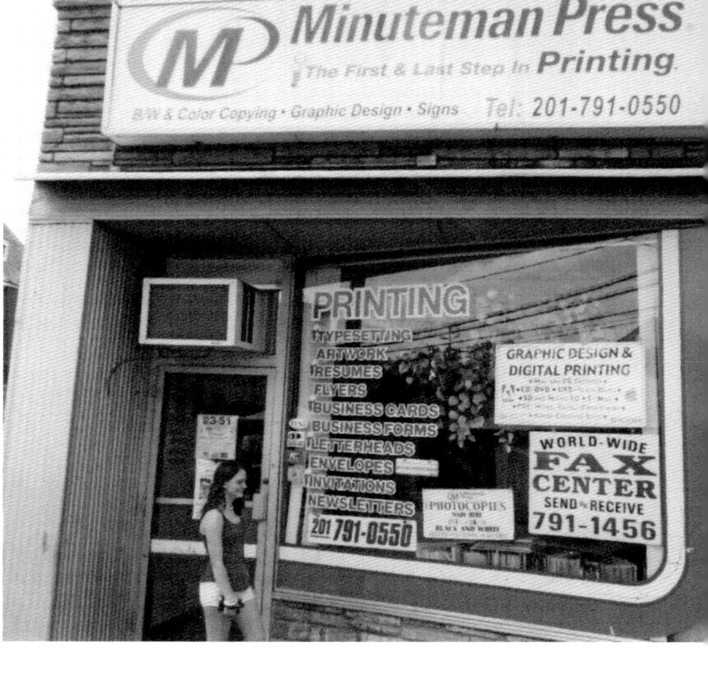

High-Speed Copying and Printing
Minuteman Press is family owned and operated by Mitch Palin (right) and his son Matt Palin (left), who have season tickets to New Jersey Devils hockey games. The print shop has been at its current location since 1983 and does everything from black-and-white copies, business cards, full-color postcards, brochures, wedding invitations, and promotional merchandise. It also offers services such as graphic design, professional finishing, lamination, embossing, cutting, binding, foil stamping, perforation, folding, and pickup and delivery. Fair Lawn residents find Minuteman Press to be a convenient place to get some quick photocopies.

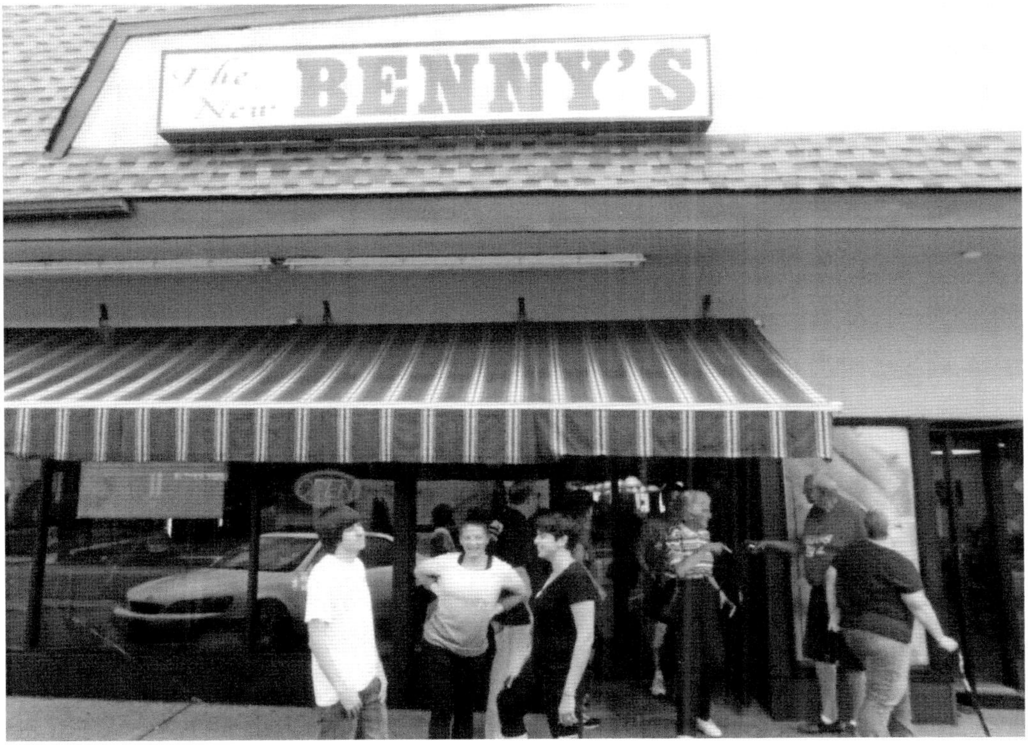

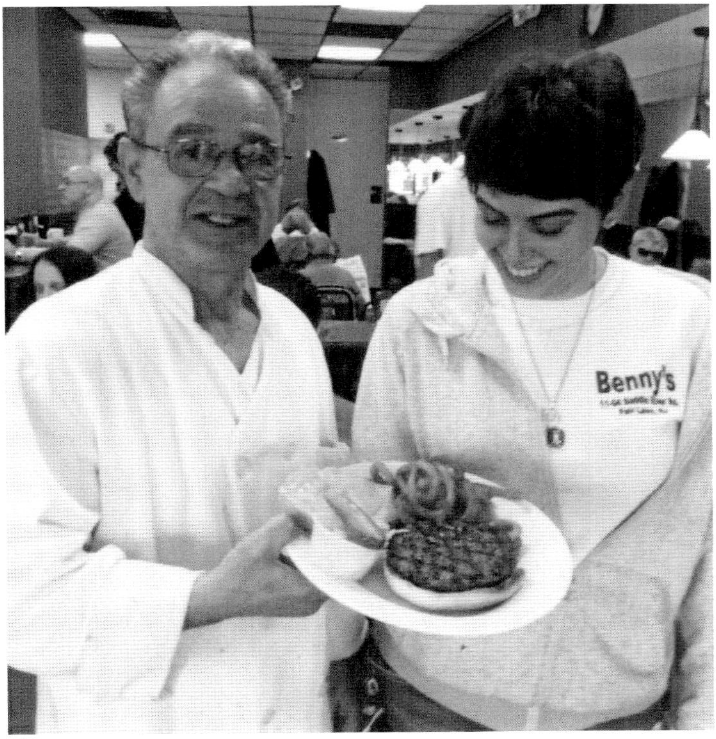

Best Breakfast Spot in Fair Lawn

Opened in 1984, Benny's Luncheonette is now owned and operated by Tony D'Ascoli and Diana Stella (both pictured). Benny's offers a variety of baked goods as well as its popular overstuffed sandwiches, including its famous pastrami sandwich. Each morning, Diana Stella bakes fresh pastries and the popular oatmeal cookies. Take-out and delivery are also available, and Benny's provides catering. There is an old-style counter where residents enjoy sitting. The chocolate chip pancakes are recommended.

Benny's was named Best Breakfast Spot in Fair Lawn by a poll of *Patch* readers.

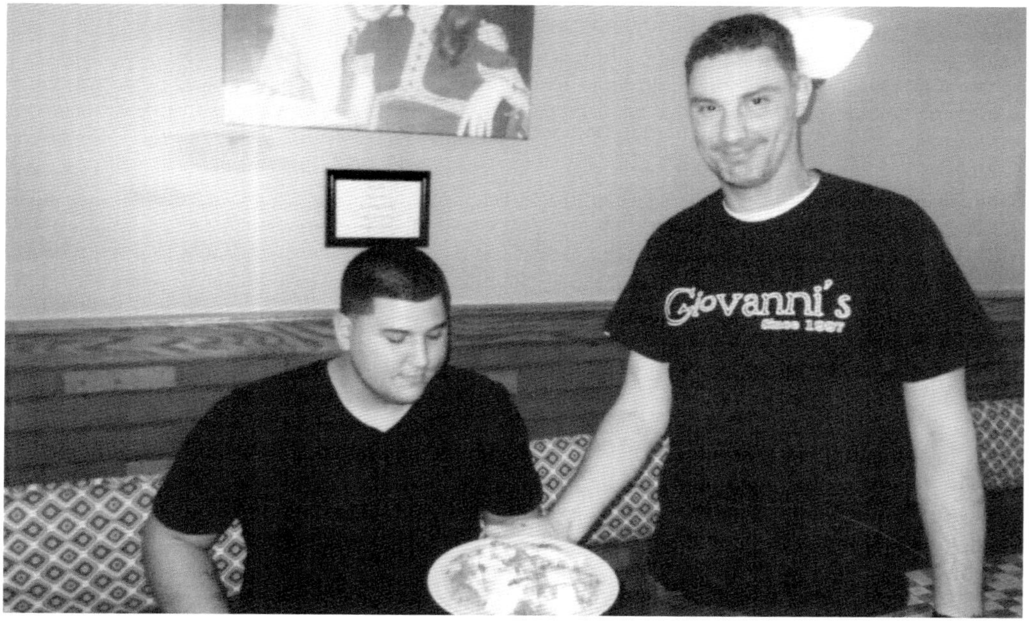

Best Deli in Town

Pictured below is Giovanni's Deli co-owner Sandy Aluotto, who began the business with her husband. They both created the recipes, and she is now the chief cook. The above photograph is of their son, co-owner Anthony Aluotto, who serves one of their popular dishes, pink vodka sauce over penne pasta. Beginning in 1997 with Italian-deli roots, the business has expanded into other cuisines including Mexican, barbecue, and vegetarian. The deli is also famous for its No. 57 wrap, which is breaded chicken, pink vodka sauce, and fresh mozzarella. Giovanni's was named Best Deli in Fair Lawn by a poll of *Patch* readers. The deli is a popular lunch spot for students from nearby Fair Lawn High School.

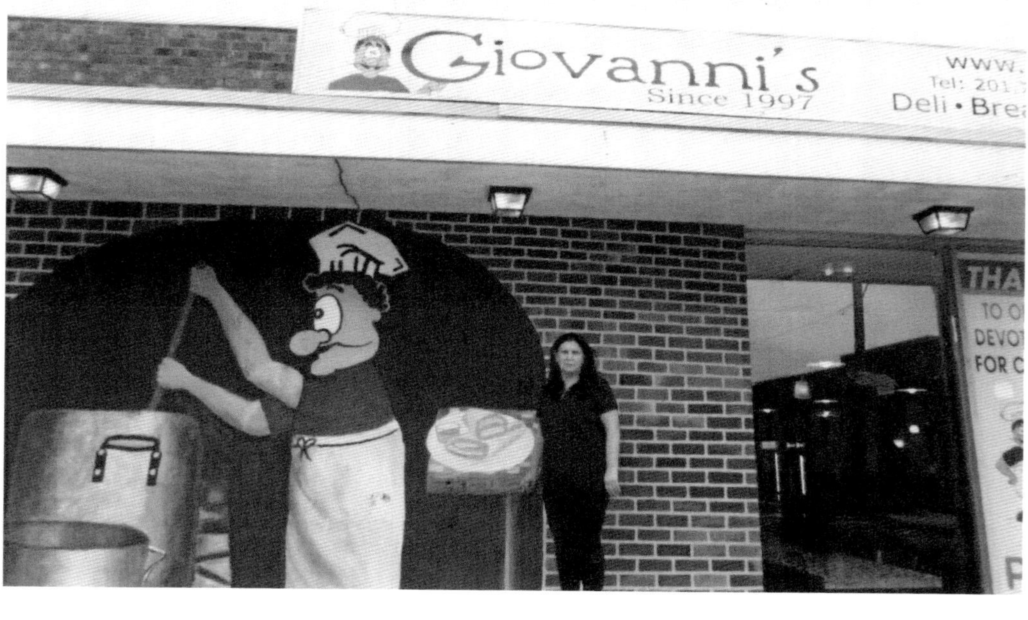

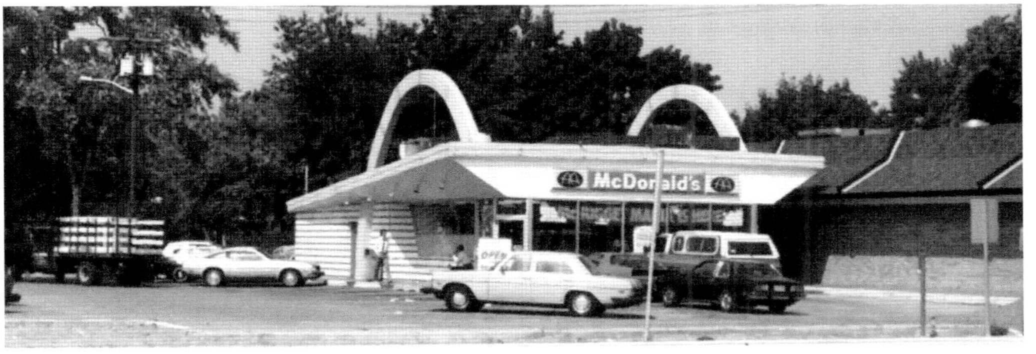

First McDonald's in New Jersey
Darren and Sebastian Lentini take great pride in being the current owners of Fair Lawn's oldest established fast-food eatery, started in 1957. The original building, with the "golden arches" intersecting the roof, was one of the last of the famous 1952-designed McDonald's before it was torn down in 1983. The present building with indoor seating replaces it.

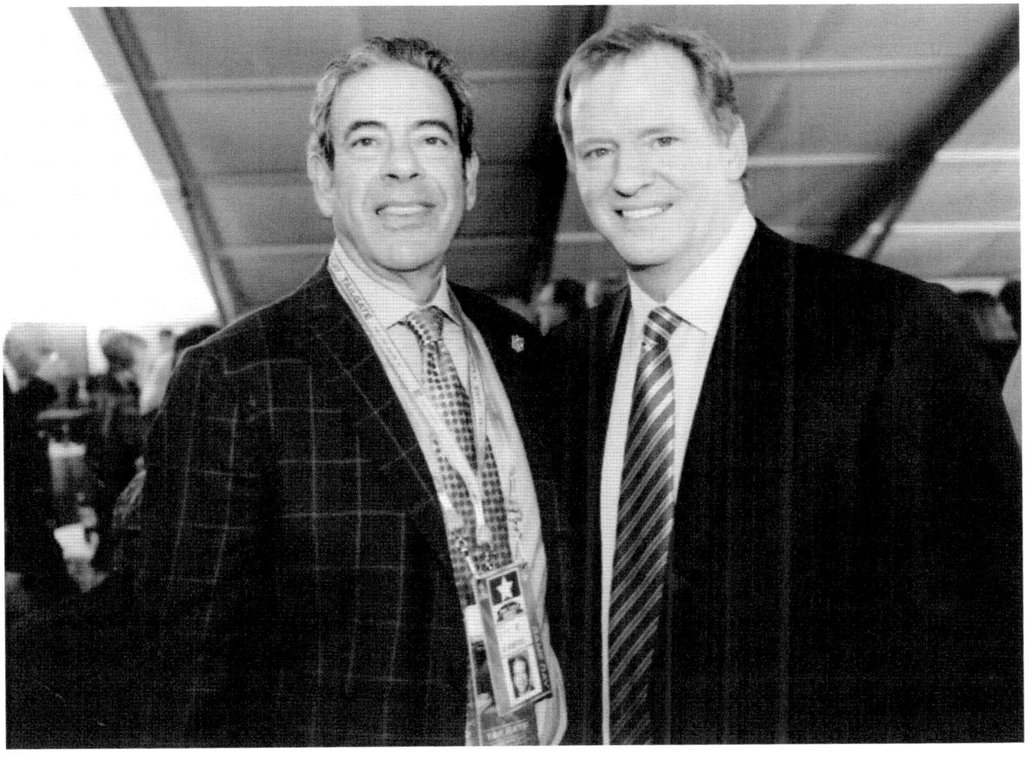

Cable Television Pioneer
Julian and Marge Bornstein, the founders of the Fair Lawn Jewish Center (see page 30) raised an outstanding son, Steve Bornstein (pictured at the left with NFL commissioner Roger Goodell), in Fair Lawn. Bornstein joined ESPN in 1980 and rose to become ESPN's youngest president and chief executive officer in 1990 at age 38. He went on to become chairman/chief executive officer of ESPN as well as president of ABC Sports and then president of ABC, Inc., the parent company. Bornstein is currently the founder and chief executive officer of the NFL Network. (Courtesy of Steve Bornstein.)

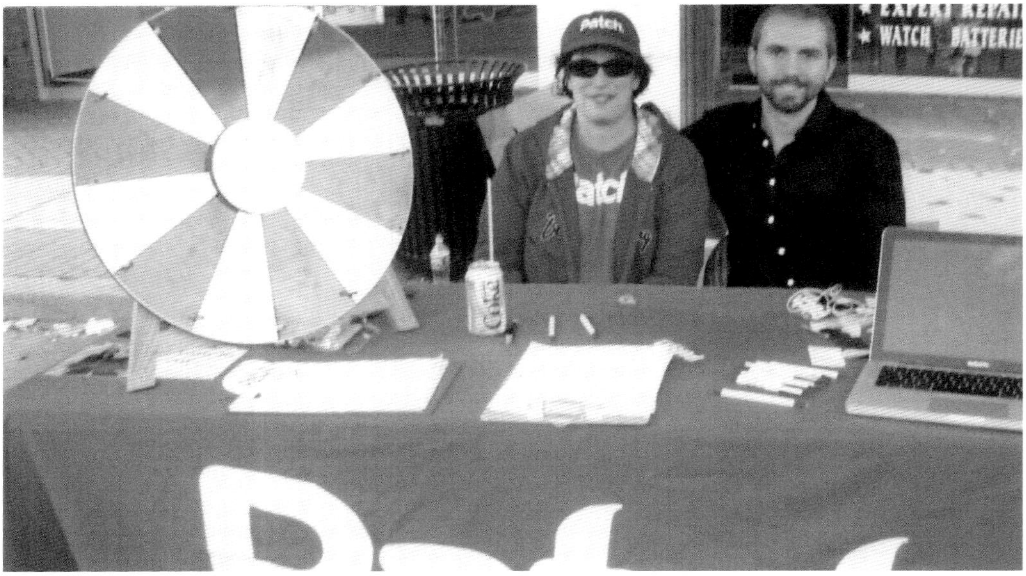

Our Town's Online News Service

Zak Koeske has been editor of *Fair Lawn–Saddle Brook Patch* since August 2011. Koeske is a Pittsburgh native who now lives in Fair Lawn. He wrote for the *Pittsburgh Post-Gazette*, covering borough government, education, and the occasional community feature. *Fair Lawn–Saddle Brook Patch* is a local online news and information platform owned by AOL. The Fair Lawn site launched in September 2010. A leading contributor of videos to *Patch* is videographer Wayne Robbins, who is known all over town by his distinctive tan cowboy hat. He is the host and producer of the television program *Inside Fair Lawn*, which has aired on Fair Lawn Television for eight years. He is pictured below interviewing Joan Goldstein, a candidate for borough council.

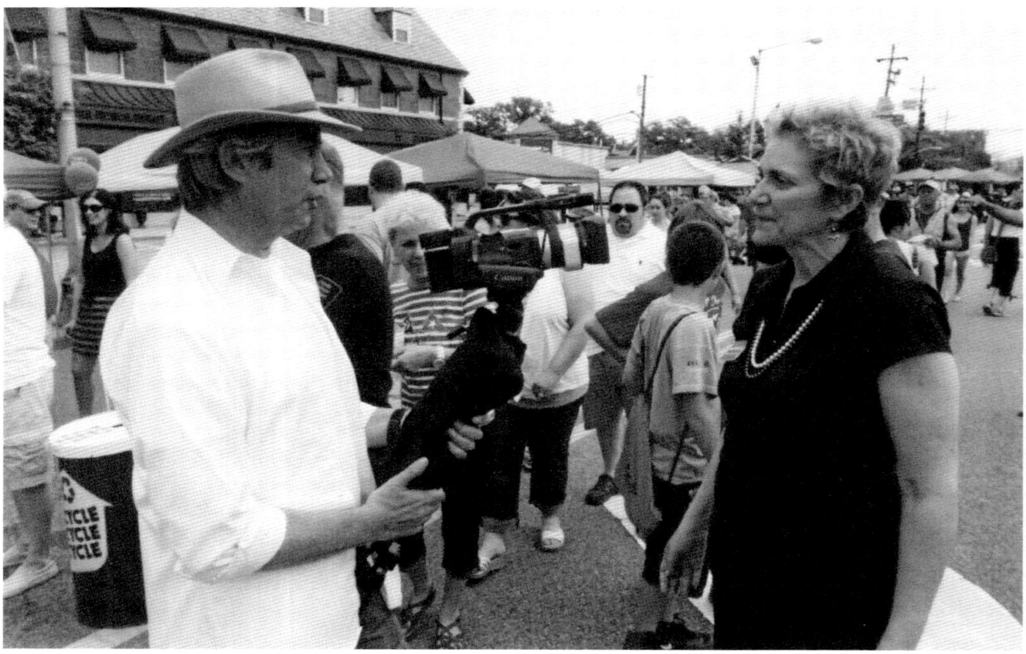

Adviser in Four Presidential Administrations

Stuart N. Brotman has served in four presidential administrations on a bipartisan basis, including roles as a founder of the National Telecommunications and Information Administration; as an inaugural appointee of the Library of Congress Copyright Arbitration Royalty Panel; as chairman of the United States–Israel Science and Technology Foundation; and as a member of the US Department of State Advisory Committee on International Communications and Information Policy.

Brotman does consulting as a senior management adviser for domestic and international telecommunications, Internet, media, entertainment, and sports clients. He provides strategic business, financial, regulatory policy, and operations counseling; due diligence evaluations; litigation support and expert testimony; and management education and executive coaching for corporate chief executive officers, presidents, and boards of directors.

Stuart Brotman served on the landmark federal task force that led to the introduction of cellular telephone and direct broadcast satellite services in the United States, and to the development of e-mail as a commercial service. He also was an architect of the competition/deregulation policy paradigm that governs today's communications marketplace.

Brotman also found time to serve as president and chief executive officer of the Museum of Television & Radio, where he oversaw museum operations in New York City and Los Angeles and enabled the museum to make major strides in its transition from a bicoastal 20th-century museum to a 21st-century institution with global reach. He was an executive producer of *Funniest Families of Television Comedy: A Museum of Television & Radio Special* that aired on the ABC Television Network.

In 2000, Brotman was named the first USA Telecommunications Eisenhower Fellow. He also served as chairman of the American Bar Association's International Communications Law Committee. His four books include *Communications Law and Practice*, the leading treatise on electronic mass media and telecommunications. Brotman is a faculty member at Harvard Law School and in the Harvard Business School Executive Education Program. He was the first concurrent digital media fellow at Harvard and MIT.

In this photograph, from left to right, are Henry Kissinger, Brotman, Merv Griffin, and Barbara Walters at a Museum of Television and Radio event. (Photograph by permission of Patrick McMullan.com. Image copyright Patrick McMullan.com.)

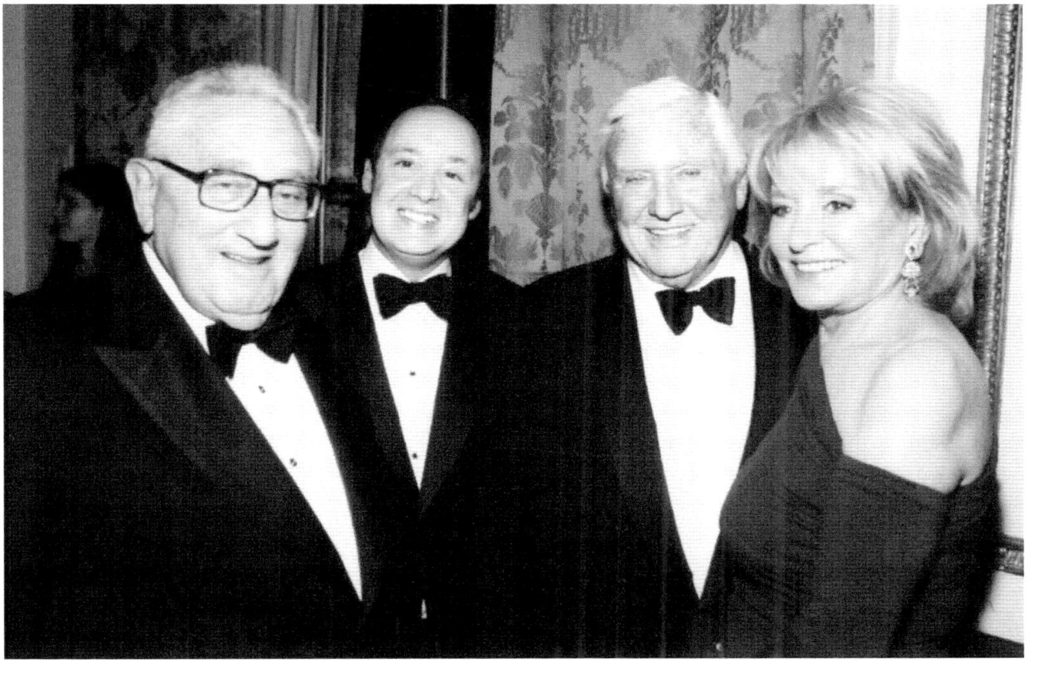

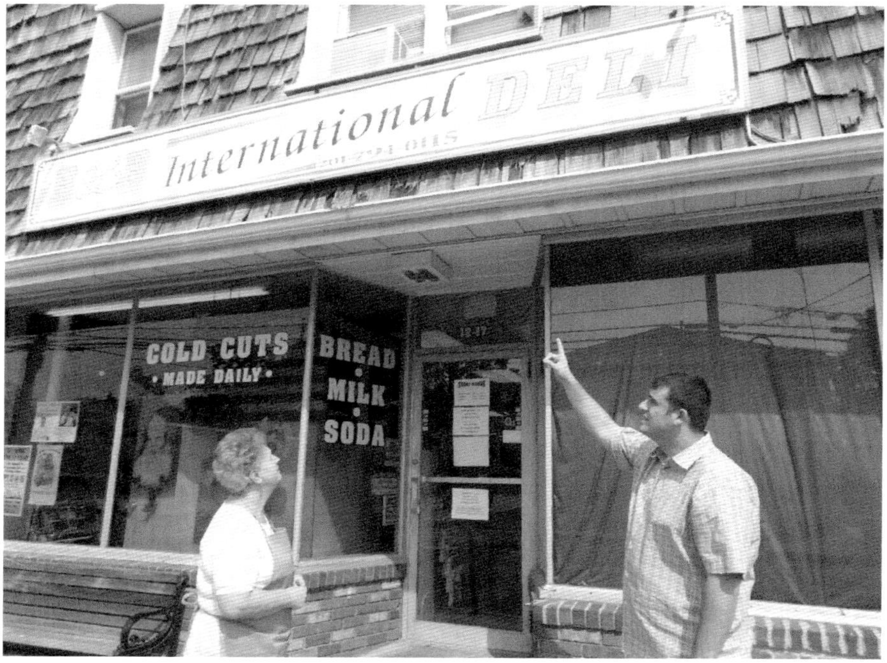

Catering to the Town's Russian Population

Charles Yalovitser (pictured above and below), the manager of B & B International Food, is the nephew of owner Felix Belferman, whom he calls "a driven, hard-working businessman who is also a great family man." Felix came from Russia with his parents, Mera and Boris Belferman, and started the store 25 years ago. It specializes in homemade Eastern European and Russian foods, making it popular with Fair Lawn's large Russian population. Felix also owns B & B Wine and Liquor. Both stores are located on River Road.

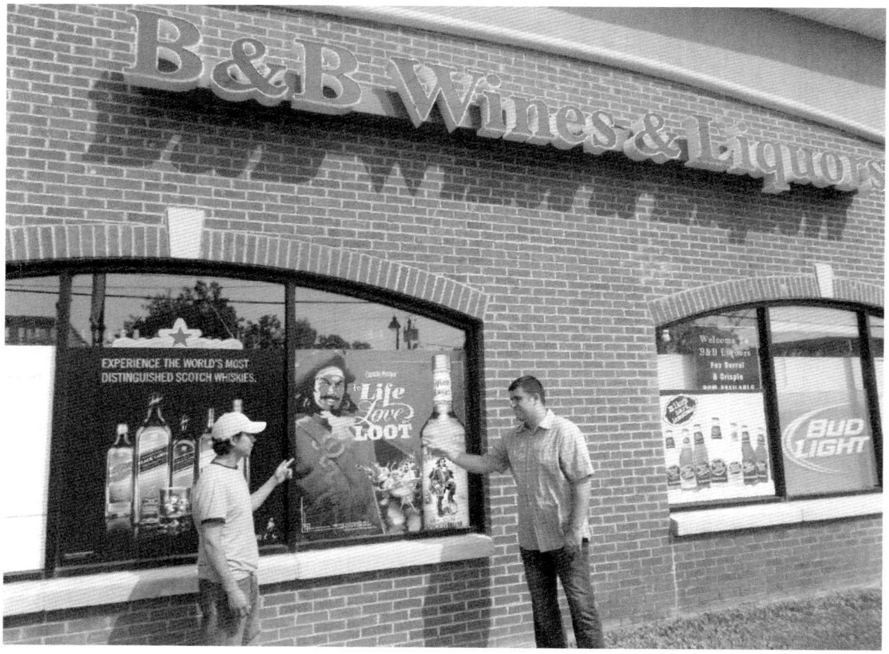

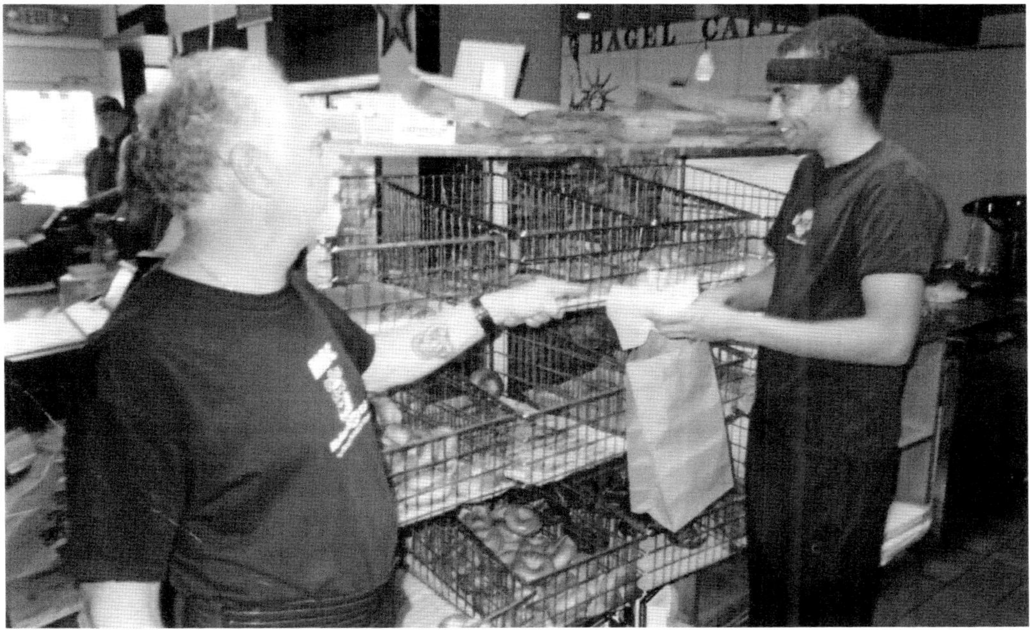

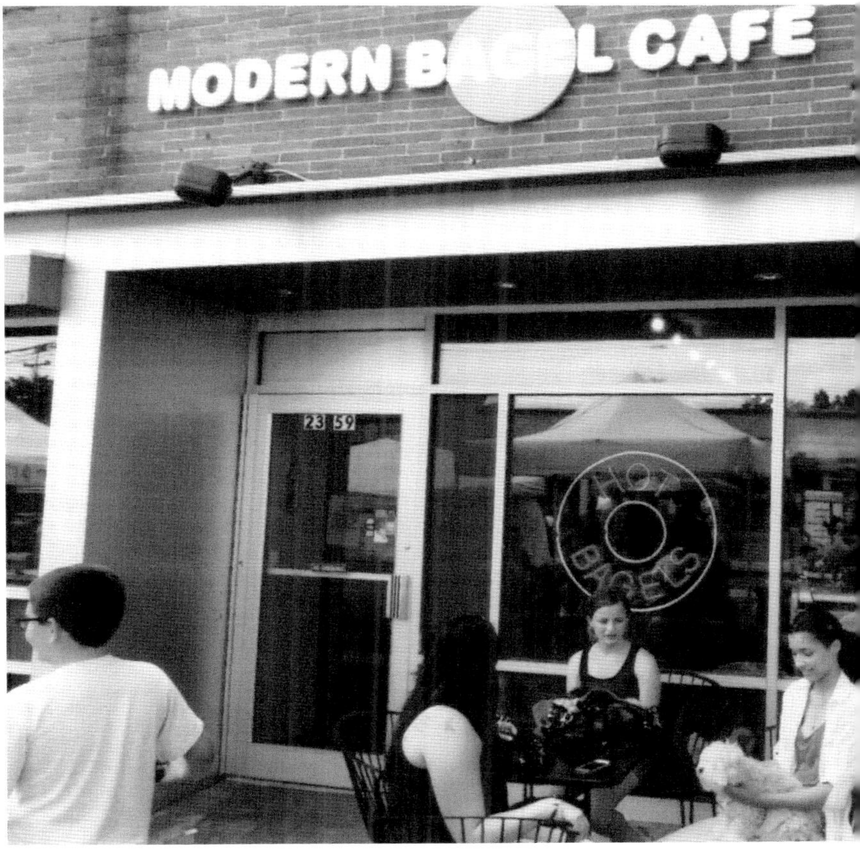

Best Bagels in Town
Modern Bagel Café has been owned and operated by Billy Barell (left) since it opened in Radburn in 1990. Barell likes to ride his motorcycle to New Milford, where he owns a horse and goes horseback riding. The café is more than just a bagel shop; it also serves coffee, deli sandwiches, and paninis. It has a full deli with customer favorites such as tuna salad, German potato salad, crunchy cole slaw, and some of the best sliced turkey sold in town. Customers may sit in the indoor dining area or at sidewalk tables in the warmer months. The store is packed on Sunday mornings when bags of bagels are carried out the door. Modern Bagel was named Best Bagels in Fair Lawn by a poll of *Patch* readers.

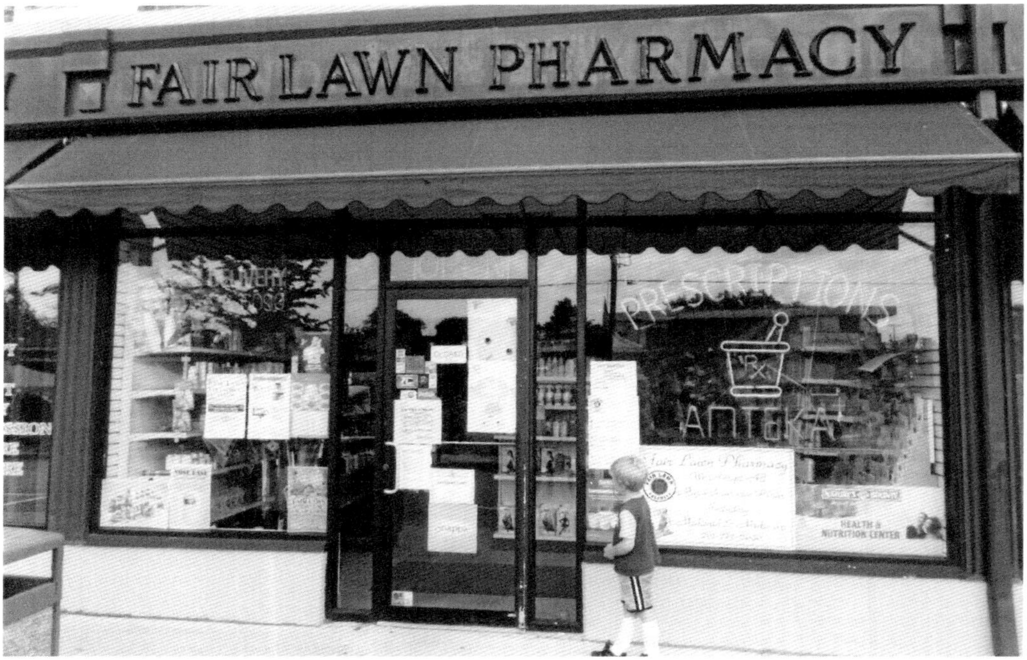

Located in the Historic Radburn Building

Fair Lawn Pharmacy is a family-owned, full-service pharmacy, managed by Alex Beda (left), that offers helpful assistance to town residents looking to have their prescriptions filled and questions answered. Beda likes to do martial arts with his children and is working for his black belt at Shido-kan Karate Dojo. In addition to the standard pharmacy services, Fair Lawn Pharmacy also offers a variety of natural medicine and homeopathic remedies, including a large selection of vitamins and herbs for those seeking alternative treatments. Since the pharmacy's staff is fluent in Russian, they are able to help local Russian seniors in their native language. Employee Shital Patel is pictured with Beda.

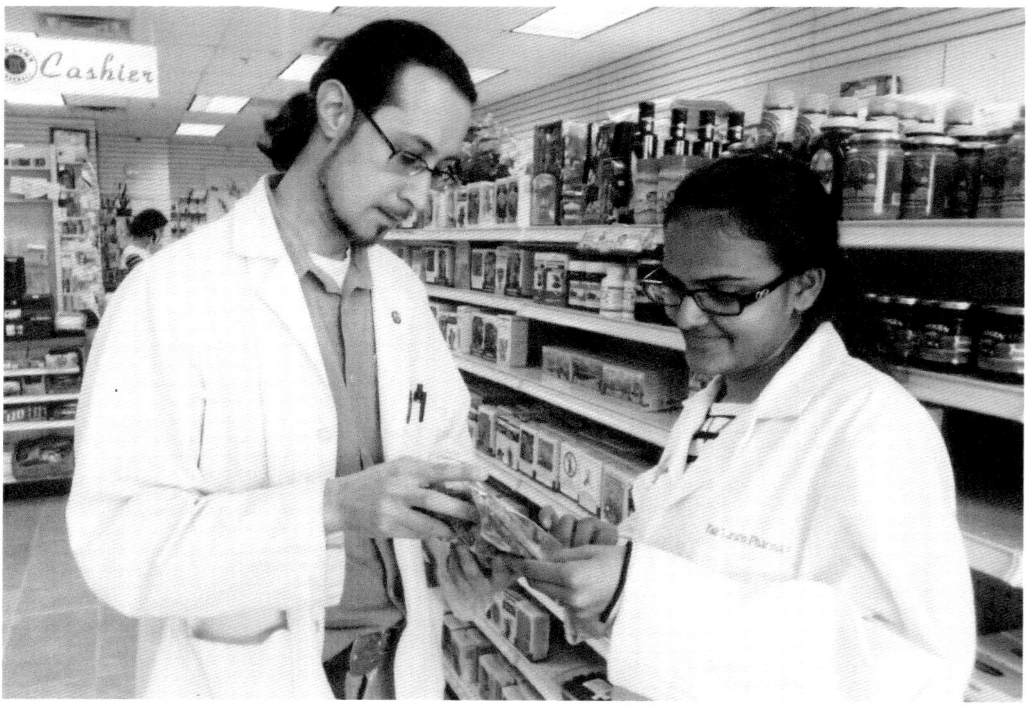

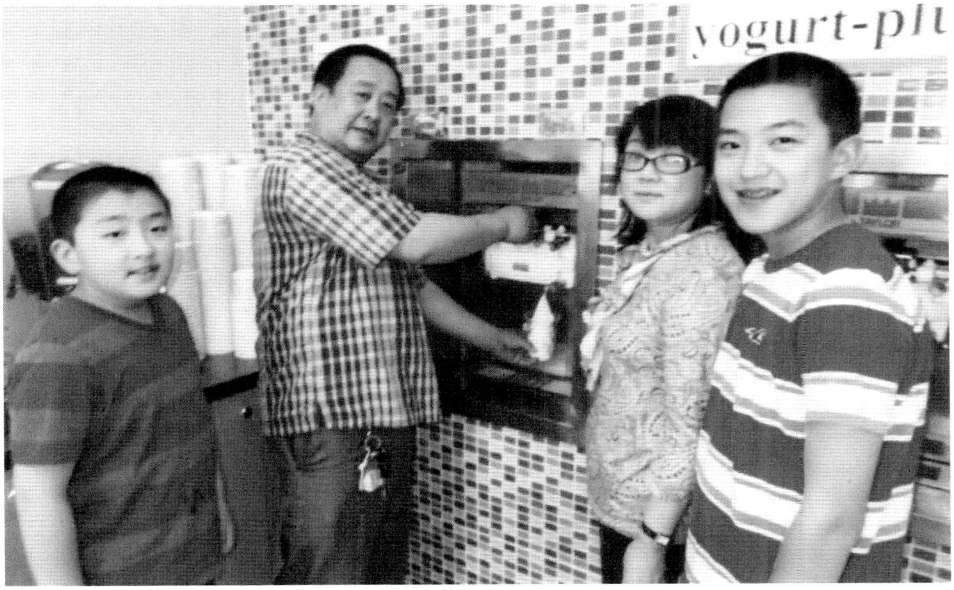

Best Yogurt in Town

Stephen Chen and his wife, Kelly, own and operate Yogurt Plus in the Radburn Plaza Building along with their sons Justin (left) and Joshua (right). They miss their oldest son, Jesse, who is in the US Air Force. Chen and his wife were born and schooled in China before coming to the United States 30 years ago. They have self-serve kosher frozen yogurt with 30 topping options from sprinkles and chocolate sauce to nearly every kind of fruit. The store also sells ice cream, smoothies, parfaits, shakes, bubble teas, yogurt cakes, ice cream cakes, and yogurt pies. The Chens say that yogurt is an excellent source of protein, calcium, and B vitamins and contains active and live cultures. Yogurt Plus was named Best Yogurt in Fair Lawn by a poll of *Patch* readers.

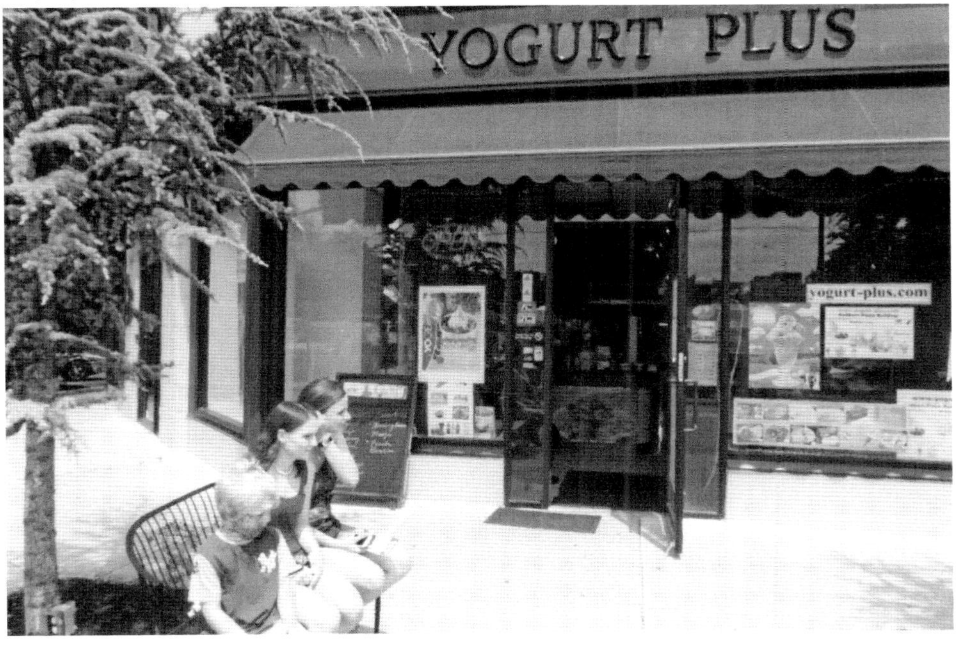

INDEX

INDEX